Gendered Places

WILLIAM J. SCARBOROUGH

Gendered Places

THE LANDSCAPE OF LOCAL GENDER
NORMS ACROSS THE UNITED STATES

TEMPLE UNIVERSITY PRESS
Philadelphia • *Rome* • *Tokyo*

TEMPLE UNIVERSITY PRESS
Philadelphia, Pennsylvania 19122
tupress.temple.edu

Library of Congress Cataloging-in-Publication Data

Names: Scarborough, William, author.
Title: Gendered places : the landscape of local gender norms across the
   United States / William J. Scarborough.
Description: Philadelphia : Temple University Press, 2023. | Includes
   bibliographical references and index. | Summary: "This book analyzes the
   difference in gender norms between different metropolitan regions across
   the United States. In so doing, it untangles the relationship between
   local culture and differences in how gender impacts employment and
   family expectations"— Provided by publisher.
Identifiers: LCCN 2022029591 (print) | LCCN 2022029592 (ebook) | ISBN
   9781439922033 (cloth) | ISBN 9781439922040 (paperback) | ISBN
   9781439922057 (pdf)
Subjects: LCSH: Sex role—United States. | Metropolitan areas—Social
   aspects—United States. | Social norms—United States. | Pay
   equity—United States. | Sociology, Urban—United States.
Classification: LCC HQ1075.U6 S33 2023 (print) | LCC HQ1075.U6 (ebook) |
   DDC 305.30973—dc23/eng/20221017
LC record available at https://lccn.loc.gov/2022029591
LC ebook record available at https://lccn.loc.gov/2022029592

Printed in the United States of America

9 8 7 6 5 4 3 2 1

For Emily, Otto, and Charlie

Contents

Acknowledgments

This book would not be possible without the remarkable support provided by countless individuals, groups, and communities. Emily, Otto, and Charlie, for whom this book is dedicated, are my inspiration and joy. The central ideas in this book were originally developed in long conversations with Emily during our nightly walks with our dog, Busika, while the contents of each chapter were refined as we eventually added a stroller to the mix. I am so grateful to experience life with you. There is no doubt that our time living in six cities across three states and two countries (surely more to come) helped develop an interest in, and awareness of, local culture. Little did we know what life had in store for us when we sat next to each other as undergraduates in an introduction to sociology course. You mean so much to me. My son, Otto, joined us when this project was only a dissertation. Caring for him has been the most meaningful thing in my life. Otto, I love your sense of humor and creativity. Your love of books has certainly motivated me as I wrote this one. My youngest, Charlie, arrived as this book went to publication and filled our family with joy and wonder. I love you so much, Otto and Charlie.

Barbara Risman and Catherine Fobes have been incredibly thoughtful, caring, and inspiring mentors. They have each provided models for the type of sociologist I aim to be—one who values care for others above all else. Barbara was my chair when this project started as a dissertation. I could not have had a better adviser. Barbara's "yes, and" approach to social theory provided an empowering model for mentorship that fostered innovation and creativity. In the many years between this project starting as a dissertation and being transformed into a book, Barbara has provided feedback on numerous drafts and had countless brainstorming sessions with me. Her feedback was crucial in developing the book, as well as encouraging me to keep pushing on during difficult periods. Catherine Fobes taught my first sociology course and has been a mentor and close friend ever since. Catherine inspired me to become a sociologist by showing me how the field can be used to address social inequality. Further yet, she modeled this impact by showing care and compassion for her students while also challenging them to expand their understanding of society. Catherine set me on a trajectory toward becoming a sociologist, and I am forever grateful.

This book has also benefited from numerous scholars, mentors, and friends who generously read previous versions and offered insightful feedback. I am grateful for Bill Bielby, Erin Cech, Leslie McCall, Barbara Risman, and Moshe Semyonov, who served on my dissertation committee and offered fantastic advice that substantially improved the theoretical and methodological approaches I use in this book. Several other scholars generously read portions of this book and offered valuable feedback. Thanks to Maria Charles, Shelley Correll, Christin Landivar, Cecilia Ridgeway, Leah Ruppanner, and Katie Sobering for your thoughtful recommendations on improving this work. Thanks to Alice Evans, who introduced me to the idea of contextual and compositional effects that I explore in Chapter 4. I greatly appreciate Bill Bielby's recommendation to use confirmatory factor analysis, which led to a major breakthrough in my conceptualization of local gender norms. Erin Cech's recommendation to explore Twitter data way back in 2016 led me on a fruitful pursuit of examining culture in discourse. Christin Landivar introduced me to the wonderful world of dot plots that I use throughout this text, particularly Chapter 4. I also thank Christa Lim for her thoughtful suggestions in designing the bar graphs presented in Chapter 3. Tom VanHeuvelen noted the advantages of labor sheds in a brief email exchange years ago, which ended up being the perfect spatial unit for this project. Ray Sin prompted me to think about norms as multidimensional, and I have not looked back since. I am also grateful to the participants of the 2018 Pathways to Gender Equality Conference at American University who provided critical feedback on my prior measurements and prompted me to incorporate a new, more valid, set of cultural indicators. Among many things, this book represents the generosity of scholars in sociology (as well as several economists and geographers) who kindly provided thoughtful suggestions that had a tremendous impact.

The Department of Sociology at the University of Illinois at Chicago was a perfect home for me to start this project. The department's focus on inequality and space made a major impression on me. I also learned a great deal from my graduate cohort, Rowena Crabbe, Allison Helmuth, Kylee

Joosten, Sarah Moberg, and Sarah Steel. The Survey Research Group, run by Allyson Holbrook and Tim Johnson, provided invaluable opportunities to receive feedback on my analytic strategies and measurements used throughout this book. While at UIC, I was fortunate to work at the Institute for Research on Race and Public Policy, where I had the opportunity to contribute to a series of reports with Amanda Lewis, Iván Arenas, and Faith Kares. With their mentorship, I refined my ability to write for public audiences and also learned how to work on large-scale collaborative projects.

If UIC was the ideal place for me to start this book, the University of North Texas has been the perfect place to complete it. It is an honor to be able to work with the amazing students at UNT. I am continuously struck by the empathy and care they show for one another. The Department of Sociology at UNT has been incredibly supportive as I have finished this book. Donna Barnes, Gabe Ignatow, and Dale Yeatts have provided insightful mentorship. I am very lucky to have been hired the same year as Ron Kwon, who has become a close colleague, collaborator, and friend. Katie Sobering provided tremendous guidance as I embarked on my first book project. I am grateful for her advice on this book and many other academic endeavors.

Several other individuals have provided crucial encouragement as I finished this book. The "Belden Ave. Crew" was always there to celebrate success or pick me up when I needed inspiration. Thanks so much, Leslie Pokoik, Mary Pokoik, Nancy Cohen, and Norm Christopherson. Many pages of the first draft of this book were written at the Writers Workspace in Edgewater. I deeply appreciate Amy Davis for fostering that community and providing the space for me to work through my ideas. Caitlyn Collins, Christin Landivar, and Leah Ruppanner have been amazing collaborators and shaped my understanding of how local policy intersects with gender norms. I am inspired by the enthusiasm they bring to our work.

I owe a tremendous thanks to my parents. I now understand how challenging, as well as how wonderful, being a parent can be, and I'm amazed at how good they were at it. It is without doubt that this book was influenced by them. My parents have never visited a village, town, or city that they did not like. Their fascination with the unique characteristics of places has surely rubbed off on me. I remember, as a child, sitting through numerous city meetings when my dad served on the planning commission. It was in those meetings where I first learned the importance of local culture and policies. My mother helped me translate those interests by fostering an appreciation and love of writing. Thanks also to my sisters, Corey and Jill, for exposing me to different ideas and challenging my assumptions.

This project has received generous financial support from numerous groups for which I am tremendously grateful. I thank the Graduate College at the University of Illinois at Chicago for their support through the Dean's

Scholar Fellowship and the Provost Award. Thanks, also, to the Center for Research on Women and Gender at UIC for their support with the Alice J. Dan Dissertation Research Award, as well as the Department of Sociology at UIC. At the University of North Texas, this research was supported by the College of Liberal Arts & Social Sciences Scholarly and Creative Activity Award and the Department of Sociology.

I have thoroughly enjoyed working with Temple University Press on this book and greatly appreciate Ryan Mulligan for his guidance and editorship throughout the process. The writing and organization of this book were much improved with Ryan's input. I thank Will Forest and Gary Kramer for their recommendations on the finer points of image quality and marketing. I am also very grateful to the thoughtful reviewers who offered valuable feedback on previous versions of this book and pushed me to more deeply engage with how gender norms are experienced as well as how they intersect with other aspects of local culture.

Gendered Places

1

Introduction

Gender, Local Culture, and Inequality

Each year, tens of thousands of tourists visit the iconic Route 66 highway (Listokin et al. 2011). One of the first major highways in the United States, Route 66 spans over 2,400 miles from Illinois to California. Visitors along the stretch cherish the cultural diversity of U.S. towns and cities. The route moves from the hustle and bustle of Chicago to the flat plains of the Midwest before jutting to the ranchlands of Oklahoma and Texas. From there, travelers enter the deserts of New Mexico and Arizona, passing through adobe landscapes as well as the national parks surrounding Flagstaff. Continuing into California, Route 66 encounters the traffic of Los Angeles before ending at the beaches of Santa Monica. Indeed, one of the primary highlights of Route 66 is that each city and town along the way holds something unique. From the Airstream diners in Missouri to the cattle ranches in Texas, travelers of Route 66 revel in each location's unique charm and cultural flair.

The diverse reputations of U.S. cities and towns extend well beyond Route 66. Travelers of all sorts relish the quirky attributes of the places they visit. In fact, city leaders often go to great lengths to promote their area's cultural reputation in order to increase tourism. We travel to the Big Easy for laid back vibes, New York for big-city buzz, and Miami for the beach and nightlife. Beyond their entertainment value, however, urban scholars and economists have argued that cities' cultural reputations are valuable assets that can be used for economic growth and innovation (Florida 2012; Ottaviano and Peri 2005, 2006). Public art and museums inspire creativity, while parks, bars, and coffee shops facilitate social exchange between diverse populations—leading to the emergence of new ideas and economic innovation (Florida 2012; Lucas 2009).

Beneath places' popular reputations and cultural flair, however, exist another layer of difference. In addition to being known as the "Big Easy," New Orleans also has a substantial gender wage gap, where women are paid 23 percent less than men. In contrast, the gender wage gap in the "Magic City" of Miami is 14 percent. Honolulu has one of the smallest gender wage gaps in the country, where women are paid 12.5 percent less than men. Meanwhile, the wage gap is over three times as large in places like Lake Charles, Louisiana. Just as locations vary in their cultural reputations, they also differ in levels of gender inequality. Travelers passing through locales along Route 66 traverse an undulating landscape of inequality, with the gender wage gap ranging from nearly 30 percent in Oklahoma City to 15.5 percent in Los Angeles (see Figure 1.1). Because the gender wage gap represents the difference in hourly pay between women and men after accounting for work, family, and human capital characteristics, this measure serves as an indicator of local levels of gender inequality more broadly. Why, after all relevant reasons have been accounted for, are women paid less than men? And why does this vary so dramatically across the United States?

Researchers have devoted a great deal of attention to uncovering the determinants of gender inequality. In general, scholars agree that the factors

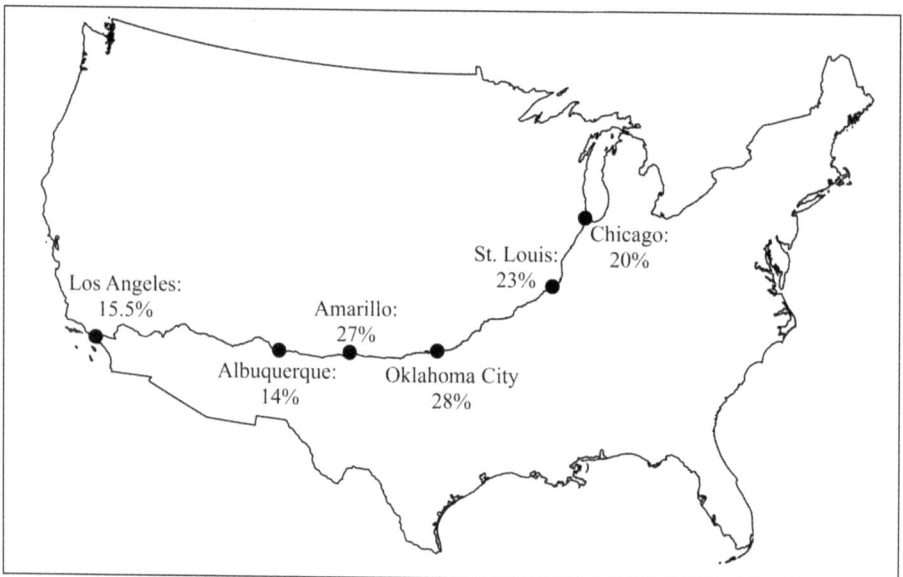

Figure 1.1 A Tour of Gender Wage Gaps along Route 66

Note: Gender wage gaps calculated with data from the 2018 American Community Survey (Ruggles et al. 2021) using equations described in Chapter 5.

contributing to gender inequality span multiple social arenas (Lorber 1995; Risman 2018). The tendency for women and men to have different educational and career preferences, as an individual-level attribute, has been found to be one reason for existing levels of occupational gender segregation and gender wage gaps, as the jobs women often prefer pay less than the jobs men tend to prefer (Cech 2013; England 2016). But this leads to the question: Why are women's preferred jobs valued less? Here is where macro-level cultural norms enter the picture, as the devaluing of women-majority occupations—even those requiring as much skill and education as occupations held mostly by men—represents a broader cultural ideology whereby women's work is rewarded less than men's (Levanon, England, and Allison 2009). Even if women and men are in the same occupation in the same firm, however, interpersonal dynamics among them, colleagues, and supervisors may further reproduce gender inequality if women experience sexual harassment, slights, or are not treated equally (Ridgeway 2011). Synthesizing the multiple mechanisms across various levels of society that reproduce gender inequality, Barbara Risman (2018) has developed the theory of gender as a social structure to explain how individual-, interactional-, and macro-level social phenomena occur in a dynamic system where patterns of inequality at one level reinforce patterns of inequality at another.

Considering gender as a social structure, and not just an individual-level attribute, has prompted sociologists to "find" gender in many seemingly mundane aspects of social life. Through this process, the term "gender" becomes a verb to describe the process of reinscribing gender dynamics through action ("gendering") as well as an adjective used to highlight how the quality of something reinforces the gender structure ("gendered"). Parents engage in "gendering" their infants when they dress girls in pink and boys in blue to indicate their sex, which would otherwise be indiscernible at such a young age. As a result, the children themselves are unwittingly "gendered" into a certain character of being masculine or feminine. Even inanimate objects can be gendered. Despite it being totally unnecessary, we have women's deodorant and men's deodorant, girls' pink bicycles and boys' blue bicycles. Bic even sells pastel-colored pens "for her." The process of gendering and the quality of being gendered illustrate how the gender structure is perpetuated beyond individual-level identities or choices but also through the inundation of messages from our social environments that remind us of what it means to be a woman or a man, how we should treat women and men, and the valuation of things, jobs, and practices that are considered to be feminine or masculine.

If inanimate objects like pens and deodorant can be gendered, can cities? And does conceptualizing geographic spaces as gendered help us explain why inequalities vary so much between them? Let us return back to places' well-known reputations. For many, thoughts of life in Dallas, also known as "The

Big D," may conjure images of cowboys and southern belles. Indeed, such depictions were common in the popular 1980s soap opera *Dallas* and continue to be conveyed in the reverence of the local football team (the Dallas Cowboys) and their famous cheerleaders. Contrast this with the thoughts that emerge when thinking of life in New York, where the prototypical woman resident may be imagined as an upwardly mobile professional. Meanwhile, women and men alike in Portland, Maine, may be characterized as wearing flannel and rejecting passivity in this place known as the "Forest City." Considering the different images of women and men associated with cities' predominant reputations, we can start to view how places' cultural context may itself be a part of the gender structure.

Beyond associating cities' cultural reputations with their gendered environments, we may also consider how individuals' personal experience varies when moving from place to place. I moved from Chicago to Dallas when my son was just under a year old. In Chicago, we were young parents in our early thirties. We knew very few people our age who had children, with most waiting until their late thirties or early forties. Arriving in Dallas, we were surprised to find that many people our age had started families years ago and typically had two or three children already! Through our move, we went from being young parents in Chicago to old parents in Dallas. Such a transition reflected the very different ideal family norms between our old home and our new home. Similar experiences have been recorded by research in other parts of the United States. In interviews with trans men, Miriam Abelson (2019) found that they were more comfortable expressing nondominant forms of masculinity in San Francisco than in places throughout the South where more mainstream forms of manhood were highly valued. In another study, lesbian women interviewed by Japonica Brown-Saracino (2017) were more likely to express butch or masculine personality traits in Portland, Maine, than in Greenfield, Massachusetts.

This book delves deeper into the distinctly gendered aspects of places that influence the way individuals feel, their interactions with others, and, in particular, large-scale patterns such as the gender wage gap. I argue that if we look beneath the surface of widely known cultural reputations associated with places, we find another, more consequential characterization of local culture that is distinctly gendered. Variation in levels of inequality, such as the gender wage gap and occupational gender segregation, are symptomatic of different gender norms across locations that convey a powerful force on local gender structures, providing differing sets of opportunities, rewards, and incentives for women and men residents. From this perspective, we can impose a more critical lens on cities' culture that acknowledges both the assets of egalitarianism while also directly addressing regressive norms that reinforce power imbalances between women and men. In other words, viewing cities as gendered recognizes local culture as not value neutral but as a crucial part of the gender structure that perpetuates, or challenges, gender inequality.

Attention to local culture has proliferated in recent decades. Most of us are inundated with news and tourism links ranking the "top ten cities" for things like food, music, hipster vibes, entrepreneurship, raising a family, and romantic getaways. Among those with the means, discussion of local culture and favorite places to visit are frequent cocktail party conversations. But beyond this topical interest, local culture has also received a great deal of scholarly attention. People like Richard Florida (2012) have argued that cities' cultural features play a large role in attracting and retaining talented workers. Florida is less concerned with gendered aspects of cities. Instead, by characterizing local culture with measures like the "coolness factor" (Florida 2002b) or the "bohemian index" (2002a), Florida finds that places with vibrant nightlife (high coolness factor) and a large concentration of artists (high bohemian index) have had the most growth in highly lucrative tech industries. Marketing scholars have also examined local culture, but through a lens of "place branding" that examines how communities actively construct their cultural reputation in efforts to attract tourism and investment (Cleave and Arku 2017; Scarborough and Crabbe 2021). Such efforts came to the forefront in 2017 when over two hundred municipalities across North America submitted proposals to host Amazon's second headquarters (HQ2). While tax incentives were weighed heavily in the choice of where to locate the retail giant's second headquarters and its anticipated twenty-five thousand jobs, a central component in the company's decision, as described in the call for proposals,[1] was "cultural community fit" and "community/quality of life," each emphasizing unique cultural environments with enjoyable "living, recreational, and educational opportunities" and a "compatible cultural and community environment." As was displayed in a drawn-out and widely publicized selection process, cities proudly marketed their unique cultural attributes as local assets that would entice Amazon. Nashville advertised its reputation as the "Music City," Denver its livability, and Philadelphia its history and museums. Ultimately, Amazon chose two locations to dual host HQ2 (Crystal City near Washington, D.C., and New York City). Importantly, these were not the areas that offered the largest tax incentives, highlighting the importance of other, nonmaterial and cultural, factors that shape local investment.

From an economics perspective, place matters. Companies succeed or fail depending on where they locate. This is one reason why Amazon put so much effort into choosing a location for their second headquarters. Places with a hip cultural reputation have an edge over other locations. A different look into these patterns, however, begs the question of how gender is implicated in the construction of "hip" places. As described earlier, places' cultural reputations are often subtly infused with gendered imagery or meanings. Nashville, for example, emulates the density and vibrancy that Richard Florida argues is vital to a "hip" culture that attracts talent and investment. The city's particular brand of music is most notably associated with Taylor Swift and Garth Brooks, two country music stars who became famous while performing and recording in Nashville. While extremely talented, both of these artists also convey (whether intentionally or not) prototypical gendered images of masculinity and femininity. Blond and slender, Taylor Swift personifies many qualities of the southern belle style of femininity, while Garth Brooks's scruffy goatee and wide-brimmed cowboy hat convey a rugged style associated with masculinities of the South and Southwest. To the extent that Swift and Brooks are emblematic of Nashville's music scene, the city's particular brand of local culture seems bound with gendered imagery of southern and country forms of masculinity and femininity. From this perspective, it is no surprise that Nashville was recently named by CNN as the bachelorette party capital of the world (Lastoe 2019).

There has been an incredible amount of interest in local culture and reputation. "Place making" is now a key component in urban planning across the United States as municipalities make intentional efforts to create a social and cultural atmosphere that improves quality of life, attracts investment, and retains talent. Yet, despite all this buzz, there has been no consideration of local gender norms. This remarkable omission is only possible through the widespread assumption that gender somehow exists outside the more "public" realms of economics, politics, and city planning. However, thinking of gender not only as an individual-level attribute but as a social structure akin and interrelated with other social structures such as the economy and politics, we can no longer ignore the centrality of gender across all dimensions of society, including our individual lives, the interactions we have with others, and the economic viability of our communities.

Viewing gender as a social structure prompts a critical set of questions examined in this book on the gendered features and consequences of the geographic spaces where people live and work. First, do places across the United States have different gender norms that convey a varying set of expectations for women and men? This allows us to examine whether cities are, indeed, gendered. Analyzing a set of cultural indicators for places across the United States reveals that local gender norms are multidimensional—meaning that areas can have egalitarian norms of gender equity in some respects, while being traditional in others. More specifically, places contain four dimensions of gender norms. The first dimension conveys expectations toward *women's advancement*. Places with egalitarian norms on this dimension support women's professional mobility to a similar extent as men's, while in more traditional locations men are more advantaged than women in career advancement. The second dimension, *public sphere gender essentialism*, relates to beliefs that women and men have naturally different, but not necessarily unequal, skills. Areas with traditional norms on this dimension have widespread beliefs that women are better suited for nurturant or care work while men are more inclined to perform technical work, such as engineering. The third dimension of gender norms relates to *intensive mothering*. Traditional places in this dimension believe that mothers should not work and instead focus primarily on childcare; in contrast, egalitarian places do not view motherhood and careers as conflicting. Finally, the fourth dimension of local gender norms pertains to *private sphere gender essentialism*, which describes beliefs around the division of household labor. In egalitarian places on this dimension, women and men share caregiving and homemaking work, while in traditional locales, women are expected to perform most of this labor. Gender norms vary widely both across the United States and between the four dimensions within specific places. Mapping the dynamic terrain of gender norms across the United States, this book reveals the incredible diversity of local culture, highlighting the gendered environments we navigate and experience as we move from place to place.

Recognizing the gendered character of places in the United States provides the opportunity to ask additional questions regarding the source of these local cultural attributes and their consequences on patterns of gender inequality. Principally, where do gender norms come from and how are they sustained? Two possibilities exist, both of which are explored in this book. Local gender norms may reflect the particular demographic composition of residents, a mechanism known as *compositional effects*. Because college educated individuals are more supportive of gender equality and feminism (Scarborough, Sin, and Risman 2019), it is possible that areas with a more educated population have more egalitarian gender norms. From this perspective, it is the characteristics of residents that shape local gender norms. Another possibility, however, is that the experience of residing in a particular cultural environment makes people hold certain values and behave in ways consistent with local norms. This mechanism, known as *contextual effects*, proposes that norms are sustained through shaping the character of people. As I illustrate in later chapters, contextual effects play a larger role than compositional effects in sustaining gender norms. As the adage goes, "It's not where you're from, it's where you're at." Local gender norms shape us. We are not controlled by them, but they nonetheless steer our preferences and decisions in subtle ways that reproduce local cultural dynamics and shape many aspects of social life.

If gender norms play such a large role in individuals' lives, how do they relate to patterns of inequality? Sociologists studying variation in levels of gender inequality across the United States, such as gender wage gaps, have focused almost exclusively on local economic characteristics related to industry composition, job casualization, and occupational segregation (Gauchat, Kelly, and Wallace 2012; McCall 2001). These scholars have found, for example, that women's concentration in lower-paying jobs than men is one of the largest contributors to the gender wage gap (Blau and Kahn 2017). But why are women and men so often employed in different occupations? Here is where cultural logics come in. Existing research has shown that different career preferences between women and men are one factor contributing to occupational gender segregation (Cech 2013; England 2016). Another is discriminatory tastes on the part of hiring managers who, often subconsciously, are biased against employing women applicants for male-dominated jobs (Correll et al. 2017). These individual-level dynamics reflect prevalent cultural gender norms. Yet, as I show in this book, these norms vary from place to place. Therefore, an examination of how local norms shape patterns of inequality provides vital new insight into not only the ideological foundations behind disparities such as the gender wage gap but also how certain local cultural environments can reduce these types of inequalities.

In short, this book deals with three overarching questions: Do places in the United States have different gender norms? How are these different gender norms sustained? And what are the consequences of these local norms? These questions assume, however, that culture and norms are meaningful aspects of our everyday life. Yet we are all capable of resisting these local ideologies. Why, then, do they merit our attention? And why would we believe that norms are so impactful on social life?

Local Culture, Gender Norms, and Navigating Social Life

Sociologists have studied the mechanisms through which cultural norms influence individuals' sense of self, preferences, habits, interactions with others, and values. As opposed to a unidirectional process of direct socialization where people internalize the cultural norms of the society within which they exist, scholars have shown how individuals are keenly aware of predominant social values, patterns of interaction, and expectations and strategically invoke such cultural knowledge throughout the course of their daily lives (Bourdieu 1990; DiMaggio 1997; Sewell 1992; Swidler 1986, 2001). From this perspective, macro-level norms are both constraining and liberating. Without widely acknowledged norms, social interaction would be impossible or, at least, extremely frustrating (Ridgeway 2011). At the same time, norms can limit the degree to which individuals may imagine patterns of behavior that are nonnormative (Bourdieu 1990) or constrain their ability to perform actions that will be socially condemned for violating cultural expectations (Connell 1995). In describing the liberating and constraining quality of cultural norms, Swidler (1986, 2001) refers to them as "cultural tool kits." We can deploy the tools in our cultural tool kit as we navigate social settings and interactions, but there are a limited set of tools at our disposal determined by the particular time and place within which we exist.

Gender scholars have provided a great deal of insight into the types of cultural tools that shape patterns of inequality. Researchers using an intersectional framework have shown, for example, how young women strategically conform to or reject dominant stereotypes of femininity depending on which is most advantageous in a given context (Bettie 2003; Garcia 2012). Others have shown how men use objects, such as cars or motorcycles, or activities, such as sports and weightlifting, to convey cultural meanings about their masculinity (Connell 1995; Messner 1990). These pursuits are guided by common understandings of what it means to be a successful woman or man (Connell and Messerschmidt 2005). Raewyn Connell describes such predominant ideal types as hegemonic masculinity and emphasized femininity (Connell 2013; Connell and Messerschmidt 2005). These culturally prescribed notions change over time but constitute the criteria by which women and men are often judged. In traditional contexts, for example, a man may be looked down upon if he chooses to be a stay-at-home father while his wife works to provide household income. In the same setting, a working mother may be shamed for spending too much time away from her children. Thus, each is judged against a hegemonic standard of masculinity or femininity that prescribes ideal social roles for men to be breadwinners and women to be nurturers. These hegemonic conceptions are subject to social change, allowing for the standards of masculinity/femininity to shift over time and to potentially become more egalitarian (Connell and Messerschmidt 2005).

Hegemonic notions of masculinity/femininity may also be described as one type of third-order belief—attitudes about what "most people" in their society value (Correll et al. 2017; Ridgeway and Correll 2004). Even if an individual may not personally believe that masculinity should be measured against hegemonic ideals of physical strength, for example, their understanding of how "most people" define masculinity (third-order belief) will guide them to continue to associate masculinity with strength. The concept of third-order beliefs allows for an extension of gendered cultural norms beyond the realm of defining masculinity/femininity and into the way that gendered assumptions are implicated in multiple forms of common knowledge. Beliefs around occupational fit, for example, are framed around common assumptions of the types of characteristics needed for a particular job. Police officers need to be calm under pressure, teachers need to have strong communication skills, and nurses should be attentive to detail and nurturant. The degree to which occupational characteristics are gender typed depends on predominant gender norms. In an experiment by Shelley Correll and colleagues (2017), study participants were asked to select a police chief in a conservative town in Kansas or a progressive town in Massachusetts. Despite the candidates' equivalent qualifications, participants were less likely to select a woman to be the police chief in Kansas than in Massachusetts. The reason for this difference is that the presumed gender conservatism of Kansas provided the criteria people used when choosing who to hire. Over and above individual beliefs, perceptions of how "most people" feel in a society play a significant role in shaping behavior and the degree to which it challenges or reproduces gender inequality.

Hegemonic notions of masculinity and third-order beliefs are each more specific concepts used to define the way cultural norms frame how we interpret the social world, assign value, and make decisions (DiMaggio 1997; Ridgeway 2011; Sewell 1992). Scholars have argued that gender is one of the most consequential normative frames individuals use in social life (Lorber 1995; Ridgeway 2011). During any given social interaction, behavior is coordinated based upon individuals' perception of their own gender and the gender of those around them (Ridgeway 2011). Upon meeting a woman, people may take a softer tone because of their implicit framing of women as being more receptive to nurturing behavior. The opposite may be true when interacting with a man, where gendered cultural frames may prescribe a more detached emotional demeanor. Beyond social interaction with others, however, gender norms associated with objects, occupations, or industries frame the actions of decision makers in multiple ways. Research on labor force stratification has found that hiring managers often infer that women candidates may lack agency while men may be less willing to work on teams (Bielby and Baron 1986; Tomaskovic-Devey and Stainback 2007). Applicants themselves may view their skills through a gendered lens. Studies have found that women underestimate their skills in male-dominated fields, such as math and computer science, while men often overestimate theirs (Catsambis 1994; Cech 2014; Correll 2001). Such differences result in women being more likely to exit STEM (science, technology, engineering, and mathematics) fields than men, regardless of performance (Cech 2014; Correll 2001).

Gender is a powerful cultural force shaping individuals' perceptions of themselves and their interactions with others. Yet the frames of gender vary across time and place. Gender attitudes have changed considerably over the past forty years, with women's labor force participation now widely supported (Scarborough, Sin, and Risman 2019). Consistent with this, women are now nearly as likely as men to be employed, although usually in separate occupations and for less pay (Stainback and Tomaskovic-Devey 2012). Gender attitudes also vary significantly between nations, with women's employment being widely supported in Sweden, Ireland, and Austria and more strongly opposed in nations such as Italy and Hungary (Budig, Misra, and Boeckmann 2012). Such differences have major implications on levels of gender wage equality and occupational segregation (Charles and Grusky 2004).

Gendered frames, predominant attitudes, third-order beliefs, and hegemonic notions of masculinity/femininity each constitute aspects of gender norms that shape patterns of behavior and interaction. These cultural components have been found to vary between nations and over time. Yet research has not yet examined whether places across the United States also have different gender norms. If norms are reflected in varying levels of inequality, then variation in the gender wage gap across the United States would suggest that places also have different cultural conditions that are more or less conducive to inequality.

Are Places Gendered?

When traveling across cities and towns in the United States, do we also experience a different set of gender norms along the way? Popular media would strongly suggest that we do. Sitcoms set in New York, such as *Sex and the City*, *Friends*, and *Seinfeld*, often have female leads embracing single life and independence. Meanwhile, shows set in the Midwest, such as *Home Improvement* and *Step by Step*, feature families with breadwinning fathers and nurturant mothers. The portrayal of "southern belles" provides a rather explicit ideal of femininity associated with the South (e.g., *Dukes of Hazzard*), while gendered beach bodies are portrayed as the norm along California's scenic coast (*Baywatch*).

Television may reflect local gender norms to some extent, but it is far too removed from our day-to-day lives to be taken as empirical evidence. Currently, however, there is little academic research on how gender norms differ from place to place across the United States. Studies of gender attitudes have uncovered regional differences, with the Northeast being the most egalitarian and the South having the most traditional views (Scarborough, Sin, and Risman 2019), but few have explored whether places themselves contain varying norms around gender. Exceptions exist in case studies focusing on particular locations. Brenda Parker's (2017) research on Milwaukee, for example, explored how gendered and racialized sets of cultural norms were infused within political campaigns for local leadership and the pursuant policy actions around urban development, housing, and transportation. In Milwaukee, the interests of upper-class White men were privileged in the municipality's efforts to attract investment, further disadvantaging women and people of color in the city. This work suggests that gender norms influence the inner workings and policy priorities of cities. Other research mentioned earlier in this chapter—by Miriam Abelson (2019) and Japonica Brown-Sar-acino (2017)—suggests that individuals' expression of their gender and sexual identity often depends on how they perceive the local norms where they reside. These cutting-edge studies represent some of the few analyses of more local gender norms and their effect on social life. But the case study method used in each is unable to identify the broader structure of gender norms across the United States as a whole and their widespread consequences on patterns of inequality.

While we do not yet know if cities have different gender norms, a growing body of work has identified other aspects of local culture that differ between cities. In fact, interest in local culture has permeated across the social sciences. As discussed earlier, urban scholars such as Richard Florida have examined how cities differ in cultural attributes related to nightlife and vibrancy, market researchers have focused on the construction of cultural reputations in place branding, and economists have studied the economic benefits of local cultural diversity measured through language variety, immigration density, and racial/ethnic composition. In political science, researchers have found a growing spatial divide in political ideology as rural places become increasingly conservative and urban centers embrace liberal ideals (Scala and Johnson 2017). Even the field of psychology, which is primarily concerned with individual-level phenomena, has examined how personality traits are clustered in certain geographical areas (Rentfrow, Gosling, and Potter 2008). Extraverts are concentrated in Wisconsin and Washington, D.C.; conscientiousness is more common in New Mexico and North Carolina; and neuroticism is highest in West Virginia and Rhode Island (Rentfrow 2010).

Collectively, social science has reached a general consensus that places in the United States do have distinct cultural environments that span nearly every aspect of social life. Knowingly or not, when we differentiate places using their common reputations (i.e., Philadelphia as the "City of Brotherly Love" or San Diego as "City in Motion"), we are actually touching on an empirical reality of places' unique culture. Harvey Molotch, William Freud-enburg, and Krista Paulsen (2000) refer to this collective setting as a location's place character, which they describe as the structure of feeling in a particular place that influences how people perceive themselves and their community. Such feelings of place character have major consequences on individual and collective behavior. Comparing the cities of Santa Barbara and Ventura, California, for example, Molotch and colleagues argue that the local place character of environmentalism in Santa Barbara motivated residents' action to preserve the shorefront from oil drilling—drilling that locals tolerated to a much larger degree in Ventura, where environmentalism was not part of the cultural fabric. Thus, local culture, while composed of values, feelings, and sense of place, can have real material consequences.

Place character is a part of all our communities. Social scientists have examined how these local attributes are composed of economic conditions, political environments, and even personality traits. But are they also gendered? Given that culture varies on numerous other dimensions, it is plausible that the gendered components of local character also differ by place as well. However, this has yet to be determined. Even more uncertain is how gender norms may vary from place to place. What are the different components of gender norms? What is the best way to describe these ideological aspects of local environments? Another interesting question relates to the ways these differences in local gender norms are sustained. Are egalitarian gender norms shaped by the types of people who reside in certain locations? Or do norms instead shape residents' perspectives, attitudes, and behaviors? Most importantly, what role do these gender norms play in levels of gender inequality across the United States, such as the gender wage gap? Might spatial variation in these cultural aspects help explain patterns of inequality and inform our solutions to improve women's access to opportunities and resources relative to men?

From Global to Local Studies of Gender Norms

We do not yet know the landscape of gender norms across places in the United States. However, a great deal of research has examined cross-national variation in gender norms across European countries. These studies have leveraged the fact that nations provide intuitive boundaries within which norms exist. Not only are nations separated by political boundaries, but they often coincide with marked differences in cultural attributes such as language, ethnicity, and heritage. Studying whether variation in gender norms makes up another component of national culture, researchers have found that country-level gender norms contain multiple dimensions and that these norms influence the way individuals navigate structural conditions related to job opportunities and family policy (Budig, Misra, and Boeckmann 2012; Charles and Grusky 2004; Knight and Brinton 2017). Carly Knight and Mary Brinton (2017), for example, analyzed gender attitude questions from the European Values Survey to argue that there are four dimensions of nation-level gender norms. Traditional norms convey a strong belief in men's leadership and the gendered division of labor, egalitarian familism norms support women's labor force participation but continue to endorse their primary responsibility for family caregiving, flexible egalitarianism emphasizes free choice without necessarily challenging traditional gender norms, while liberal egalitarian norms challenge gendered divisions of labor and support women's advancement. With these four dimensions, Knight and Brinton identify how nations like Italy have high levels of egalitarian familism while places like Denmark embrace the feminist ideals of liberal egalitarianism. Other research performed by gender scholars has uncovered how these countrywide norms influence residents' navigation of policy and economic environments. Nations with women-friendly public policies like paid parental leave only improve women's labor force participation if accompanied by progressive norms of gender egalitarianism (Boeckmann, Misra, and Budig 2015). Thus, cultural norms that mothers should not work and instead should focus on childcare are a major reason why maternal employment is much lower in Italy than in Germany and France, despite these nations having similar public policies around paid family leave (C. Collins 2019).

Cross-national research on gender norms has greatly advanced our understanding of how these cultural aspects of the gender structure vary geographically and their consequences on patterns of gender inequality. These studies take a macro-comparative approach through examining variation across the large-scale unit of nations. Yet, aggregating to such a broad level disregards within-nation heterogeneity. While this may be less problematic in smaller, more homogeneous countries like some found in Europe, the United States is both geographically large and highly diverse. This point emerges prominently in exploring variation in the gender wage gap between European nations and across commuting zones in the United States. In Europe, the wage gap spans from a low of 3 percent (women are paid 3 percent less than men) in Belgium to a high of nearly 26 percent in Estonia, a range of about 23 percentage points (see Figure 1.2, International Labour Organization 2018; Kremer 2018). In the United States, data from 2018 show that places like Burlington, Vermont, have a gender wage gap of 14 percent, while the wage gap is 39 percent in Lake Charles, Louisiana—a difference of 25 percentage points.

To the extent that variation in gender inequality reflects underlying cultural differences, the comparison of United States commuting zones to European nations suggests that diversity within the United States is comparable to that across Europe. However, within-nation heterogeneity in gender norms has been given far less attention. There are at least two reasons for this gap in existing research. First, it is much harder to specify the geographic units by which local norms vary within a nation than it is to rely upon well-established political boundaries in cross-national research. Second, measuring norms at a more local level presents challenges to current methodological approaches that have relied on survey data that provide large enough sample sizes within nations but are often too small to examine more detailed geo-

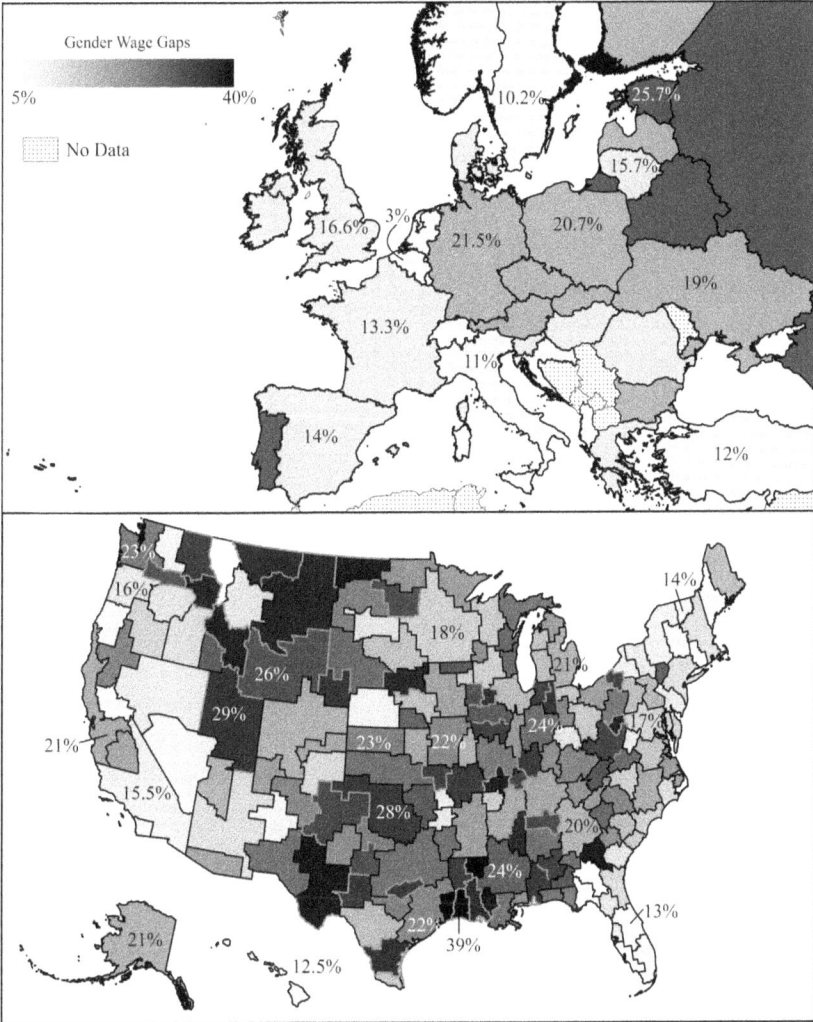

Figure 1.2 Gender Wage Gaps across European Nations and U.S. Commuting Zones

Note: U.S. and European wage gaps adjusted for human capital (except for Austria, Croatia, Denmark, Germany, Greece, Iceland, Ireland, and Belarus due to data limitations). Data on European wage gaps come from the International Labour Organization (2018). Data for Belarus are from the World Bank (Kremer 2018). Data on U.S. wage gaps are from the 2018 American Community Survey (Ruggles et al. 2021), calculated with equations discussed in Chapter 5.

graphical units. Addressing these two methodological conundrums makes it possible to explore the research questions posed here.

Focusing on the first challenge of specifying within-nation spatial units relates to the fundamental question of what, exactly, we mean by local. Research on inequality and economic growth has used a number of spatial units, including city boundaries, local labor markets, metropolitan areas, commuting zones, counties, states, and regions (Rice and Coates 1995; Davis and Dingel 2019; Florida 2012; McCall 2001; Ruppanner 2020; Scarborough and Sin 2020; Sutton, Bosky, and Muller 2016). Each unit offers different advantages and limitations. City boundaries, for example, have direct policy relevance for local municipalities. Yet, focusing primarily on those who live within a particular city leaves out the significant share of individuals who commute to cities but reside in outlying suburbs. Metropolitan areas do a better job of capturing this level of integration. However, the delineations of metropolitan areas are centered around central "cores"—densely populated urban centers. As a result, most rural or semirural areas of the United States are left out of studies using metropolitan areas. States and counties offer another set of political boundaries that scholars have used to focus on spatial variation. States are ideal for examining policy dynamics at this level of analysis, while counties offer a more detailed delineation that has remained relatively consistent over time, making it ideal for longitudinal analysis. Yet both of these boundaries impose arbitrary divisions between populations in cases where large commuting zones span several state boundaries and encompass numerous counties (e.g., Chicago, Kansas City, Memphis, New York, Omaha, Portland, St. Louis, and Washington, D.C.).

Geographers have led the way in uncovering the benefits and limitations of different spatial units of analysis. A recent study by Christopher Fowler, Leif Jensen, and Danielle Rhubart (2019) highlights the utility of three geographical units and argues that researchers should choose one depending on the purposes of their study. First, *metropolitan areas* are ideal for research focusing on dynamics occurring within and around a central urban core and an integrated periphery. This is made possible by neglecting areas of the United States that are not near a major city. Second, *local labor markets* provide greater nationwide coverage and are ideal for studies focusing on economic connection in wages and employment. Yet the focus on economic dynamics in these units often overlooks commuting patterns whereby someone lives in one labor market and works in another. Third, *labor sheds* provide, by far, the greatest measure of containment defined as the share of residents who live and work within the same geographical area. In 2010, for example, Fowler and colleagues found that 93 percent of residents lived and worked within the boundaries of a labor shed, higher than the definitions for local labor markets (86 percent) or metro areas (80 percent).

For this book, I have weighed the benefits and limitations of various geographical units for the study of local norms. Because local culture both influences and is constructed by a collectivity of people who live, work, and interact with one another, I have chosen to prioritize containment in the selection of labor sheds as the unit of analysis. This measure minimizes the degree to which local residents regularly travel across spatial borders. With fewer opportunities to interact with people from different labor sheds, the likelihood for distinct norms to develop within these units is maximized. Indeed, the analyses presented in later chapters illustrate major differences between neighboring labor sheds in local gender norms. I use the most recent definitions that demarcate 179 labor sheds across the United States (see Figure 1.3). Henceforth, I refer to labor sheds as commuting zones to emphasize the fact that they are designed to capture high levels of containment between residents' homes and place of work.

In her study of patterns of inequality across the United States, Leslie McCall (2001: 17) writes "the question of how to delimit a labor market spatially will perhaps never be answered to anyone's satisfaction." The same statement is true here. Although I have taken care to intentionally adopt a spatial unit that most readily captures local culture, many will argue that the unit is too broad, others will contend that it is too specific, and certainly many will seek

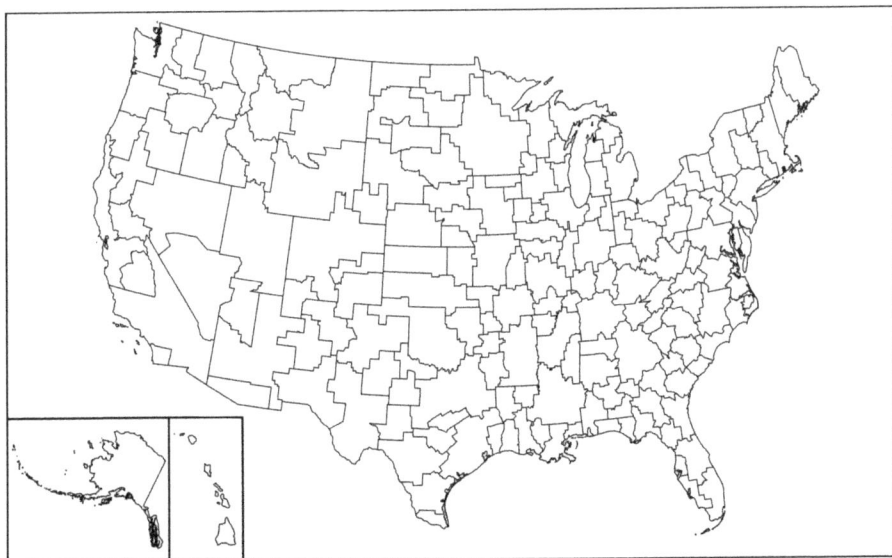

Figure 1.3 U.S. Commuting Zones

Note: Commuting zone delineations based on Bureau of Economic Analysis labor sheds (Fowler, Jensen, and Rhubart 2019).

out their community on the map and argue that its unique culture is not well represented by the associated commuting zone. I do not necessarily disagree with these arguments, but I do contend that they do not undermine the usefulness of commuting zones to study local culture. It is clear that focusing on commuting zones aggregates norms from more localized neighborhoods and cities that have important cultural differences. However, the differences between these more detailed units are less pronounced and consequential than the differences between commuting zones. Chicago's creative and eccentric Logan Square neighborhood may hold a unique space in the city's cultural milieu, but Dallas's funky Deep Ellum community occupies a similar niche within its wider geographical context. Surely there are differences between Logan Square and Deep Ellum, but these are inherently related to their ecological location within separate commuting zones. Additionally, the more detailed conceptualization of local culture, the less impact it likely has on individuals' lives since people travel through multiple neighborhoods, cities, and towns on a regular basis. Commuting zones, in comparison, are much more encompassing. The cultural characteristics of a commuting zone will be experienced by individuals while at home, at work, and during their leisure. To this end, not only do commuting zone norms have a greater role in social life, but they also consist of elements that are common across the range of geographical locations people move through in their daily routine.

Ultimately, this study does not focus on determining which geographical unit is best for the study of culture. Such work is better oriented to the expertise of geographers, who have, for their part, done an excellent job of pointing me in the direction of commuting zones as an advantageous unit for my purposes. Therefore, throughout this book I define "local" to mean the commuting zones where we live, work, and rarely exit in the course of our daily lives. The individuals occupying this shared space collectively contribute to, reproduce, and/or challenge local norms.

How Do We Measure and Observe Gender Norms?

Having defined the "local" component in the study of local culture, the second methodological challenge is determining how we measure culture at this level of analysis. Cross-national research has relied on large-scale surveys that ask respondents' attitudes about various items related to gender, such as whether a child suffers if their mother works or if men should be entitled to scarce jobs during periods of economic recession. These studies aggregate average responses to survey items for respondents from each country to calculate nation-level measures of gender norms. A strength of this approach is that it focuses on individuals' attitudes, which make up a major component of culture. Yet attitudes are not the only aspect of local culture, as individuals may hold certain values that their behavior does not align with. For example, a person may report that women are just as well suited as men for leadership positions but still exhibit cognitive gender bias against women applicants for a managerial position in their company. This is because cultural norms also manifest on a subconscious level in implicit stereotypes that frame how we interpret the behavior and performance of others (Ridgeway 2011). Such manifestations may not be readily observed in attitudinal surveys, but psychologists have developed implicit attitude tests that measure the extent to which a person holds implicit gender associations.

The many elements of culture pose challenges for quantitative research endeavoring to map the terrain of local norms and examine their consequences. Cross-national research has approached this challenge at a country level but has relied primarily on large-scale survey data, which often capture only a single aspect of culture (attitudes) and ignore within-nation heterogeneity. Even if we were to accept the limitation of focusing only on attitudes, a similar approach to studying local norms in the United States would not be possible since there is no single survey that captures all possible dimensions of gender and culture. This is one reason why most research on local gender norms in the United States has been qualitative. It may be that qualitative research is better positioned to capture the complexity and contradictions of social phenomena such as culture. By focusing on narratives, text, and symbols, qualitative research engages directly with the many ways culture is conveyed. Japonica Brown-Saracino (2017), for example, drew insight from residents' self-presentation of hair and clothing style to infer local cultural norms around butch (popular in Portland, Maine) and feminine identities (more common in Greenfield, Massachusetts).

However well equipped qualitative research is to examine local culture, it is also limited in examining questions related to general trends. In other words, it excels at depth but not breadth. This is where quantitative research provides a suitable complement. Yet, quantifying local culture is inherently difficult because culture is, by definition, immaterial in its source, becoming observable only through expression in art, attitudes, discourse, and practice. Leveraging the ubiquitous character of local culture and its effects on multiple aspects of social life, this book quantifies the presence and multiple dimensions of local norms through combining a diverse set of indicators that each capture a different manifestation of gender norms. Each indicator has been used independently in previous research but never in combination with others. By combining a large set of indicators and linking them to local commuting zones, I identify how the full collection of these cultural markers differs from one place to the next, thereby measuring spatial variation in local gender norms.

I use eight indicators that together cover the way norms manifest in attitudes, cognitive bias, public discourse, and behaviors. To measure how norms are conveyed through attitudes, I use four questions from the General Social Survey (Smith et al. 2018) that report attitudes toward women's leadership (one question), support for working mothers (two questions), and views toward the gendered division of family labor (one question). Details on question wording are provided in Chapter 2. These items have been used extensively in research examining longitudinal cultural change for the United States as a whole (Cotter, Hermsen, and Vanneman 2011; Scarborough, Sin, and Risman 2019) and have recently been applied to study local norms (Scarborough and Sin 2020; Ruppanner et al. 2021).

Although attitudinal surveys provide one reflection of culture, norms also manifest in the subtle ways that cognitive bias influences decision-making and assessments. To measure this aspect, I use data from two implicit association tests measuring gender bias against women in careers and women in science. Implicit association tests (IATs) are the most common method used to measure implicit stereotypes—individuals' subconscious associations toward different groups of people (Pratt and Crosina 2016). Unlike attitudinal survey items, which record explicitly stated opinions, IATs are designed to measure the extent to which individuals hold stereotypical views they may not openly express or act upon but are nonetheless oriented toward (Greenwald, McGhee, and Schwartz 1998). Scholars have argued that these implicit attitudes reflect one's cultural settings, as stereotypes become internalized within individuals' subconscious over time (Xu et al. 2018). The largest set of IATs is conducted through Project Implicit (Xu et al. 2018), where researchers have developed numerous tests of implicit attitudes toward identities such as race, gender, disability, sexuality, and age. Two IATs measure implicit gender bias. The Gender-Career IAT measures stereotypes against women in careers, and the Gender-Science IAT captures stereotypes against women in the physical sciences. These tests are publicly available online and have been completed over one million times since their launch in 2005 and 2003, respectively.

In addition to expressed attitudes or implicit bias, norms also manifest in everyday behaviors. One need only to log on to their social media account to see cultural production in real time as users express their views, comment on public issues, and share their interests. Indeed, researchers have taken advantage of the cataloging of discourse on social media to study multiple aspects of culture, such as public sentiment, social networking, and activism (Earl and Kimport 2011; Mejova, Weber, and Macy 2015). Gender scholars have directed much attention to social media in the study of feminism, as movements like the Women's March and #MeToo were organized and publicized in online spaces (Crossley 2017). Drawing on the way culture is reflected in public discourse as well as the growing importance of social media to feminism, I also include a measure of local sentiment toward feminism expressed on Twitter in each commuting zone as an additional indicator of local gender norms.

Last, I examine gendered patterns in college major selection as an indicator of gender norms manifesting through individuals' preferences for certain fields of study as well as the subtle directives they receive from others that may push them out of subjects that are atypical for someone of their gender. Comparative research has used gender segregation in college graduates' field of study as an indicator of gender norms (Charles and Bradley 2009). Scholars have argued that the association of women with nurturance is reflected in their predominance in expressive fields of study, such as the humanities or liberal arts, while the stereotype of men as agentic leads to their overrepresentation in the physical sciences, where the manipulation of objects plays a more central role (Cech 2013). Therefore, as a final indicator of culture, I examine differences between commuting zones in the gender segregation of field of study among those with a college degree.

Collectively, I use eight different variables from four different data sources to measure the various ways gender norms are reflected. I provide more detail on each variable in Chapter 2, where I apply them in developing a quantified measure of local gender norms. Integrating such a diverse set of indicators, each of which has been used independently in previous research on gender and culture, also allows me to explore whether local gender norms contain multiple dimensions. It is possible, for example, that places may have egalitarian norms around the division of family labor but still maintain widespread beliefs that women and men are suited for different types of work in the labor force. Thus, combining such a diverse set of cultural indicators not only allows for comprehensive measurement of the way norms manifest but also enables me to examine whether local gender norms are multidimensional. Including a range of indicators also has methodological benefits to measuring norms. As discussed at length in Chapter 2, each single indicator reflects both the influence of gender norms as well as other aspects of commuting zones. Segregation in college graduates' field of study, for example, may reflect norms as well as economic opportunities. By focusing on correlations between indicators, I parse out aspects that contribute to each indicator independently and instead measure the underlying factors that link indicators together: local gender norms.

The large-scale approach of measuring gender norms across all United States commuting zones is one major contribution of this book. It is important to note, however, that achieving this aim comes at some expense of capturing the uniqueness of each place's history and background. For example, Chapter 3 illustrates how local norms in Minneapolis and Boston have similar levels of egalitarianism. Despite these shared characteristics, however, these two places have distinct histories. Boston has long been a leader in the national feminist movement. It was home to the first grassroots organizing for women's suffrage in the late 1800s (Berenson 2018), the location where some of the most influential intersectional feminist groups first formed (Combahee River Collective [1978] 2014), and one of the first cities to establish women's health clinics and women's centers, many of which are still active today (Spain 2011). Feminist organizing is also central to the history of Minneapolis, but in this location, Scandinavian cultural heritage played a much larger role. According to Anna Peterson (2011), suffragist movements in Minneapolis were often built from coalitions between Norwegian and Swedish ethnic groups who advocated for the United States to follow countries like Norway in allowing women to vote. This legacy continues, as scholars such as Robert Putnam (2001) have drawn a connection between Minneapolis's high levels of social capital to values of welfare rooted in local Scandinavian culture.

In this book, I do not capture a level of detail that would differentiate the unique histories, traditions, and events shaping local culture in specific places like Minneapolis and Boston. Such an approach requires a much deeper dive into a smaller number of locations. Doing so would make it impossible to map the terrain of gender norms across the United States or examine their broader relationship to patterns of inequality. Instead, I take for granted that places have distinct histories and particularities that, despite their uniqueness, may lead them to similar outcomes in terms of contemporary gender norms. Taking these liberties allows me to make broader comparisons between a comprehensive set of locations. Whereas a more detailed approach focusing on a smaller set of case study locations is limited in making generalizable claims, the method I adopt here is ideally suited for examining not only differences between two places but broader patterns across the entire United States. I do not argue that my approach is any better or worse than one that devotes greater detail to a smaller number of places. Instead, I view this book as complementing prior studies that have used more detailed qualitative methods. Research by scholars such as Japonica Brown-Saracino, Katja Guenther, Harvey Molotch, and Krista Paulsen has documented the historical conditions that lead places to develop distinct cultures as well as the ways these local environments shape individuals' experiences and personal identity. Their case study research on specific locations has established that places have unique configurations of norms that play a large role in social life. My aim in this book is to build from this theoretical foundation to explore how these norms are geographically patterned, how this spatial variation is sustained, and the broader relationship of local gender norms to levels of inequality.

Throughout subsequent chapters, I uncover, map, and identify the consequences of local gender norms across the United States. In pursuit of these aims, I adopt a theoretical lens that focuses primarily on the gendered components of local culture and pays less attention to the many other aspects that comprise places' unique character. As discussed earlier in this chapter, previous research has identified components of local culture related to political orientation, bohemianism, tourism, and even personality traits such as conscientiousness. A focus on local gender norms does not imply that gendered components are any more important or influential than other aspects of culture. Instead, what makes local gender norms unique is that they have not yet been identified and mapped to a similar extent as other cultural features of places. Presently, local gender norms remain unidentified beyond the few locations that have been examined as case studies. Imposing a theoretical lens that focuses on gender norms simplifies the multitude of features comprising dynamic local cultures in order to identify what often goes unnoticed: the subtle, yet influential, ways that gender norms spatially vary across the United States. I do not intend to develop a fully comprehensive theory of local culture. Instead, my aim is to identify local gender norms as one critical component that has not yet been fully considered but plays a fundamental role in society.

Organization of the Book

This book includes six chapters that collectively examine three guiding questions: Do gender norms vary across the United States? How are these norms sustained? What are their consequences on social life? You are now reading the first chapter, where I review the context for this book and the driving motivations for the questions explored. Chapter 2, "Gendered Places: Local Configurations of Gender Norms," applies existing theories of gender norms to examine local variation in these cultural attributes across the United States. Some scholars have conceptualized gender norms as varying unidimensionally from traditional to egalitarian. Others have argued that norms are different when directed toward the public sphere of work and the private sphere of family, while a third set of researchers contends that norms contain a vertical component pertaining to men's access to power and leadership and a horizontal component conveying essential difference between women and men. Testing each of these theories with a set of cultural indicators that reflect various aspects of local gender norms across the United States reveals that commuting zones are characterized by a structure of gender norms that combines previous theories to identify vertical and horizontal elements occurring separately in the public and private spheres. This integrated model contains four dimensions of gender norms, described as *women's leadership, public sphere gender essentialism, intensive mothering,* and *private sphere gender essentialism*. Recognizing the multidimensional as-

pects of local gender norms allows us to consider how places may be egalitarian in some respects while retaining traditional norms in other areas.

The third chapter, "Mapping the Terrain of Local Gender Norms," extends the model of gender norms from Chapter 2 to examine the diversity
of gendered cultural environments across the United States. First, I use a series of nationwide visualizations to map each dimension of gender norms
across the United States as whole. Then, I zoom in to focus on a set of locations
that illustrate configurations of local gender norms. Boston and Minneapolis are two locations with highly egalitarian norms across all dimensions. In
direct contrast, Columbus and Salt Lake City have universally traditional
norms. Further yet, New Orleans and San Francisco have contradictory configurations of gender norms; they are egalitarian in some respects but traditional in others. When discussing each commuting zone, I contextualize
measures of local gender norms by drawing on previously published qualitative studies that have interviewed residents in each location. Interpreting
qualitative patterns with respect to local cultural environments highlights
how individuals' everyday lives differ in ways that correspond to prevailing
gender norms in the community where they reside. Chapter 3 closes by comparing sets of commuting zones that share similar economic characteristics
but nonetheless have very different configurations of gender norms. Las Vegas, Miami, and Nashville each have large service sectors oriented toward
tourism but have vastly different configurations of local norms that range
from generally egalitarian (Las Vegas), to contradictory (Miami), to mostly
traditional (Nashville). Cleveland and Detroit are both Midwest manufacturing hubs, but norms are far more egalitarian in Detroit than they are in
Cleveland. The tech sector predominates in the coastal cities of Boston and
Seattle. Yet norms are more egalitarian in Boston, particularly toward intensive mothering and private sphere gender essentialism. These initial patterns
suggest that norms are not reducible to economic composition but instead
constitute independent features of places in their own right.

If norms are a core characteristic of places, where do they come from
and how are they sustained? This is explored in the fourth chapter, titled
"What Sustains Local Gender Norms?" In this section of the book, I examine two possible mechanisms driving variation in gender norms across the
United States. These mechanisms, compositional and contextual effects,
were discussed earlier in this chapter. Compositional effects drive variation
in gender norms through differences between places in the demographic
characteristics of the people who live there. Contextual effects, in contrast,
occur when areas' gender norms influence the attitudes and behaviors of
residents. Examining the extent that these two perspectives help explain
local variation in gender norms shows that context plays a larger role than

composition. It is the cultural features of places that shape residents, rather than the demographic characteristics of residents that shape places. This is particularly true in areas with traditional gender norms, where those who would usually espouse gender egalitarian beliefs (such as the college educated) hold more conventional attitudes.

If gender norms shape individuals' attitudes and behaviors, what relation do they have to patterns of gender inequality? Chapter 5, "Culture's Consequences: The Relationship of Local Gender Norms to Inequality," examines this question by investigating the link between the four dimensions of gender norms and levels of the gender wage gap across United States commuting zones. Egalitarian norms toward women's advancement, public sphere gender essentialism, and private sphere gender essentialism are related to lower gender wage gaps. After establishing this general relationship, I then explore two possible mechanisms driving this pattern. First, norms may shape wage gaps through the *occupational sorting* of women and men into different jobs with varying pay. In traditional environments, women may more commonly prefer jobs in the care sector, which have lower wages than jobs that men conventionally prefer. In addition, hiring managers may be more likely to discriminate, either explicitly or implicitly, against women applicants in high-paying male-dominated occupations in commuting zones with traditional norms. Together, these cultural processes operate to sort women into lower-paying and men into higher-paying occupations, therefore leading to larger gender wage gaps. The second possible mechanism is *within-occupation valuation*. Differences in the value placed on women and men holding the same occupation often result in gender wage gaps between workers in the same role. Norms conveying women as essentially suited for caregiving tasks can make it difficult for supervisors to notice their broader contributions while also fostering expectations that women workers perform the majority of "office housework," such as administrative and planning tasks, that do not directly lead to raises, bonuses, or promotions. Through these processes, gender norms may shape the differential value placed on women and men holding the same occupation.

Focusing on four key occupations capturing varying levels of pay, gender composition, and required skills shows that gender norms operate through both occupational sorting and within-occupation valuation, but under certain conditions. Egalitarian gender norms support women's entry into high-paying managerial and STEM occupations as well as men's entry into office administration roles, which reduces women's concentration in this low-paying job. As a result, one way that norms relate to wage gaps is through facilitating the occupational sorting of women out of lower-paying feminized jobs and into higher-paying positions. Yet egalitarian gender norms also facilitate women's entry into low-paying, male-dominated blue-collar occupa-tions, indicating that gender norms shape patterns of occupational segrega-tion in ways that may not always translate into increased earnings but nonetheless facilitate more integrated labor markets. Within occupations, local gender norms only facilitate more equitable valuation of women's and men's labor in occupations with a substantial share of women workers, such as management (43 percent women) and office administration (73 percent women). Male-dominated STEM (70 percent men) and blue-collar (83 per-cent men) occupations, in contrast, constitute employment settings where local norms of egalitarianism are resisted and men retain wage premiums in spite of prevailing values of gender equality. These patterns reflect the fact that norms are not deterministic but can be contested based on the interests of individuals or subgroups. Nonetheless, Chapter 5 shows a strong relation-ship between local norms of egalitarianism and greater wage equality that is sustained broadly through occupational sorting and, in certain settings, within-occupation valuation. Chapter 5 closes with a discussion of the re-cursive relationship between gender norms and forms of inequality such as the gender wage gap. Norms and wage gaps constitute a reflexive and self-reinforcing feedback loop. Gender wage gaps confirm norms at the same time that norms reinforce material inequalities between women and men.

The concluding chapter, "Advancing Equality at the Local Level," first summarizes key points from the book and reflects on important areas of research still to be done. This book adopts a theoretical framework that highlights the gendered aspects of local cultural environments, but these norms are also deeply connected to structures of racial inequality and cul-tural norms characterizing patterns of racism. I theorize on the ways local gender norms intersect with local structures of racial inequality with the aim of supporting future work that incorporates this level of complexity.

The final chapter also discusses the book's implications for social policy and efforts toward achieving gender equality. This monograph is designed to inform residents in communities across the United States about the role of local gender norms in social life. With an awareness of the cultural envi-ronments we live within and navigate, we can be intentional about choosing actions that contribute to local norms and advance social policies that pro-mote equality. For those in positions to enact policy change at a local level, the book is a call to action. Egalitarian gender norms promote the well-being of local communities, but these norms need to be complemented by policy conditions that cement egalitarian ideals. Increasing funding for childcare programs, thinking critically about how school-day lengths affect parents, and ensuring, at a minimum, that men and women who work for the gov-ernment and government contractors are paid equally are the types of pol-icies that can be done by local governments to improve gender equity and residents' lives. Some municipalities and states throughout the United States have instituted these types of programs. This work is highlighted throughout the chapter as models for other communities to follow. Directing efforts to local change creates new opportunities to advance gender equality. Areas with progressive gender norms can leverage local consensus to build support and implement policies that assist families in pursuing gender egalitarian ideals. There is no need to wait for federal legislation when such change can occur much faster in our local communities. Implementing these types of policies at a local level can also prove their effectiveness, building a stronger argument for national implementation through federal legislation.

This book serves as a reminder of the important work done by social movement activists and advocacy groups who are leading cultural change. By questioning cultural assumptions around gender, feminist activists have continually advanced gender norms of egalitarianism. Whether individuals identify as feminists or not, we are collectively influenced by the new ideas and ways of perceiving gender that are advocated by these groups of change makers.

This book is also written for researchers and scholars in the social sciences. By introducing a framework for describing the multidimensional structure of local gender norms, this book advances a way of conceptualizing how places can exhibit traditional tendencies on some dimensions while being egalitarian in others. In other words, places are not simply more or less egalitarian but differ in complicated ways across various cultural components and aspects of society. This framework may be useful in research contextualizing the dynamic way cultural environments shape individuals' lived experiences. It also makes visible the important role of local culture in patterns of inequality. While more difficult to quantify than economic conditions, local gender norms have profound effects on disparities between women and men. A major goal of this book is to make these relationships visible so that interventions can be made in fostering local cultures that promote equality.

Motivations

There are two major motivations for this book. First, I hope to reveal to readers the ubiquitous context of gender norms that we navigate each day and how these vary from place to place. By presenting empirical evidence for the presence of gender norms and providing a theoretical lens to conceptualize them, my hope is that individuals may rearticulate the challenges they face in life not as stemming from individualized troubles but as inherently related to the social context within which they reside (Mills 2000). My second motivation is that, with an understanding of gender norms, we can intentionally challenge norms that make people's lives harder and support those that progress us toward social equality and well-being. As I show in the following pages, gender norms that convey women as less agentic, less independent, and essentially different from men undermine their opportunities in the labor force and foster inequality in families. But norms are not immutable. Norms both influence patterns of human behavior and are reinforced by that very behavior. Therefore, an awareness of problematic norms can break the cycle as individuals consider how their taken-for-granted cultural assumptions are related to inequality.

To a large degree, social activist groups have had great success in questioning widespread cultural patterns that reproduce inequality. The civil rights movement challenged de jure racial discrimination under Jim Crow through protests and demonstrations showing the harmful effects of racism and racist institutions on African Americans throughout the country. Today, the Black Lives Matter movement does similar work. By proclaiming that Black lives matter, these activists enact a discursive agenda intended to shed light on the many ways in society that Black lives are physically harmed and culturally erased. In relation to gender, the feminist movement has played a tremendous role in altering gender norms over the past century. Feminist writers like Simone de Beauvoir, Angela Davis, and Shulamith Firestone challenged women's role as a complementary support to men. Feminist activism from the 1970s through today has continued to challenge traditional gender norms and inequality. Public demonstrations and consciousness-raising groups organized by feminist activists have the explicit aim of shedding light on the challenges posed by gender norms that constrain women's opportunities. While we have not fully achieved the goal of gender equality, the feminist movement was, and continues to be, successful in advancing these aims. In 1950, only about a third of women participated in the labor force, but by 2020 women's labor force participation rate had grown to 58 percent (U.S. Census Bureau 2020). In 1980, women were paid 36 percent less than men, but by 2018 the gender wage gap had fallen by almost half to 18.9 percent (Hegewisch and Hartmann 2019). In education, there has been even greater transformation. In 1967, men were nearly twice as likely to receive a college degree than women, but since 2015 women now slightly surpass men in college degree attainment (Ryan and Bauman 2016).

It is without question that we have made major strides toward gender equality. But the unfortunate truth is that we still have a long way to go. Women's labor force participation rate, while at an all-time high, remains ten percentage points less than men (U.S. Census Bureau 2020). The gender wage gap is smaller than it was in 1980, but it has not improved much at all in the past decade and remains substantial (Hegewisch and Hartmann 2019). Furthermore, the gender wage gap for Black and Hispanic women is even greater than that for White women. In 2018, White women earned eighty-two cents for every dollar earned by White men, while Black women earned sixty-five cents and Hispanic women sixty-two cents (Hegewisch and Hartmann 2019). Even in the field of education, where we have seen major progress in women's overall levels of achievement, inequality remains through the stark segregation of women and men into different educational fields. Presently, less than 25 percent of bachelor's degrees in the fields of engineering and computer science are awarded to women (Catalyst 2020). These challenges have only grown worse during the COVID-19 pandemic, which has disproportionately affected women. Although we have yet to uncover the full extent that the pandemic has set us back in terms of reaching gender equality, early evidence has shown that women's labor force participation has fallen precipitously alongside a reversion to traditional family arrangements where women have taken on the majority of housework, caregiving, and home-schooling tasks in the context of pandemic lockdowns and school closures (C. Collins et al. 2021).

Gender inequality remains a defining characteristic of U.S. society. In this book, I argue that focusing on change at a local level offers a strategic advantage in advancing efforts toward greater equality between women and men. Although federal legislation is the route for the largest and most far-reaching impact, long-standing gridlock at the federal level has prevented any real comprehensive legislation from passing over the last several decades. Despite overwhelming public support for issues like gun control and immigration reform, the U.S. Congress has failed, repeatedly, to pass any comprehensive bills on this issue. The record on gender is not much better. Despite passing both the House and the Senate in 1971 and 1972, the Equal Rights Amendment (ERA), which would amend the constitution to guarantee equal rights to women and men, failed to garner enough state ratifications by the original deadline of 1977. Renewed feminist activism has generated new support for the ERA, with resolutions recently passing in Nevada, Illinois, and Virginia. Yet it is unclear whether these state ratifications are symbolic, as they occurred long past the original deadline. Nonetheless, the ERA was introduced to Congress in 1971 and did not receive the necessary number of state ratifications until 2020. Federal legislation for gender equality is necessary and important, but five decades to pass an amendment with broad support is too long.

Despite its challenges, we should continue to push for change at the federal level that supports gender equality. At the same time, however, we can advance change in our communities. Local governments have constituents who are more likely to hold similar political and social views, making consensus easier to achieve. In instances where disagreements arise, they are more likely to be resolved as they are less entrenched in long-standing partisan feuds and more firmly based on issues pertaining to the well-being of the community. Bruce Katz and Jeremy Nowak (2017) argue that these qualities of local governments make them pivotal actors in the future of the United States. Increasingly, municipalities are the "testing ground" for progressive policies that are too risky or controversial to pass at a federal level but receive broad support at a local level. Washington, D.C., for example, recently passed a policy for paid parental leave providing mothers and fathers eight weeks of leave while receiving up to 90 percent of their salary. As this program runs successfully, other municipalities may follow suit, helping build a case for broader, nationwide implementation.

Making local change starts with recognizing and shifting local norms. It is no surprise that Washington, D.C., passed such gender-progressive policy. As I show in later chapters, the nation's capital has some of the most egalitarian gender norms in the country. In other areas with more traditional norms where women are expected to stay home to perform childcare, it is unlikely that a community will pass a policy for paid parental leave. However, residents are not merely subject to local norms. Instead, they are active participants in the reproduction, or transformation, of their local cultural environments. In a traditional context, for example, each time a man passes a baby with a dirty diaper to a nearby woman, they are reproducing norms that childcare is women's work. When schools habitually call mothers instead of fathers to inform parents of a sick child, they reinscribe gendered divisions of labor. When managers ask a woman supervisor, but not a man supervisor of equal rank, to take notes at a meeting, they perpetuate norms around the type of work women and men are suited for. By viewing each of these instances as not only individual acts but reflections of broader cultural norms that reproduce gender difference and inequality, we can empower ourselves to change those norms through intentional behavior. Dads, uncles, and grandfathers can take a larger part in diaper duty, managers can be sure that administrative work is shared equally among colleagues, and schools can disrupt gender norms by more commonly calling fathers to communicate information and make requests, such as when a sick child needs to be taken home.

The purpose of this book is to shed light on the invisible, yet highly consequential, structure of gender norms that we live within and negotiate on a daily basis. For only through noticing these norms and recognizing their consequences can we take intentional efforts to change them. By focusing on the places where we live and work, this book intends to be relevant for all readers interested in improving their communities—asking them to take notice of the subtle actions that reproduce local norms and question whether they advance social equity or impede it.

2

Gendered Places

Local Configurations of Gender Norms

In the film *The Beverly Hillbillies*, based on the popular television series from the 1960s, a humble family from Missouri discovers a massive oil deposit on their property and sells it to an energy company for millions. With their new fortune, the family—which includes Jed Clampett; his daughter, Elly May; his mother-in-law, Granny; and his nephew, Jethro—decides to move to Beverly Hills, California. The Clampett family purchases a mansion like many others in the affluent suburb of Los Angeles, but their riches cannot hide the many ways in which they do not belong. Jed's preference for carrying around a massive shotgun and Granny's tendency to pick up roadkill to cook for supper give them away as out-of-towners whose family culture is quite different from the norm in Southern California. One of the primary plots in the film highlights Elly May's adjustment to her new high school. On her first day, Elly May dresses in a tight-fitting and low-cut denim outfit, donning a straw hat over her long blond hair. The neighbor boy giving her a ride to school is speechless on arrival, as Elly May's southern style emulates his version of attractive hyperfemininity that contrasts sharply with the more casual fashion of most girls at the local high school. If her uniquely feminine style did not make her stand out enough, Elly May soon challenges the captain of the men's wrestling team, Derek, to a match after she sees him bullying another boy. In front of the whole school, Elly May easily defeats him, ending by triumphantly swinging Derek in circles and throwing him outside the wrestling mat and onto his back.

The Beverly Hillbillies film grossed $57 million and topped the weekend box office earnings shortly after its release. The television series was even more popular, ranking as the number one show in the United States for its first two seasons. The fumblings of a family navigating a new culture in a new home struck a chord with the American public. Certainly, many of us have felt out of place when relocating or traveling, if only to a lesser extreme than the Clampetts. My first time in New York, I felt like I was going to be run over on the sidewalk for walking too slow! When visiting San Diego, I was constantly feeling overdressed in what I thought was casual attire of jeans and a button-up, in stark contrast to the flip-flops and beach shorts that were the more common style. After moving to Chicago, I quickly learned I would have to adjust my commute to account for time talking to neighbors on their stoop, something I did not encounter much at all while living in Grand Rapids, Michigan.

Beyond trivial familiarities, however, adjusting to local culture also has gendered elements. This was most visible in Elly May's transition to her new school and friends. On one hand, Elly May's personal style was much more feminine than the other girls at her school. Emblematic of country and southern forms of femininity, Elly May wore more makeup and revealing clothes than was usual for young women in Southern California. On the other hand, Elly May's physical strength and aggressiveness, illustrated in her wrestling match with the school bully, revealed another aspect of difference between Elly May's conceptions of femininity and those of women in her new home. In Missouri, it was common for women, even ones as pretty as Elly May, to perform physically strenuous work, hunt, or even wrestle a bear (as one scene depicts). Such displays of strength were so unusual for women in Southern California that students filled the gymnasium to watch Elly May defeat Derek in wrestling. Viewed from this perspective, Elly May's adjustment to her new school reveals dynamic and multiple ways that gender is infused with local norms. While Elly May's style was much more feminine than other girls, her strength and willingness to take on a fight embodied traits more common among men, and far less common among women, in Beverly Hills.

While we cannot say with certainty whether Elly May's experience is common or representative (it comes from a fictional movie and television series, after all), it does pose some important questions about the gendered aspects of local culture. Sociologists and urbanists have long studied the role of locally bound cultural environments in people's lives. To this end, research has established that areas do have unique cultural settings that become embedded in individuals' personalities and patterns of behavior. As discussed in the introductory chapter, sociologists have referred to this as "place character"—the set of traditions, values, and rituals that define and continually reinscribe the immaterial aspects of an area and the identities of the people who live there (Molotch, Freudenburg, and Paulsen 2000; Paulsen 2004). Only recently, however, have scholars started to pay closer attention to the gendered elements of local culture and place character. In one example, Elizabeth Bruch and Mark Newmann (2018) analyzed data from an online dating website to find that both women and men, but especially men, use more words and are more positive when sending messages to potential dates in Seattle than in Boston. Other research focusing on college campuses has found that feminist groups receive more support in cities in the Northeast than the Midwest (Reger 2012). While studies such as these suggest that local cultural elements related to gender shape interactions between women and men and the viability of feminist activism, they do not directly examine the contextual conditions of local gender norms as distinct attributes of place character.

This chapter examines whether places in the United States have different gender norms that are reflected in patterns of residents' behaviors and attitudes. First, I dig a bit deeper into research on local culture more broadly, reviewing the ways that place character has been found to shape social life and individuals' sense of self. Then, I outline what we already know about gender norms and their applicability to local culture. While many studies focus on the way norms relate to individual-level behavior, our understanding of gender norms is primarily restricted to its nation-level manifestations. Using this research as a foundation to examine norms at the more local level of commuting zones, I outline three frameworks that have been used to describe the structure of gender norms in cross-national studies. Some scholars view gender norms as unidimensional, ranging along a single cultural scale from traditional to egalitarian (Inglehart and Norris 2003). Others have examined gender norms through the lens of "separate spheres," where gender attitudes, expectations, and behaviors are differentiated between the two social realms of work and family (Scarborough, Sin, and Risman 2019). A third conceptualization of gender norms argues that they have two dimensions: a vertical dimension describing norms around men's power, privilege, and authority over women and a horizontal dimension reinforcing the notion that women and men are inherently different and therefore should be found in separate (but not necessarily unequal) social positions (Charles and Bradley 2009; Charles and Grusky 2004). After reviewing these existing theories on the structure of gender norms, I introduce a fourth approach that combines public/private and horizontal/vertical frameworks by examining how vertical and horizontal elements exist within both private and public spheres.

I illustrate the applicability of each of these four frameworks using a set of eight theoretically informed cultural indicators. Comparing the strengths of the different frameworks in describing the relationship between this set of indicators reveals that an integrated model conceptualizing local gender norms as being composed of four dimensions with vertical and horizontal components in the public and private spheres provides the most accurate description of the gendered components of local culture. By recognizing local gender norms as multidimensional across these four components, we can better account for instances such as Elly May's, where her Missouri roots made her much more traditional than her new Southern California peers in some aspects while simultaneously challenging conventional gender norms in other respects.

Culture and Social Life

The sociological study of culture asks two fundamental questions: How does culture affect social life? How is culture maintained, challenged, and/or transformed by social action? The investigation of these questions examines the many taken-for-granted assumptions we use while navigating our daily lives. Subtleties in human interaction, seemingly trivial traditions or habits, and even patterns of speech and language formation can reflect and reinforce widespread cultural ideologies that steer patterns of behaviors and shape our relationships with others. Of course, we are not totally controlled by cultural conditions. Indeed, many individuals react against cultural norms. But even in these cases, no one can fully avoid the culture they live within, they can only respond to it.

While a cornerstone of social theory is that culture structures social life in patterned ways (Griswold 1994), there is far less agreement about how this occurs. Theorists from the mid-twentieth century, including Talcott Parsons, argued that culture is a system of norms and values shaping individuals' attitudes and behaviors through direct socialization (Parsons [1951] 1991). By merely existing in a certain place and time, we unwittingly internalize prevalent cultural norms and assume corresponding ways of behavior. While this perspective predominated in the mid-twentieth century, it remains only somewhat popular today, with scholars like Geert Hofstede (1984: 9) stating that culture is "the collective programming of the mind." Instead, many theorists have critiqued this heavy-handed socialization approach for perceiving individuals as passive recipients of cultural instructions, rather than agentic actors who engage more intentionally with local norms, values, and traditions (Wrong 1961). As stated by Harold Garfinkel (1991: 68), this classical understanding views an individual as a "cultural dope," "who produces the stable features of the society by acting in compliance with pre-established and legitimate alternatives of action that the common culture provides." In other words, there is no individual agency or choice in these classical socialization-based models of culture, only the collective following of cultural directives.

Socialization approaches to culture, despite their limitations in accounting for human agency, shed important light on the tremendous role of culture in social life. Critiques of this classical approach also helped form the foundation for contemporary sociological theories of culture. Today, while there is agreement that culture generates social patterns, there is debate over the mechanisms involved. Pierre Bourdieu (1984) also proposed a "strong arm" theory of culture, albeit to a lesser degree than Parsons, by arguing that culture provides a constrained set of identities, tastes, and activities that are imaginable at a given time and place. He used the term "habitus" to describe the unconscious patterns of behavior associated with one's origins in a certain cultural environment. Bourdieu's theory of culture is designed to help explain the reproduction of power and inequality by examining how social class distinction is composed not only by economic resources but by a set of cultural norms that differentiate upper, lower, and working classes. In applying Bourdieu's theory of culture, Julie Bettie's (2003) ethnography of California high schoolers showed how working-class youth adopted raggedy clothing styles and informal ways of speech that were explicitly class coded. While it helped form group solidarity, it also clearly differentiated them from upper-class students who wore name-brand clothes, took honors classes, and spoke more formally (particularly with teachers). Not only did working-class youth feel uncomfortable acting any other way, but the boundaries of class culture were policed by peers' claims that students were "posing" if they dressed less casually or spoke with greater acumen.

Bourdieu's theory of culture expands from traditional conceptions by highlighting variation in cultural expectations and values across social class. As a result, this approach better conceptualizes how culture reinforces differences between groups and plays a role in reproducing inequality. Yet, many have argued that this conception still does not allow for individual agency and the ability for people to react against their cultural environment. As a result, additional theories have been proposed to better account for individuals' freedom of action. Some view culture's internalization as creating a schema by which those in a shared society attach meaning to social objects and interactions (DiMaggio 1997; Sewell 1992). From this perspective, culture frames the choices we make by attaching values to certain outcomes. Others attribute far less causal power to culture's effect on human behavior by arguing that its primary influence comes into play as individuals make post hoc justifications for prior behavior (Boltanski and Thévenot 2006). From this perspective, people are adept cultural navigators and draw upon available tropes, turns of phrase, and sometimes contradictory sets of values to justify their choices and achieve their desired ends. A personal example illustrates how cultural knowledge may be used to justify personal action. In explaining our decision to move from Chicago to Dallas, over one thousand miles from our family, my wife and I used different justifications for each of our parents that would appeal to their cultural values. For my in-laws, we spoke of the job opportunities we both received that offered fulfilling work with students at a public university. For my parents, we focused on the lower cost of living that allowed us to afford a more comfortable home to raise our son. Far from being cultural dopes, we strategically invoked different justifications based upon our understanding of each parents' values.

If individuals draw upon their cultural knowledge to navigate life, interpret observations, and justify their decisions, where does this knowledge come from? It is not as though each of us is born with an endless understanding of cultural nuance. Ultimately, even if we adopt a more flexible approach to conceptualizing culture that emphasizes human agency, we must still acknowledge the preconditions set for us by our cultural environment in shaping the options we have for action and our ideas of how our behaviors may be interpreted by others. In theorizing both the constraining and enabling effects of culture, Ann Swidler (1986, 2001) uses the metaphor of a "tool kit." The cultural tool kit describes the host of cultural knowledge we carry with us that helps us navigate social interactions and dynamics. The items in our tool kit are a function of the cultural environments we are familiar with. Thus, drawing important points from Bourdieu's approach, individuals' do not possess total knowledge of cultural nuance. But neither are they culture dopes. Instead, considering both how cultural conditions set the basis for what types of action are even imaginable, as well as individuals' agency in choosing cultural values to inform their action, the notion of a cultural tool kit integrates culture as constraining to the extent that each of us has a limited set of cultural "tools" to draw upon while also recognizing culture as enabling in the ways that individuals have choice over which cultural tools they wish to use.

The tool kit approach to culture allows for an understanding that individuals are not passive recipients of culture while at the same time acknowledging that culture does have tremendous effects on social life. Such dynamics were illustrated in Nikki Jones's (2010) research on young Black women in Philadelphia. The women interviewed by Jones were well aware of the stereotypes they faced and the threat of their actions placing them in one of two cultural archetypes: good or ghetto. Some young women even toed the line between these personas—drawing from their cultural knowledge to display a "good" identity in one context and a "ghetto" one in another depending on which was most advantageous and, in many circumstances, offered the most protection. Jones's interviewees expressed agency in the types of ideals they expressed and the characteristics they conveyed, but their choice of available repertoires for identity was predetermined by macro-level factors related to larger cultural ideologies and stereotypes around race, gender, and class.

Cultural tool kits and common understandings of norms and values allow us to navigate social interactions and contexts—that is, until they do not. As comically illustrated with the example from *The Beverly Hillbillies* that opened this chapter, when we move from place to place, we often discover that our cultural tool kit is missing several necessary items and contains others that are no longer relevant and may even get us into trouble. Such awkward interactions suggest that there is a strong geographical component to the way that culture shapes social life. Indeed, sociologists have found major differences between the geographies of cities, metro areas, and nations in local culture and collective sense of place. Studying intellectuals across Italy, Norway, and the United States, Wendy Griswold (2008) identified distinct regional cultures reflected in book readers' adoration of literature conveying aesthetics associated with a particular place. Carl Sandburg's poetry, for example, has become a central part of Chicago's identity, as the city's moniker as the "City of Big Shoulders" was first coined in Sandburg's 1914 poem describing the rough-and-tumble atmosphere of the rising industrial hub. Studying local culture in Memphis, Zandria Robinson (2014) observed how Black residents construct distinct regional identities through drawing on differences in food, music, and fashion from Northern cities. Other studies have examined the way regional identities surface in popular music. Nashville is associated with country music, Detroit with Motown, and New Orleans with jazz. But these associations are more than just novelties, as Nashville's country music scene emulates the areas' broader country-western cultural identity (Wynn 2015). Regional cultural differences between New York and Los Angeles surfaced prominently in the 1990s feud between rappers Notorious B.I.G. and Tupac Shakur, where the high-paced tempo of New York rap (B.I.G.) contrasted markedly with the laid-back, conversational style of the L.A. rap scene (Tupac), emulating differences in local cultural identities and ways of life between these artists' respective cities (Jago 2017).

Japonica Brown-Saracino defines the collection of stories conveying local culture as place narratives, "the stories residents tell about their city to themselves." She continues to explain that these narratives "offer models for who and how to be in a place" (2017: 15). The intangible characteristics of a place's reputation equip residents' cultural tool kits with a particular set of repertoires that, while not completely determinative, incentivize certain behaviors and deter others. In studying lesbian, bisexual, and queer (LBQ) women across Ithaca, New York; San Luis Obispo, California; Portland, Maine; and Greenfield, Massachusetts, Brown-Saracino finds that local place narratives help construct norms that have implications on the expression of women's sexual identity. Ithaca's reputation as a small, safe, college town helped shape an "integrationist" presentation of sexual identity among LBQ residents who did not outwardly display their sexuality. In contrast, LBQ residents in San Luis Obispo embraced a politics of identity where their sexuality was a core part of how they saw themselves and who they chose to interact with. Reputations of San Luis Obispo as the "happiest place on earth," combined with LBQ residents' exclusion from social groups covertly oriented toward heterosexuality, helped foster a close-knit lesbian community with definitive markers of belonging.

Brown-Saracino argues that places have distinct "sexual identity cultures" that convey messages around what it means to hold a particular sexuality. Her research suggests that the predominant narratives and reputations we associate with places also have elements that shape highly personal parts of one's sexual identity. But her study also generates new questions. If places have sexual identity cultures, do they also have race cultures? Class cultures? Central to this book, do places have distinct gendered cultures? Additionally, Brown-Saracino's work examines only four locations across the United States known for having large LBQ communities, leaving it unclear how local cultures and norms vary on a more universal level. If local culture is distinct between Ithaca and San Luis Obispo, what about Ithaca compared to Buffalo? Albany? Or even other college towns like Bloomington, Indiana?

Social Contexts, Gendered Cultures

We currently know little about the gendered components of local gender norms in places across the United States. This is not to say, however, that scholars have ignored the role of gender in culture. In fact, the study of these macro-level cultural components of the gender structure has attracted a great deal of attention, even if their local variation has been relatively ignored. Much research has examined the role of gender norms in sustaining patterns of difference and inequality between women and men. While culture, writ large, consists of discourse, patterns of behavior, artistic expressions, and modes of justification, *norms* are a component of culture that relate specifically to widespread expectations of what is appropriate to do, say, or feel within a setting (Horne and Mollborn 2020). *Gender norms* pertain to the set of expectations differentiating conduct between women and men (Pearse and Connell 2016). Consequently, gender norms have been studied extensively as a source of gender inequality. Widespread beliefs that women are better caregivers than men, for example, constitute powerful norms resulting in women's greater time spent providing childcare and their disproportionate representation in care occupations (Ridgeway 2011). Norms of intensive mothering that frame full-time careers as incompatible with attentive parenting have also been found to undermine mothers' employment because employers are often biased against hiring mothers, whom they perceive as less committed workers, and because mothers themselves face pressure to abandon their careers in order to fulfill ideal parenting expectations (Ruppanner et al. 2021). Whereas gender norms often convey mothers as primary caregivers, research has shown that men are commonly expected to be breadwinners. As a result, men are less likely to take on domestic tasks, even during periods of unemployment (Legerski and Cornwall 2010).

Although research has extensively studied the role of gender norms in social life and their consequences on inequality, a smaller body of work has focused on their spatial variation. Here, scholars have primarily examined cross-national differences in gender norms, as opposed to within-nation heterogeneity. This approach leverages the fact that nations have discrete borders and identities that can be used to compare gender norms. Focusing on differences between nations, scholars have not only identified national differences in gender norms, but recent work has proposed frameworks for understanding the multidimensionality of these norms, as nations may be egalitarian in some respects but traditional in others. However, cross-national research is unable to capture within-nation heterogeneity where gender norms vary between places within the same country. While this may pose less of a problem in research on smaller, more homogeneous countries, the United States is neither of these things. Studies of gender attitudes in the United States have consistently found significant regional differences (Scarborough, Sin, and Risman 2019), providing initial evidence for important within-nation spatial variation. As noted in the introductory chapter, urban scholars and psychologists have argued that places throughout the United States not only have different cultures but even different "personalities" (Rentfrow, Gosling, and Potter 2008) and norms around interpersonal exchange (Fritsch and Wyrwich 2018). If there is substantial variation across the United States in these additional components of culture, it would stand to reason that gender norms also vary on such a local level.

Much of what we know about spatial variation in gender norms comes from cross-national research. While this body of literature disregards more local variation, it does provide an excellent foundation for conceptualizing the way gender norms differ from place to place. Three frameworks have been used in cross-national research to describe the cultural expectations conveyed by gender norms. I describe these in greater detail in the following. I then propose a fourth framework that integrates insight from previous theories to outline a four-dimensional model of gender norms. Collectively, these four frameworks are used to guide my analysis examining the configurations of local gender norms across the United States.

Unidimensional Gender Norms

Studying over seventy nations, Ronald Inglehart and Pippa Norris (2003) conceptualized nation-level gender norms as unidimensional and ranging from traditional to egalitarian. Traditional norms prescribe strict gendered divisions of labor where men are decision makers and breadwinners while women tend to home and children. On the other side of the spectrum, egalitarian norms convey equality in both decision-making and the division of labor between women and men. Examining the relationship among culture, economic change, and inequality, Inglehart and Norris found that economic growth does not result in improved gender equality unless accompanied by egalitarian norms. This unidimensional conception of gender norms is also prevalent, if not explicitly stated, in studies on gender attitudes in the United States where multiple indicators are often combined into an overall scale of gender egalitarianism used to identify general patterns in this cultural construct (Bolzendahl and Myers 2004; Brewster and Padavic 2000).

The unidimensional framework is the simplest but also most widely used model for conceptualizing gender norms. Broadly characterizing places as varying between traditional and egalitarian provides an easily interpretable tool to efficiently describe the cultural qualities related to gendered values, expectations, and patterns of behavior. The unidimensional model also offers methodological advantages. By virtue of its simplicity, researchers can conceptualize unidimensional norms using few indicators. Therefore, even when the data are less than comprehensive, researchers can still infer some qualities of the local gendered environment. However, these strengths are made possible through simplifying a more complex reality. It is possible, for example, that the aggregation of cultural indicators into a single construct obscures important differences between the dimensions of gender norms. Indeed, two additional frameworks have shown that there are important differences between gender norms directed at separate aspects of society.

Gender Norms across Public and Private Spheres

Despite the common use of unidimensional scales to measure gender egalitarianism, a large body of research suggests that cultural meanings around gender differ substantially across the public sphere of work and the private sphere of family. Sociologists first characterized this public/private split in the structural functionalist theories of the mid-twentieth century, which argued that women's focus on the private sphere and men's on the public sphere was a rational arrangement for the fulfillment of personal needs (Parsons [1951] 1991; Parsons and Bales 1955). This approach has since been rejected by feminist scholars who argued that the functionalist perspective on the public/private split legitimated gender inequality and divisions of labor (Lopata and Thorne 1978). Instead, contemporary theorizing about the public/private split examines how there are distinct cultural meanings attached to these realms of society. Recent research on individuals' gender attitudes, for example, has found that people hold different attitudes about gender in the family from gender at work (Scarborough, Sin, and Risman 2019). Studying gender norms across seventeen European nations, Carly Knight and Mary Brinton (2017) found that a large share of the population in Hungary, Slovenia, Czech Republic, Estonia, and Italy supported gender equality in the public sphere of work but continued to feel that women should be primarily responsible for family and home duties.

Although there is limited spatial-comparative research on gender norms toward the public and private spheres within the United States, qualitative research provides early evidence that norms may differ between these two cultural realms. In interviews with a diverse group of young adults in the New York City metro area, Kathleen Gerson (2009) found that these individuals envision different life paths when it comes to work and family. While many aim for egalitarian partnerships, when pressed on how they would adjust to the difficulties of balancing work and families, young men are more likely to say that they would prefer traditional family arrangements where they work and their wife stays at home, while young women state that they would rather remain single and independent. Barbara Risman (2018) finds a similar dynamic among millennials residing in Chicago. Among the 116 people interviewed in her study, 48 (41 percent) held contradictory views about gender—they supported equality in some ways but often fell back on traditional gender norms within personal relationships.

Unlike the unidimensional approach that theorizes norms as unified across all aspects of society, a public/private sphere framework accounts for instances where gender norms may differ across the social domains of work and family. Research has long indicated that support for gender equality in the public sphere is greater than support for gender equality in the family (Mason and Lu 1988), but now researchers find a substantial number of individuals who support gender equality at work but oppose it in the home (Scarborough, Sin, and Risman 2019). Furthermore, research on multiple indicators of gender equality has found that we have made much more progress in the public sphere than in the private sphere (Goldscheider, Bernhardt, and Lappegård 2015). Women's advances in education (where they now outperform men in most measures), labor force participation, and managerial representation far exceed the shifts we have observed toward gender equality in childcare and housework, where much of the shrinking gender gap has been driven by women's decreasing time spent on household chores rather than an increase in men's contributions (Bianchi, Robinson, and Milke 2006).

Conceptualizing differences in gender norms between the public and private spheres allows us to better recognize the cultural components behind the differential pace of change toward gender equality between work and family. However, other models have also been proposed to describe the multidimensionality of gender norms.

Horizontal and Vertical Dimensions of Gender Norms

In their examination of occupational gender segregation across developed nations, Maria Charles and David Grusky (2004) identify two independent cultural forces driving different patterns of segregation. First, a vertical component, which they call male primacy, manifests when men are found in the most powerful and highest-paying occupations while women are located below them in the occupational ladder. Second, the horizontal dimension of culture, what these scholars refer to as gender essentialism, perpetuates the notion that women and men are inherently different but not necessarily unequal. According to the logic of gender essentialism, women's propensity for nurturance allows them to succeed in the service sector, where people-centered skills are valued, while men's agency lends itself to thing-centered occupations emphasizing the manipulation of objects and decision-making.

Analyzing cultural processes through the framework of vertical and horizontal dimensions sheds light on some of the dynamic and contradictory patterns of gender inequality in the new economy. Even in situations with high levels of women's labor force participation and general support for gender equality, horizontal segregation is often maintained through a logic that women and men are different and therefore better suited for jobs in separate industries or occupations (Charles and Grusky 2004). In the United States, this is most apparent in the dynamic changes we have observed in management. While there has been a major increase in women's representation in management since the 1980s, most of this change has been concentrated in feminized fields such as education, medical services, and real estate (Scarborough 2018b). In other words, there has been a decline in vertical segregation alongside an increase in horizontal segregation. Contradictory trends in vertical and horizontal cultural dimensions have also been found in education, where women now obtain a larger share of college degrees than men but there remains high levels of gender segregation by field of study, with STEM fields like engineering and computer science being dominated by men while women are concentrated in the liberal arts (Charles and Bradley 2009).

The vertical/horizontal framework offers yet another two-dimensional model for conceptualizing gender norms. Like the public/private sphere framework, this approach recognizes how norms can be dynamic and contradictory, with egalitarian aspects in some ways but traditional components in others. Diverging from the public/private sphere model, however, this framework pays less attention to social spheres and emphasizes, instead, the cultural mechanisms that separate women and men into unequal positions.

Integrated Model: Horizontal/Vertical Dimensions within Public/Private Spheres

Previous research has conceptualized gender norms as either unidimensional, differentiated between the public/private spheres, or containing vertical/horizontal dimensions. There is substantial evidence that each of these approaches captures a meaningful aspect of gendered cultural environments. It is therefore possible that a combination of frameworks provides the most comprehensive model.

While there has yet to be a study that explicitly explores the relationship between public/private and vertical/horizontal aspects of culture, previous research strongly indicates the presence of horizontal/vertical dimensions of gender norms located in both the public sphere and the private sphere. Maria Charles and David Grusky's (2004) initial formulation of vertical and horizontal dimensions was based on an analysis of cultural processes taking place in the public sphere that manifest in vertical segregation (representation of women in managerial/professional positions) and horizontal segregation (segregation of women and men into different occupational fields). Other studies using the vertical/horizontal framework have also focused on the public sphere by examining trends in educational attainment alongside segregation of academic field (Charles and Bradley 2009).

In the private sphere, the horizontal/vertical framework has been used less explicitly but can be neatly applied to existing findings. The vertical dimension may be most readily apparent in intensive mothering norms that convey women's careers as incompatible with parenting. Although research has documented widespread support for women's employment, expectations that mothers are primarily responsible for child-rearing remain common and are driven by pressure on mothers to provide time-, energy-, and resource-intensive care for their children (Dernberger and Pepin 2020). Sharon Hays (1998) described these cultural expectations as the *ideology of intensive mothering*. As defined by Hays (1998: 8), this cultural ideology pressures mothers to provide "copious amounts of time, energy, and material resources on their child." This means sacrificing work obligations or aspirations whenever necessary. Grounded in family and caregiving expectations, intensive mothering norms have been shown to have major consequences on mothers' career advancement. Beliefs that mothers are less devoted to work than nonmothers or fathers can bias hiring managers against employing mothers or paying them equally (Correll, Benard, and Paik 2007). Indeed, such expectations toward mothers have been found to be among the largest barriers to women's overall labor force participation (Ruppanner et al. 2021) as well as a major contributor to gender wage gaps (England 2005).

Research on families also indicates that horizontal norms are present in the private sphere. Specifically, beliefs about the proper roles of husbands/fathers as breadwinners and wives/mothers as caregivers reflects cultural norms of gender essentialism (Cotter, Hermsen, and Vanneman 2011). These common expectations for women and men in the family manifest in persistent gendered divisions of household labor. Despite convergence in recent decades, women continue to spend nearly twice as much time as men on housework and childcare, while men spend upward of ten additional hours in paid work a week than women (Parker and Wang 2013).

Viewed as a whole, we can clearly see how public/private and vertical/horizontal frameworks for understanding gender norms can be integrated by identifying vertical and horizontal dimensions within both public and private spheres. Instead of equating vertical norms across the public and private spheres, for example, this approach accounts for the fact that vertical conditions in the public sphere of work may exist separately from vertical conditions in the private sphere of the family. Along the same lines, this integrative approach accounts for cultural heterogeneity within the public and private spheres—providing for instances where norms of essential difference in the public sphere are separate from views toward women's leadership. In sum, the intersection of vertical/horizontal and public/private cultural frameworks results in a multidimensional model containing four separate components. Summarized in Table 2.1, I label the vertical component of the public sphere as *women's advancement*, the horizontal component of the public sphere as *public sphere gender essentialism*, the vertical component of the private sphere as *intensive mothering*, and the horizontal component of the private sphere as *private sphere gender essentialism*.

Summary of Frameworks

Existing research provides three frameworks to describe local cultural environments: a unidimensional model describing gender norms as ranging from traditional to egalitarian, a public/private sphere model that differentiates gender norms in the realms of work and family, and a vertical/horizontal model that separately conceptualizes norms of women's advancement from norms around gender separation. In addition, I have proposed a fourth model where vertical and horizontal elements take place separately in the public and private sphere. The first three frameworks have been applied in cross-national research or in longitudinal studies of the United States as a

TABLE 2.1	INTEGRATIVE MODEL OF GENDER NORMS		
		Vertical/horizontal dimensions	
		Vertical dimension	*Horizontal dimension*
Public and private spheres	Public sphere	Women's advancement	Public sphere gender essentialism
	Private sphere	Intensive mothering	Private sphere gender essentialism

whole, while the fourth framework is newly proposed here. Therefore, we do not yet know how these apply to places across the United States. In the next section of this chapter, I address this gap. Using a unique set of cultural indicators covering all aspects of the four theoretical models highlighted previously, I illustrate how well each framework describes the structure and variation of gender norms across United States commuting zones. First, I define my approach to measuring gender norms. Then, I compare how well each theoretical model describes the relationship among cultural indicators to identify the best framework for describing variation in gender norms across the United States.

Measuring Local Gender Norms

One reason why within-nation variation in gender norms has received less attention by scholars is because this topic presents a methodological challenge for researchers. Unlike economic characteristics for which census and administrative data provide readily available measures, gender norms are ideological characteristics of local contexts that are not directly observable in commonly used forms of survey or administrative data. While gender norms are difficult to measure, however, their effects are not. Local gender norms shape the paths people pursue, the choices they make, and their attitudes toward a variety of topics. By virtue of being reflected in a number of observable ways, norms are an ideal example of what statisticians and quantitative social scientists call a *latent construct*. According to Timothy Brown (2015: 13), a latent construct is "an unobservable variable that influences more than one observed measure and that accounts for the correlations among these observed measures." In other words, while we cannot see latent variables such as gender norms directly, we can triangulate their presence through examining their influence across a set of indicators. Because the indicators are, theoretically, only related through their shared influence of the latent variable (gender norms, in this case), we can define the latent variable by focusing specifically on the shared patterns across indicators. This process of defining the latent construct through the interrelationships of indicators is known as latent modeling or factor analysis. Another way to think about this approach is by considering it as a type of statistical archaeology. We may not be able to directly see the thing we want to measure (gender norms), but we can define it by identifying its "footprint" and the many impressions it leaves in society.

Before getting into the details of the particular latent modeling method I use, I first describe the set of cultural indicators chosen to represent the impressions that gender norms leave on social life. Each of these indicators has been used to represent cultural aspects of gender in prior research but has not been examined yet as part of a multidimensional structure of local gender norms. In describing each indicator, I provide details on measurement, data sources, and which dimension of gender norms it reflects across the four frameworks outlined previously.

Gender Attitudes on Leadership

One way that cultural norms are reflected is through individuals' viewpoints and attitudes (Vaisey 2009). Gender scholars have directed significant attention to this particular type of cultural indicator in studying spatial variation in gender attitudes as well as the factors contributing to individuals' perceptions (Scarborough, Sin, and Risman 2019). Four gender-attitude questions from the General Social Survey (GSS, Smith et al. 2018) are commonly used in this body of research. I use all these items to measure local gender norms,[1] but I first describe one item related to women's political leadership because it reflects views toward women's public sphere advancement. In nearly every wave of the survey, the GSS has asked respondents if they agree or disagree with the statement: *Most men are better suited emotionally for politics than are most women.* Previous research has used this item to measure cultural expectations toward women's leadership capabilities (Meagher and Shu 2019). Specifically, the question taps a common gender stereotype—that women lack the emotional competency for leadership and that such roles are better suited for men. While this surfaces prominently in politics, gendered assessments of leadership also have implications in the workforce, as similar gender stereotypes play out in biases against women in managerial roles (Eagly 2007). Consequently, scholars have used this survey question to explore gender attitudes toward leadership in the public sphere of work and politics more broadly (Scarborough, Sin, and Risman 2019). Following cross-national research that has aggregated attitudinal items to construct measures of country-level norms, I calculated the average proportion of respondents in each commuting zone disagreeing with the statement that men are better suited for politics than women.[2]

Gender-Career Implicit Association

Although attitudes are commonly used to measure aspects of gender norms, these components of culture also surface in more subtle ways. People may vocally state that they support women in leadership but nonetheless hold bias against hiring or promoting women into such roles. This common occurrence reflects what psychologists refer to as implicit attitudes that surface in the habitual, if not explicitly stated, association of men with leadership and women with nurturance. Such implicit views take place beyond the immediate perception of individuals. Instead, they frame the way they assess, evaluate, and interpret the behavior of others (Ridgeway 2011). For example, a well-known study by Claudia Goldin and Cecilia Rouse (2000) showed that women musicians were more likely to be hired after symphony orchestras instituted blind auditions. After a screen was used to conceal performers' gender, women were 50 percent more likely to advance from the preliminary round of auditions and 5 percent more likely to be hired. Comparing orchestras' different audition structures, women made up only 10 percent of new hires in those with unblinded auditions and 35 percent of new hires in orchestras with blinded auditions. This study indicates that jury members' perception of the prototypical orchestra musician may have been implicitly male typed, disadvantaging women and coloring jury members' evaluations to view men more favorably during auditions. This effect occurs even though few jury members would explicitly state a preference for men musicians.

Implicit attitudes have been found to play a large role in the workplace, where they pose particular challenges to women's occupational advancement (Heilman 2001). Although manifesting in individuals' behavior and decision-making, scholars have argued that these implicit attitudes reflect exposure to cultural environments (Arkes and Tetlock 2004). Shelley Correll and colleagues (2017), for example, found that cognitive gender bias was triggered more in settings with conservative gender norms (such as a rural town in Kansas) than in locations with more liberal gender norms (such as Massachusetts). In other words, implicit gender attitudes are not only an individual-level attribute but also an important indicator of the types of local norms individuals are exposed to.

Unlike attitudinal survey questions, which capture explicitly stated opinions, implicit attitudes are measured through tests designed to identify cognitive associations that are often beyond the perception of respondents themselves. These IATs are used extensively in the field of psychology to measure the degree to which individuals subconsciously associate social groups with various characteristics. The largest set of IATs is administered through Project Implicit (Xu et al. 2018), a collaborative research project started by scholars from the University of Washington, Harvard University, and the University of Virginia with the aim of informing the public about cognitive biases and providing a platform to measure these biases. Project Implicit currently hosts fifteen different IATs measuring cognitive associations with characteristics such as race, age, skin tone, and disability. Here, I use two IATs designed to measure separate implicit associations with gender: the Gender-Career IAT and the Gender-Science IAT. Like all Project Implicit IATs, each of these are available online for anyone to take.[3] This means that there is no systematic sampling of respondents to ensure the data are representative. This limitation is offset by the fact that Project Implicit is the only source of data large enough to produce local estimates of average implicit attitudes for places throughout the United States. Furthermore, I do not rely on IAT data to stand alone. Instead, as described previously, local gender norms are defined through their interrelationship with other indicators. Since most indicators come from nationally representative samples, any bias related to the convenience sampling in the IAT data is unlikely to be present in the other indicators and is unlikely to transfer into the latent measures of gender norms.

I used the Gender-Career IAT as one indicator of gender norms related to women's advancement in the public sphere of work. In this test, online participants are instructed to place words into two bins (using keyboard strokes), across two conditions. In one condition, participants place male names and career words into one bin and female names and family words into another. In the second condition, they are instructed to place female names and career words into a single bin while placing male names and family words into a separate bin. After completing both conditions (the order is randomized across respondents), an implicit attitude score is calculated through taking the standardized difference in response times between the two conditions. Participants with high levels of cognitive gender bias report faster word associations in condition one (male/career, female/family) than condition two (female/career, male/family). Although the process is complicated, a simple way of describing this measure is as the difference in how fast respondents associate conventional gender associations (men/career, women/family) compared to unconventional associations (men/family, women/career). Aggregating to commuting zones, I calculated the average IAT score measuring implicit bias against women in careers.[4]

Gender-Science Implicit Association

In addition to the Gender-Career IAT, I also used the Gender-Science IAT to measure an additional aspect of local gender norms related to expectations that women and men are not necessarily unequally qualified for careers but rather that they are suited for different fields of work. In this test, respondents are again instructed to sort words into bins across two conditions. In the first condition, words associated with men (e.g., "father," "husband," "uncle") and science ("chemistry," "math," "geology") are placed in one bin while words associated with women ("mother," "wife," "aunt") and liberal arts ("music," "English," "history") are sorted together. In the second condition, the pairings are switched so women-related and science words are placed together, separately from men-related and liberal arts words. As with the Gender-Career IAT, the order of these conditions is randomized, and the implicit attitude score is measured as the standardized difference in the time it takes respondents to sort words between the two conditions. Commuting zone levels of implicit attitudes toward women in science were measured as the average IAT score in each location.[5]

Gender Segregation in Field of Bachelor's Degree

Explicit and implicit attitudes have been used extensively to study the way gender norms manifest in individuals' perspectives. A third way scholars have examined gender norms is through revealed preferences in behavioral outcomes. This has been particularly prevalent in studies of college major selection. In cross-national research, scholars have inferred nation-level gender norms through aggregate patterns in the tendency for women and men to study different topics at university. Maria Charles and Karen Bradley (2009), for example, used gender segregation of educational field to measure horizontal norms of gender difference across forty-four industrialized nations. Research in the United States, while focusing less on spatial variation, has studied patterns of students' college major selection to examine the role of gender essentialist beliefs in these decisions (Cech 2013). Although women's college degree attainment has grown dramatically over the past fifty years to now slightly exceed men's, these studies show how gender norms remain a powerful influence in education. To date, women account for just over a third of all college degrees in STEM fields (Catalyst 2020). The numbers are even less in engineering and computer science, where women make up a fifth of all graduates. In contrast, men make up about a quarter of graduates in education and about a third in literature and languages (Siebens and Ryan 2012). These patterns are driven both by students' preferences for different fields of study as well as their treatment by educators and peers, which may push them out of some fields and draw them into others (Cech, Blair-Loy, and Rogers 2018). Together, these processes reflect gender norms conveying expectations that certain areas of study are better suited for women or men.

To capture the way gender norms are reflected in the tendency for women and men to study different academic fields, I use data from the five-year 2018

American Community Survey (ACS, Ruggles et al. 2021)[6] to calculate the commuting zone index of dissimilarity,[7] which measures the gender segregation of field of study among college degree holders aged twenty-five years and older. The index of dissimilarity is one of the most common measures of segregation and is calculated through the summed absolute difference in women's and men's population across fields of study relative to their overall population (Taylor et al. 2019). Estimates from the index are interpreted as the proportion of women and men who would have to change educational fields for there to be perfect gender integration, with a score of zero indicating perfect integration and a score of one reflecting absolute segregation.

Attitudes toward Working Mothers' Relationship with Child

As discussed previously, gender norms have also been observed with respect to ideologies of intensive parenting that frame mothers' careers and employment as incompatible with parenting. To capture these expectations conveyed by local gender norms, I used data from the GSS to calculate the percentage of commuting zone residents agreeing with the statement: *A working mother can establish just as warm and secure a relationship with her child as a mother who does not work.* Previous research has generally treated this survey item as reflecting norms related broadly to the private sphere of the family (Ruppanner et al. 2021). Yet, considering how intensive mothering expectations may reflect a more specific aspect of family gender norms, I treat this item as directly reflecting the expectations that mothers sacrifice career aspirations for childcare, rather than gender norms in the family more broadly. As with the previous item used from the GSS, I aggregate responses to commuting zones by calculating the proportion of respondents agreeing with the statement that working mothers can establish a warm bond with their children.[8]

Attitudes toward Working Mothers and Children's Well-Being

I use a second variable from the GSS to capture an additional way norms of intensive mothering are reflected. This item measures disagreement with the statement: *A preschool child is likely to suffer if his or her mother works.* This question measures expectations that the best care a child can receive is from his or her mother, as opposed to receiving quality care from stay-at-home fathers, childcare centers, or preschools. It also directly captures views that mothers' work is incompatible with parenting. For many mothers, these expectations drive them to exit the labor force or feel guilty about their time working (Hays 1998). Aggregating to commuting zones, I calculated the proportion of respondents disagreeing with this statement as another measure of intensive mothering norms.[9]

Attitudes toward Household Division of Labor

I use one additional survey item from the GSS to capture the way gender norms are reflected in essentialist beliefs about women's and men's responsibilities in the family. The survey question measures respondents' disagreement with the statement: *It is much better for everyone involved if the man is the achiever outside the home and the woman takes care of the home and family.* Unlike the two previous survey items related to intensive mothering, this one explicitly states expectations for both men's and women's ideal family roles. Such views are rooted in norms of essential difference directed toward the private sphere of the family that men are better oriented to "providing" and women to "caring" (Cotter, Hermsen, and Vanneman 2011). Like previous items used from the GSS, I aggregate this to commuting zones by calculating the proportion who disagree with these traditional divisions of household labor.[10]

Mother's Day/Father's Day Twitter
Sentiment toward Feminism

An additional way that gender norms surface is in public discourse taking place on social media. This is most prominent in debates around feminism where issues like the gendered division of labor and gendered expectations are often explicitly debated in ways that convey cultural values and local norms. Indeed, gender scholars have argued that variation across the United States in support for feminist ideals reflects different cultural environments related to gendered expectations for women (Crossley 2017; Scarborough and Helmuth 2021; Spain 2016). Studying feminist activism on college campuses, Alison Crossley, for example, finds that much feminist organizing occurs online, even in these geographically concentrated social settings. Furthermore, the degree of support or opposition experienced by feminist groups varied largely across geographical lines, with groups in the Midwest receiving more hostility than those on the West Coast. Far from overcoming spatial boundaries, feminist discourse on social media can make them more apparent, as posts originating from different locations convey sentiment that reflects distinct local norms (Scarborough and Helmuth 2021).

With such a broad agenda, it may be unclear what dimensions of gender norms are conveyed in local sentiment toward feminism. My previous research (2018a), however, indicates that feminist discourse on Twitter is most closely tied to views about the family division of labor, with profeminist areas

TABLE 2.2   ILLUSTRATIVE SAMPLE OF TWEETS
Coded as positive
1. my mom and i are watching @HandmaidsOnHulu together and discussing feminist theory
2. Thank you to my fellow kick-ass feminist mom! h
3. 4 Year Old: I'm a GIRL doctor! Husb: Or as WE say, a doctor #dudefeminist #feminist #raisinggirls #momlife
4. Honest feminist support of moms would be an all inclusive solidarity, regardless if you agree w parenting choices (or situations).
5. Joni Mitchell, Emmylou Harris, Eudora Welty . . . moms. Hear more about feminist icons here
6. I LOVE my dad but having my moms last name was always kinda badass and cemented my feminism.
7. My dad is such a feminist and he doesn't even know it
8. today i made my dad realize how much of a feminist he is and it's the best thing that happened to me today
9. Y'all, my dad is awesome #feminist #nastywoman #heforshe #lovemydad
10. I am a proud feminist father
Coded as negative
11. As a yogi and a mom, when i became a mom, feminism let me down.
12. 3-yr-old boy wants to play with boy stuff, but his feminist mom makes BIG point she won't tolerate THAT . . .
13. Smh girls with puppies out here calling themselves mom's, surprised there hasn't been a feminist rant yet
14. Women's Rights must feed off of the blood of there non existent children to work, a cost way to high for any civilized culture
15. Idc what these feminist say . . . no kid boy wants to hear about their mom ass naked on the internet from their peers
16. Imagine having a mom with a nose ring. Feminism was a mistake.
17. feminism worst thing ever happened to families, to children
18. why does it seem like every feminist had a terrible father
19. Feminists are tired of the emasculated manchildren that feminism created
20. Feminism is a war on men. Motherhood and child bearing
Note: Tweets edited to remove usernames and identifying information.

being more likely to feel that housework and childcare should be shared equally between mothers and fathers. This is further supported by the fact that the data I reviewed in that research focused on feminist-related tweets occurring around Mother's Day and Father's Day in 2017—a period of time when statements about feminism would be more likely to be directed toward parenting and families. Table 2.2 provides a sample of tweets occurring at that time, showing how the majority of pro- and anti-feminist tweets were based on views toward the gendered division of family labor.

Leveraging the rich ways that gender norms are reflected in social media discourse on feminism, I calculated the proportion of tweets in each commuting zone that were positive toward feminism. I used the same data set of tweets I analyzed in my previous work that were collected on Mother's Day and Father's Day weekends in 2017.[11] Applying a key finding from that study, I treat these tweets as primarily reflecting sentiment toward the gendered division of family labor.

Summary of Cultural Indicators

In summary, I used eight observed variables to measure local gender norms, each of which have been found in previous research to reflect various cultural aspects of gender. I also intentionally selected indicators so that at least two variables could represent each possible dimension of gender norms pertaining to the cultural frameworks outlined previously. Table 2.3 summarizes the eight variables used to reflect gender norms, the dimension they represent across each framework, their associated data sources, and descriptive statistics.

When used alone, each measure described prior provides only a partial understanding of gender norms that may also be affected by other characteristics of local commuting zones. The gender segregation of university field of study, for example, may also reflect economic conditions as well as cultural ones. This is where the strength of latent modeling comes in. Because such diverse indicators are related with one another primarily through the shared effects of local gender norms, focusing only on the way these indicators are correlated allows us to remove aspects that do not reflect local cultural conditions. Now that I have discussed the eight cultural indicators, I provide a review of the method used to examine how they collectively reflect local gender norms.

Mapping the Impressions of Local Gender Norms

As discussed earlier, gender norms represent a prototypical *latent construct* that is not directly observable but instead detectable through its influence on numerous indicators. The previous section outlined eight indicators reflecting the effects of local gender norms. These indicators were carefully selected to not only convey the many ways norms manifest in attitudes, cognitive biases, behaviors, and discourse but also to capture the multiple dimensions comprising local gender norms. I use confirmatory factor analysis (CFA) to apply each of the four theoretical frameworks for describing gender norms (outlined prior) to the set of cultural indicators. CFA allows me to test whether each of these theories are useful or if they offer little substantive insight. This is done through statistically modeling how well latent factors (in this case, dimensions of gender norms) describe the interrelationships (otherwise known as the covariance matrix) of observed indicators.

TABLE 2.3   OBSERVED INDICATORS OF GENDER NORMS

Variable	Data source	Unidimensional	Public/ private	Vertical/ horizontal	Four dimensional	Descriptives	
						Mean	SD
1 Proportion disagree, men better suited for politics than women	GSS	Unidimensional	Public	Vertical	Women's advancement	0.763	0.026
2 Implicit attitudes toward women in careers	IAT	Unidimensional	Public	Vertical	Women's advancement	0.397	0.010
3 Implicit attitudes toward women in science	IAT	Unidimensional	Public	Horizontal	Public sphere gender essentialism	0.388	0.011
4 Gender segregation in field of university degree	ACS	Unidimensional	Public	Horizontal	Public sphere gender essentialism	0.361	0.028
5 Proportion agree, working mothers can establish warm relationship with child	GSS	Unidimensional	Private	Vertical	Intensive mothering	0.607	0.021
6 Proportion disagree, preschool children suffer if mother works	GSS	Unidimensional	Private	Vertical	Intensive mothering	0.535	0.048
7 Proportion disagree, better if man works and woman tends home	GSS	Unidimensional	Private	Horizontal	Private sphere gender essentialism	0.593	0.059
8 Proportion of positive tweets toward feminism on Mother's Day/Father's Day	Twitter API	Unidimensional	Private	Horizontal	Private sphere gender essentialism	0.775	0.062

Note: GSS = General Social Survey; IAT = Implicit Attitude Test from Project Implicit; ACS = American Community Survey.

The better the theoretical framework, the better it describes indicator relationships. We can compare frameworks with a number of statistical tests that indicate how well each one accounts for the correlations between indicators as well as whether improvements between frameworks are significant. Then, we select the framework that best describes the relationships between indicators as the ideal one for defining the structure of gender norms across U.S. commuting zones.

The basic approach of CFA is illustrated with the four models in Figures 2.1a, 2.1b, 2.1c, and 2.1d, where arrows from the ovals to the rectangles represent the way dimensions of gender norms (ovals) are reflected in the associated indicators (rectangles), while double-sided arrows between the ovals represent how dimensions of gender norms may be correlated with each other. Each rectangle also has a small circle associated with it, representing the many other factors besides gender norms that influence it (referred to as error). The premise behind CFA is that measuring common variance between indicators can parse out the error and produce a more valid and reliable construct. In instances where two indicators' error terms (the small circles) may be related due to factors besides the latent construct (gender norms, in this case), researchers can specify these error terms to be correlated.[12]

Figure 2.1a represents the unidimensional theoretical perspective on gender norms. Here, a single factor captures the interrelationships between all eight indicators. This model presumes that gender norms vary along a single dimension from traditional to egalitarian and that all indicators shift in unified fashion along this scale.

The second model presented in Figure 2.1b tests whether local gender norms have separate dimensions relating to the public and private spheres. This CFA model includes two factors representing each dimension. The first factor predicts commonalities between four observed measures relating to the public spheres of work and education: views toward women in leadership, implicit attitudes toward women in careers, implicit attitudes toward women in science, and gender segregation in university field of study. The second factor in this model pertains to the private sphere of the family and is reflected by views toward working mothers' relationship with their child, perceptions of whether young children suffer if mothers work, attitudes toward family gender roles, and the proportion of positive tweets about feminism during Mother's Day and Father's Day.

Figure 2.1c illustrates the third model, which uses two factors to test the vertical/horizontal framework. The vertical dimension is reflected by indicators pertaining to women's achievement and independence. These include views toward women's leadership, implicit attitudes toward women in careers, views toward working mothers' relationship with children, and views that young children suffer if their mother works. Reflecting the horizontal dimen-

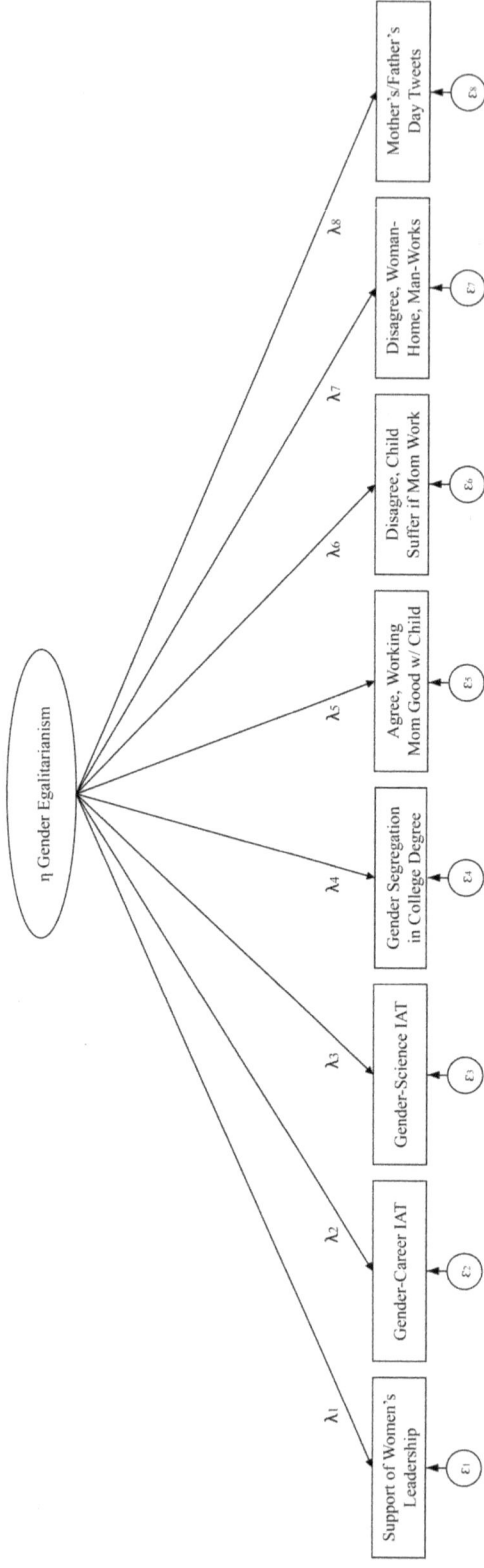

Figure 2.1 CFA Models for Each Framework of Local Gender Norms

2.1a Unidimensional Framework

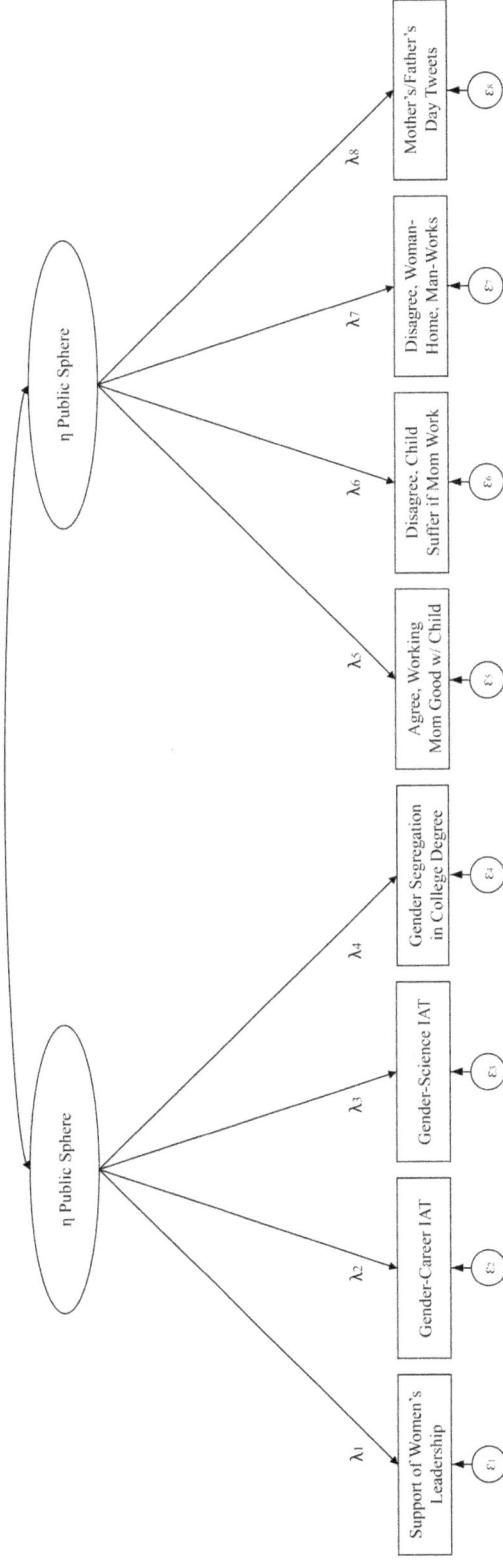

2.1b Public/Private Sphere Framework

sion are indicators for norms of essential gender difference. These include implicit attitudes toward women in science, gender segregation in field of study among college graduates, views about gender roles in the family, and the proportion of positive tweets about feminism during Mother's Day and Father's Day.

Finally, the fourth model presented in Figure 2.1d includes four factors representing the integration of public/private and vertical/horizontal dimensions. First, norms around women's advancement are reflected by views toward women's leadership and implicit attitudes about women and careers. Second, public sphere gender essentialism is observed through implicit bias toward women in science and the gender segregation in field of study among college graduates. Two additional factors represent norms around intensive mothering and gender essentialism in the private sphere. The items measuring views toward working mothers are used as observed measures of intensive mothering. Last, attitudes toward gendered divisions of labor in the family and the proportion of Mother's Day/Father's Day tweets that are positive toward feminism reflect gender essentialism in the private sphere of the family.

Each CFA model produces several pieces of information. The strength of an indicator as a reflection of local gender norms is measured by factor loadings that report how much of the variation in an indicator is predicted by the latent construct. These are represented by λ in Figures 2.1a, 2.1b, 2.1c, and 2.1d. Factor loadings were substantial and significant for all indicators across all four of the CFA models. Therefore, I do not discuss factor loadings here, but I report them in Table 2.4, located at the end of this chapter. Instead, I focus on model fit statistics that tell us how well the different frameworks describe the overall relationship between variables and therefore provide a measure of which framework best captures local gender norms. The most commonly used model fit statistic is the root mean square error of approximation (RMSEA). The benefit of the RMSEA is that it penalizes models with extra parameters—meaning that it only improves if the benefits to describing gender norms outweigh the added complexity of extra cultural dimensions. Lower values of the RMSEA indicate better model fit. Generally, scholars use a cutoff of 0.08 for acceptable fit—meaning that CFA models with a RMSEA below 0.08 are viewed as sufficiently measuring the latent construct through observed indicators (Acock 2013). Ideal fit occurs when the RMSEA is not significantly different from 0.05 (Acock 2013; Brown 2015). Applied to my analysis, I can say that one of the four frameworks adequately describes local gender norms when the RMSEA is below 0.08 and is not significantly different from 0.05. Because the RMSEA is the most widely used diagnostic for testing the usefulness of CFAs, I focus on this statistic. Other model fit statistics such as the chi-squared and comparative fit index are

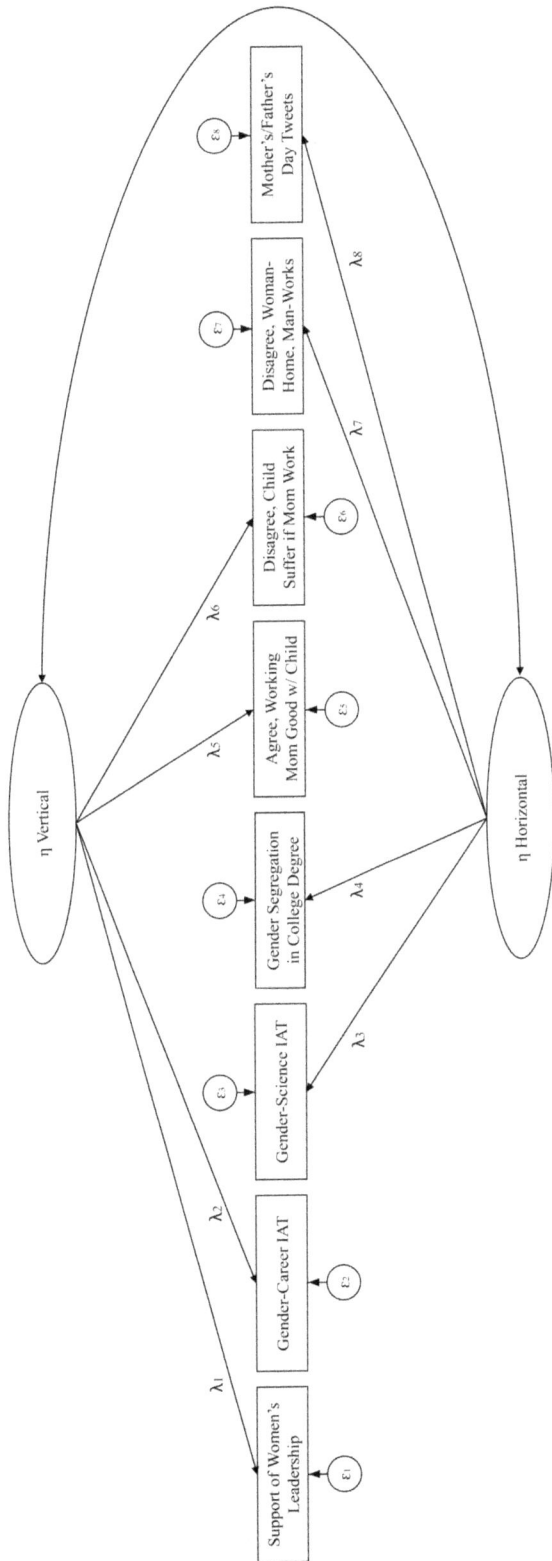

2.1c Vertical/Horizontal Framework

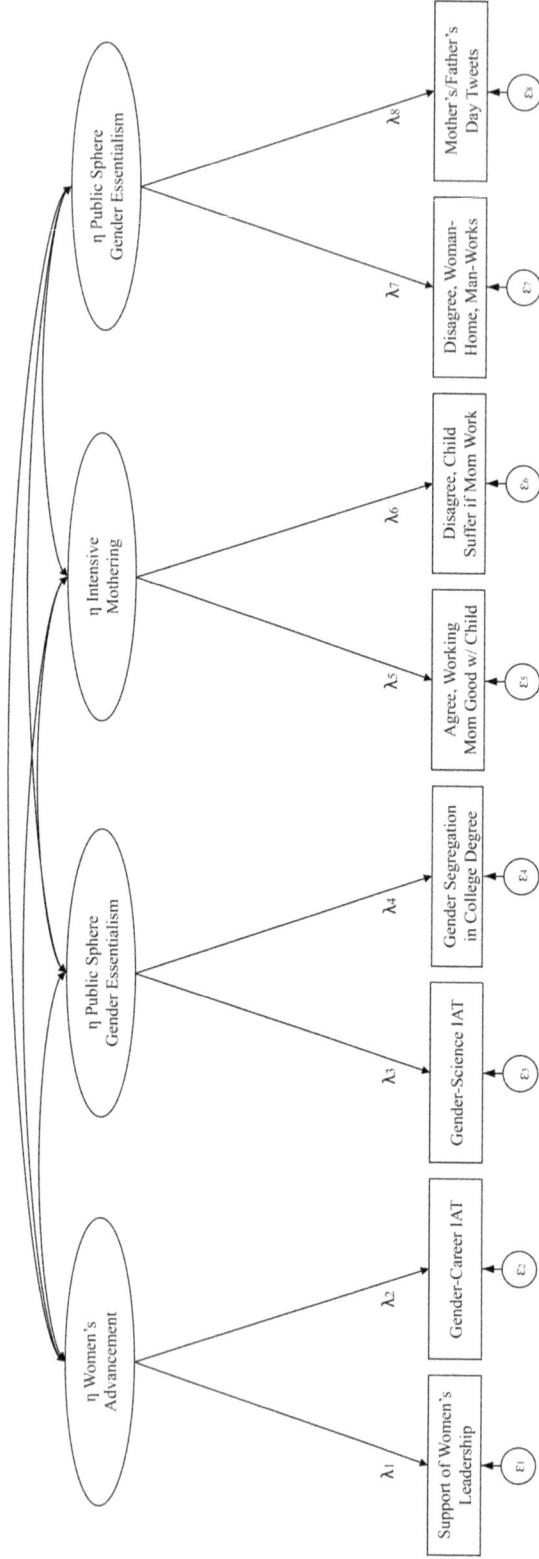

2.1d Integrative 4-Dimensional Framework

Diagram elements (as labeled):

- η Women's Advancement
  - λ_1 → Support of Women's Leadership (ε_1)
  - λ_2 → Gender-Career IAT (ε_2)
- η Public Sphere Gender Essentialism
  - λ_3 → Gender-Science IAT (ε_3)
  - λ_4 → Gender Segregation in College Degree (ε_4)
- η Intensive Mothering
  - λ_5 → Agree, Working Mom Good w/ Child (ε_5)
  - λ_6 → Disagree, Child Suffer if Mom Work (ε_6)
- η Public Sphere Gender Essentialism
  - λ_7 → Disagree, Woman-Home, Man-Works (ε_7)
  - λ_8 → Mother's/Father's Day Tweets (ε_8)

reported in Table 2.4, located at the end of this chapter. Findings from these statistics point to the same conclusion reached when focusing only on the RMSEA.

Which Framework Best Describes Local Gender Norms?

In this section, I show how well each framework describes local gender norms. I present the RMSEA as a statistical diagnostic reporting the degree to which each framework comprehensively describes the interrelationships of cultural indicators. In addition to the RMSEA, I also show how each framework describes local gender norms using an illustrative set of twenty commuting zones. This provides a more practical tool for observing the strengths and limitations of each framework by showing how they apply in characterizing a concrete set of locations. I used the CFA models illustrated in Figures 2.1a, 2.1b, 2.1c, and 2.1d to calculate continuous measures for each dimension of gender norms pertaining to each framework. The scales are standardized and range from traditional (lower values) to egalitarian (higher values), with a score of zero reflecting the average. Each unit on this scale corresponds to a standard deviation difference in local egalitarianism. For interpretation, I label these values as being very traditional if the score is –2, traditional if –1, average if 0, egalitarian if 1, and very egalitarian if 2. For the multidimensional frameworks, each dimension has a separate scale, allowing us to observe how levels of traditionalism/egalitarianism may differ across these dimensions.

RMSEA values are illustrated in Figure 2.2 and discussed in the following sections for each of the four frameworks. Comparing the RMSEA reveals clear evidence that some frameworks are better than others in describing the configurations of local gender norms.

The Unidimensional Framework

The RMSEA for the unidimensional model indicates that this simplified approach does not provide a very detailed description of local gender norms. At 0.092, it is above the 0.08 threshold for acceptable model fit and significantly different from 0.05. Yet some researchers still view RMSEA values below 0.1 to be somewhat useful, if less than ideal (Hooper, Coughlan, and Mullen 2008). Considering the simplicity of the unidimensional model and the diversity of the eight factors, this marginal RMSEA statistic suggests that there may be some utility to thinking about gender norms in a unidimensional manner where places range from traditional to egalitarian. It also provides evidence that each variable used in the CFA is a valid indicator of local

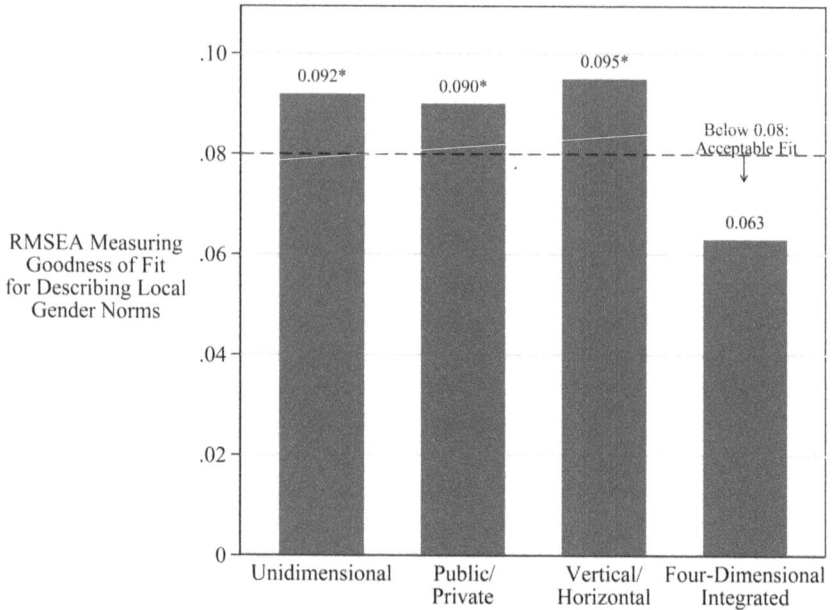

Figure 2.2 Statistical Model Fit Indicating How Well Each Framework Describes Local Gender Norms

Note: Full results, including factor loadings and additional model fit statistics, located in Table 2.4. * Indicates RMSEA is significantly ($p < 0.05$) different from 0.05. Best fitting model has RMSEA below 0.08 and not significantly different from 0.05.

gender norms because such a diverse set contains items that would only be related with one another through the shared influence of these cultural attributes.

Figure 2.3 plots twenty commuting zones along the unidimensional scale of local gender norms calculated with the first CFA model. In many ways, the placement of areas along this unidimensional scale resonates with their broader reputations. Minneapolis and New York City, for example, rank as highly egalitarian. These places are known as progressive urban hubs with liberal values. But not all populous commuting zones rank as egalitarian. Houston, the fourth largest city in the country, emerges as a more traditional area on this unidimensional measure.

While some findings from the unidimensional framework resonate with places' reputations, there are also surprises that question whether this simplified approach is missing important details. Grand Rapids, for example, is found to be an egalitarian area, while Miami is found to be more traditional. Few would assume gender norms in Grand Rapids, a major manufactur-

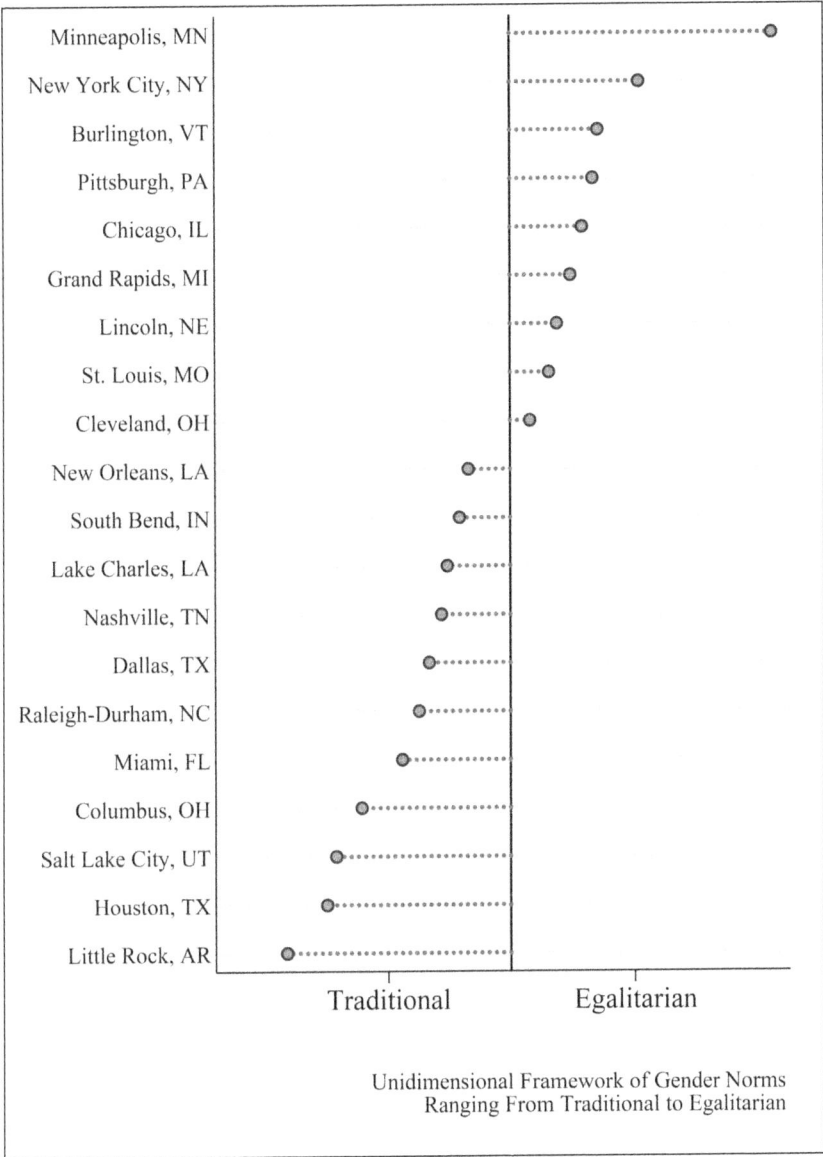

Figure 2.3 Twenty Illustrative Commuting Zones Plotted
by Unidimensional Scale of Local Gender Norms

Note: Commuting zones identified by principal city.

ing hub and regional center of political and religious conservatism, has an environment more supportive of gender equality than the diverse and vibrant metro of Miami. It is possible that further detail is needed to understand these counterintuitive trends.

The unidimensional framework of local gender norms may offer some insight in broadly differentiating traditional places like Little Rock from egalitarian places like Burlington. But there is also evidence that it neglects important details on how gender norms may differ across various aspects of society. A unidimensional framework conceptualizes places like Miami as being traditional, even if they exhibit egalitarian gender norms in some respects, and places like Grand Rapids as egalitarian, even if there remain some hints of traditionalism. The RMSEA further indicated that the unidimensional framework is limited in capturing the full story of local gender norms. With a RMSEA of 0.092, the unidimensional framework does only a marginal job at describing the way the eight indicators of gender norms are interrelated with one another. Overall, these findings suggest that a more sophisticated model of local gender norms is necessary.

The Public/Private Sphere Framework

Accounting for differences between the public and private spheres adds detail to our understanding of local gender norms. This is revealed in Figure 2.4, where the same set of commuting zones previously examined with the unidimensional measure are now plotted with the two-dimensional public/private sphere framework. In general, places like Minneapolis, New York City, and Burlington remain egalitarian across both dimensions, while Little Rock, Houston, Salt Lake City, and Columbus are traditional in both dimensions. There are, however, some important differences even among places that generally trend egalitarian or traditional. Egalitarianism in Burlington appears to be driven more by norms directed toward the private sphere than in the public sphere, whereas in Chicago, local norms are much more egalitarian with respect to the public than the private sphere. Among more traditional locales, Raleigh-Durham has more traditional norms in the public sphere than in the private sphere, while the opposite pattern is observed in Little Rock.

Differentiating between public and private spheres also adds some insight on why Miami emerged as traditional and Grand Rapids as egalitarian in the unidimensional model. Miami is shown to have particularly traditional gender norms toward the private sphere of the family, with only average levels of egalitarianism toward the public sphere. Grand Rapids, in contrast, trends egalitarian in the private sphere but reports average norms in the public sphere. This suggests that the primary point of differentiation between these areas is with respect to norms toward the private sphere of the family,

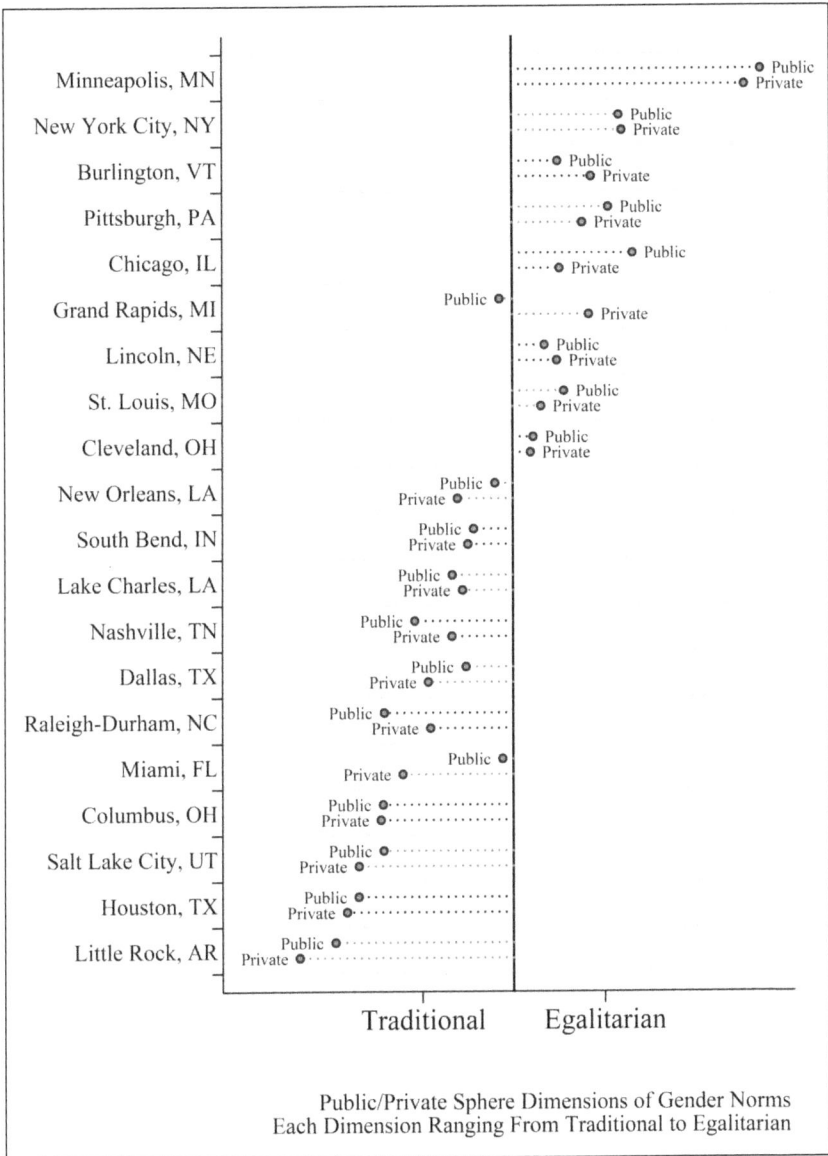

Minneapolis, MN	●···● Public ●···● Private
New York City, NY	············● Public ···········● Private
Burlington, VT	·····● Public ········● Private
Pittsburgh, PA	···········● Public ········● Private
Chicago, IL	············● Public ····● Private
Grand Rapids, MI	Public ● ·········● Private
Lincoln, NE	···● Public ····● Private
St. Louis, MO	···● Public ··● Private
Cleveland, OH	·● Public ·● Private
New Orleans, LA	Public ●· Private ●······
South Bend, IN	Public ●···· Private ●·····
Lake Charles, LA	Public ●······· Private ●····
Nashville, TN	Public ●··········· Private ●·······
Dallas, TX	Public ●······ Private ●········
Raleigh-Durham, NC	Public ●·············· Private ●········
Miami, FL	Public ● Private ●···········
Columbus, OH	Public ●············ Private ●················
Salt Lake City, UT	Public ●······· Private ●···············
Houston, TX	Public ●················· Private ●···············
Little Rock, AR	Public ●········· Private ●················

Traditional   Egalitarian

Public/Private Sphere Dimensions of Gender Norms
Each Dimension Ranging From Traditional to Egalitarian

Figure 2.4 Twenty Illustrative Commuting Zones Plotted by Public/Private Sphere Two-Dimensional Scales of Local Gender Norms

Note: Commuting zones identified by principal city.

with Miami being much more traditional. Yet, it is still rather surprising that the cosmopolitan metro of Miami leans more traditional than Grand Rapids in this two-dimensional public/private sphere framework. It is possible that further detail is needed to understand these unexpected patterns.

Many commuting zones illustrated in Figure 2.4 have some relative differences in gender norms between the public and private sphere. Others, however, have little or virtually no difference, such as Houston, Columbus, Lake Charles, and Minneapolis. Consistent with this, the general ordering of commuting zones from traditional on both dimensions (Little Rock) to egalitarian on both dimensions (Minneapolis) remains unchanged from the unidimensional model, suggesting that areas continue to be differentiated on levels of overall egalitarianism.

The public/private sphere two-dimensional framework for local gender norms provides some additional detail on local cultural environments while also hinting that further complexity may be necessary. This is confirmed with the RMSEA from the public/private sphere CFA model. At 0.090, the RMSEA is slightly better than the unidimensional model but still above the 0.08 threshold and significantly different from 0.05, suggesting that it does not adequately represent the structure of local gender norms. In other words, we still need a better model to describe local gender norms. Two frameworks remain to be tested: the vertical/horizontal and the integrated four-dimensional model.

The Vertical/Horizontal Dimension Framework

The vertical/horizontal framework for describing local gender norms argues that the structure of gender norms contains a vertical component emphasizing men's leadership, power, and advancement as well as a horizontal component conveying norms of essential difference between women and men. Levels of egalitarianism on these dimensions calculated from the CFA models are illustrated in Figure 2.5 for the twenty illustrative commuting zones used in previous sections. For most commuting zones, gender norms are quite similar across vertical and horizontal dimensions. Chicago is slightly more egalitarian on the vertical dimension, but the difference is small. Minneapolis, New York City, Lincoln, South Bend, Lake Charles, and Nashville have nearly identical gender norms across vertical and horizontal dimensions. In some areas, however, differentiating between these aspects of gender norms does capture some detail. New Orleans is somewhat more traditional on the horizontal dimension than the vertical dimension, suggesting strong norms of gender differentiation in this location. Overall, however, vertical and horizontal norms were highly correlated across commuting zones.

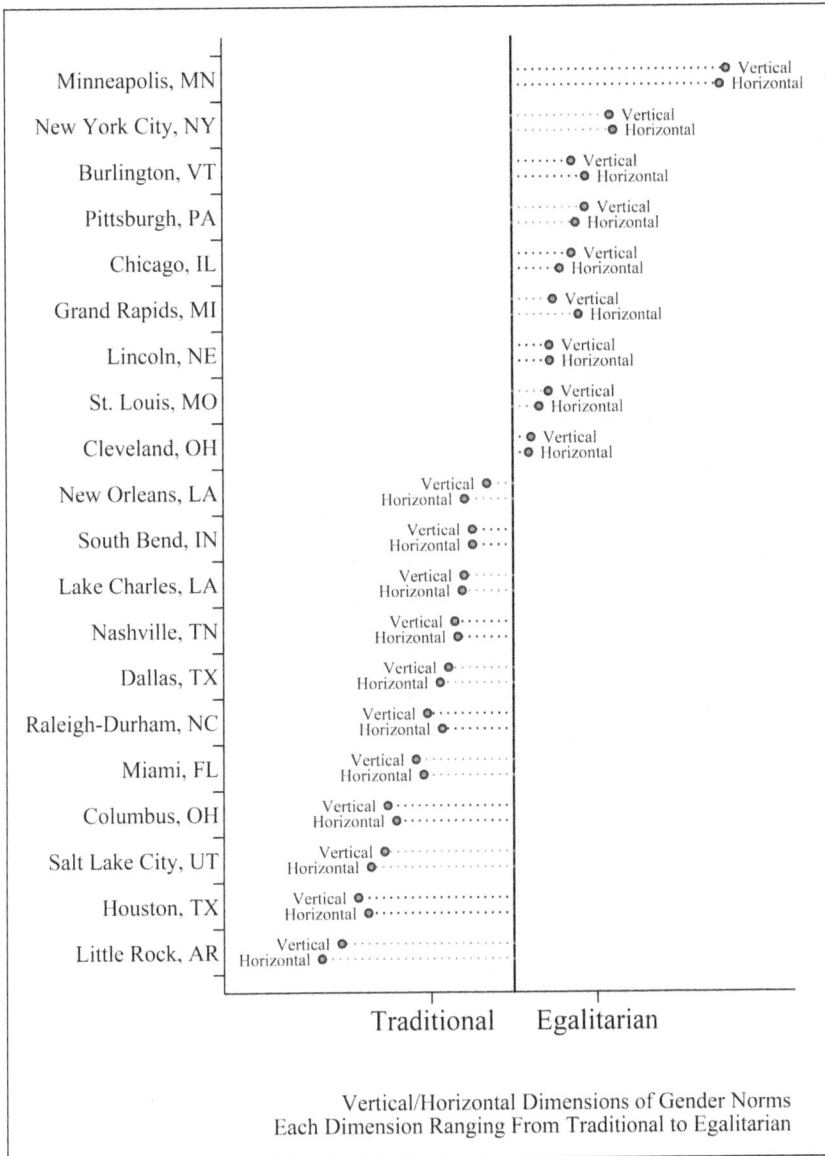

Figure 2.5 Twenty Illustrative Commuting Zones Plotted by Vertical/ Horizontal Two-Dimensional Scales of Local Gender Norms

Note: Commuting zones identified by principal city.

Empirically testing whether the vertical/horizontal framework improves our ability to describe local gender norms, the RMSEA (illustrated in Figure 2.2) reports that this model actually performs worse than both the unidimensional and public/private frameworks. At 0.095, the RMSEA is not only above the 0.08 threshold and significantly different from 0.05, but it is also larger than all previously tested models. In other words, the vertical/horizontal framework provides no additional insight on the structure of gender norms, and the additional complexity of the added dimension actually makes it more difficult to use. Although the vertical/horizontal framework has been used extensively on cross-national studies of gender norms across Europe, these findings suggest it is less applicable to the U.S. context. However, it is also possible that the vertical/horizontal framework remains useful when integrated into the public/private sphere framework to form a four-dimensional model of local gender norms—a prospect I now turn to.

The Integrated Framework

If the public/private and vertical/horizontal frameworks each provide a less than ideal description of local gender norms, does an integrated framework do any better? As discussed earlier, this integrated framework outlines four dimensions of local norms where vertical and horizontal elements take place separately in the public and private sphere. This framework allows for the possibility that support may exist for women's advancement in the public sphere, alongside continued beliefs that women and men are inherently different and, therefore, women's advancement should occur in separate fields from men (public sphere gender essentialism). It also differentiates between beliefs that women should sacrifice careers to provide intensive childcare (intensive mothering) and local endorsement for traditional divisions of labor in the family (private sphere gender essentialism).

Figure 2.6 plots the four dimensions of local gender norms calculated from the integrated CFA model across the same set of commuting zones illustrated in previous sections. Here, we see quite a different picture than what was observed in the unidimensional and two-dimensional frameworks. Nearly all commuting zones show major variability across the four dimensions. Even Minneapolis, which is egalitarian across all dimensions, is found to have particularly high levels of egalitarianism in women's advancement, suggesting that women's educational and occupational success is supported more than other aspects of gender norms in this location. In many commuting zones, we observe exceptional features that were overlooked in previous frameworks providing less detail. Burlington, for example, was found to be highly egalitarian in the unidimensional, public/private, and vertical/horizontal models. However, the integrated framework reveals that Burlington, while egalitarian on most dimensions, is only average on women's advancement. Women in this commuting zone receive less support in terms of career advancement and leadership than other similarly situated places. In Chicago, we find mostly egalitarian norms, but not with respect to intensive mothering, indicating that working moms in this city still experience major barriers and a lack of support. This is in direct contrast with New Orleans, where norms trend slightly traditional except with respect to the dimension related to intensive mothering. In New Orleans, mothers' employment is supported and viewed as not in contradiction to parenting.

The four-dimensional model also adds detail to our comparison of Grand Rapids and Miami. Grand Rapids trended mostly egalitarian when using previous frameworks, but here we find that this area is actually traditional with respect to norms toward women's advancement. In other words, women's leadership and occupational mobility are not widely supported in Grand Rapids. The remaining dimensions are slightly above average in this area. In comparison, Miami has average norms toward women's advancement and much more egalitarian norms toward public sphere gender essentialism. This indicates that women's leadership—and, particularly, equal treatment toward different educational and occupational fields—is more egalitarian in Miami than in Grand Rapids. This is consistent with these areas' respective reputations. However, Miami also has very traditional norms around intensive mothering—meaning that women's careers are only supported so long as they do not have children, which would violate expectations that mothers devote themselves entirely to caregiving. Similarly, norms around gendered divisions of family labor are also traditional in Miami, although not to the extent of intensive mothering.

The comparison of Grand Rapids and Miami highlights an important strength of the four-dimensional model. Although we may conventionally view Miami as more cosmopolitan, liberal, and egalitarian than Grand Rapids, the four-dimensional model reveals that this is true only in norms related to public sphere gender essentialism and, to a lesser extent, women's advancement. Miami is actually the most traditional of all commuting zones in Figure 2.6 when it comes to norms of intensive mothering, while also containing somewhat traditional norms toward the gendered division of family labor.

Figure 2.6 illustrates important within-commuting zone heterogeneity across the four dimensions of gender norms. Yet, we still observe a general pattern where commuting zones are organized along a diagonal axis separating broadly traditional from egalitarian areas. The relationship is imperfect but nonetheless suggests that gender norms may be complex across four

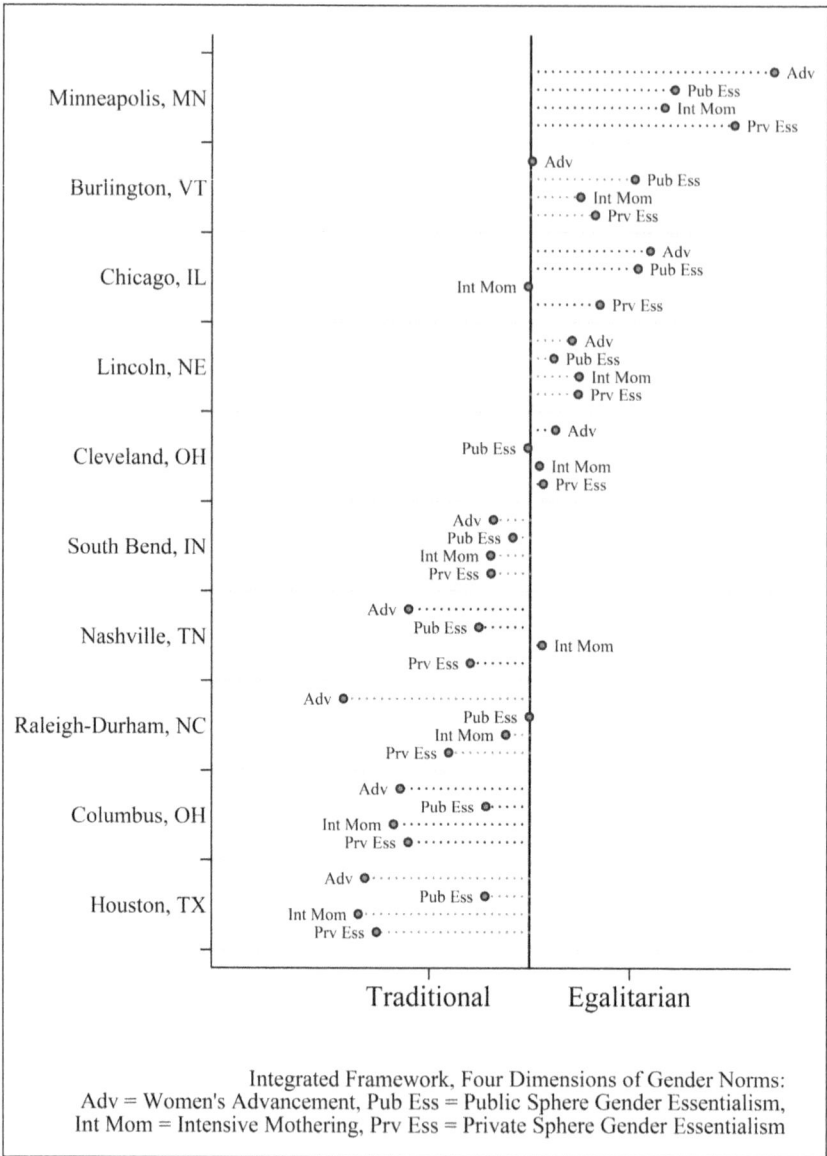

Figure 2.6a Twenty Illustrative Commuting Zones Plotted by Integrated Four-Dimensional Scales of Local Gender Norms

Note: Commuting zones identified by principal city.

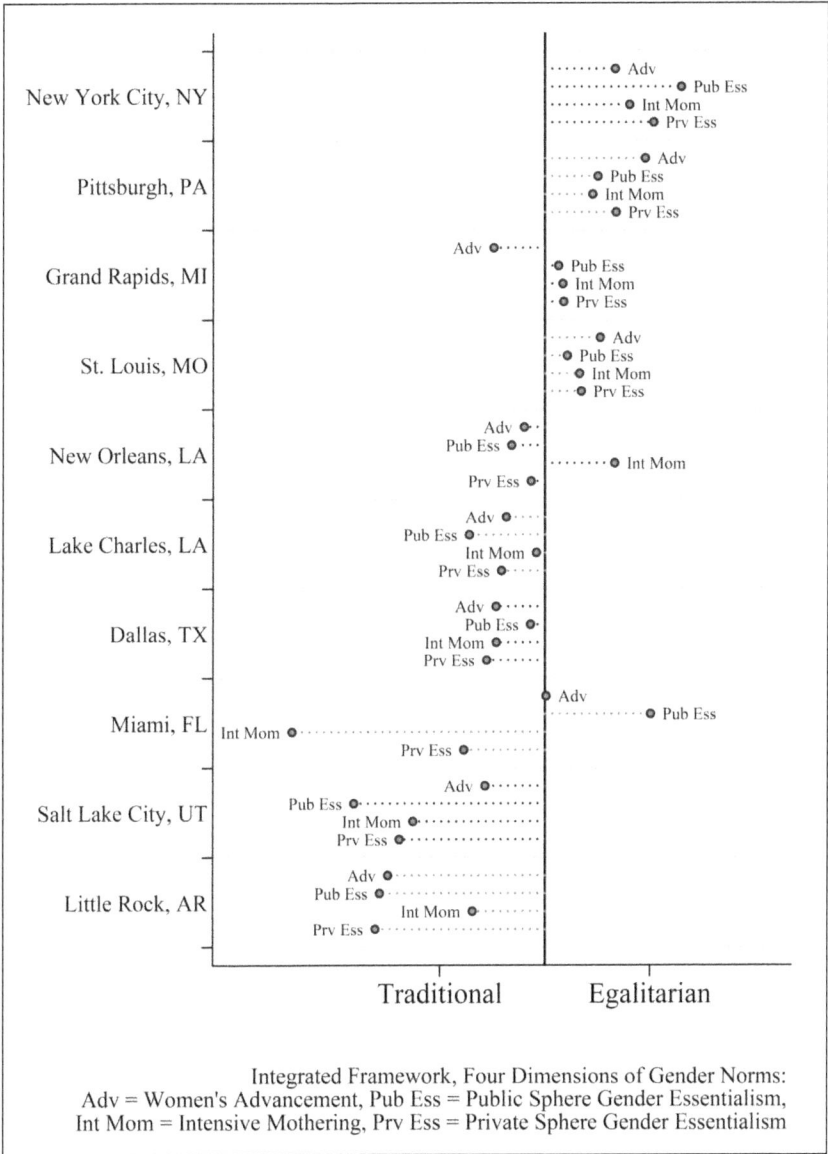

Integrated Framework, Four Dimensions of Gender Norms:
Adv = Women's Advancement, Pub Ess = Public Sphere Gender Essentialism,
Int Mom = Intensive Mothering, Prv Ess = Private Sphere Gender Essentialism

Figure 2.6b

dimensions while still being broadly differentiated between those that generally trend egalitarian and those that lean traditional.

Statistical tests of the usefulness of the integrated four-dimensional model confirm its value. The RMSEA, at 0.063, is far below what was observed for all other frameworks and is under the threshold for defining ideal model fit. It is also not significantly different from 0.05. This suggests that the added complexity of the four-dimensional framework is well worth it to explain the full detail of local gender norms. Thus, not only does the integrated four-dimensional model advance our substantive characterization of local gender norms, but there is also statistical evidence that it provides an ideal description.

Summary of Cultural Frameworks

Both the statistical diagnostic of the RMSEA and the visual comparison of local gender norms across twenty commuting zones point to the usefulness of the integrated four-dimensional framework for describing local gender norms. This framework was best suited for capturing the way areas may be egalitarian in some respects but traditional in others (such as Grand Rapids and Miami). Even among areas that trend egalitarian or traditional in all aspects, the four-dimensional model was able to identify variation in the intensity of these patterns across dimensions. Places like Minneapolis may be generally more egalitarian than most commuting zones, but this is particularly true with respect to norms toward women's advancement. In contrast, Houston has high levels of traditionalism on most dimensions except public sphere gender essentialism, where norms against women and men working in similar roles are less severe than norms that pose barriers to their occupational advancement and convey motherhood as incompatible with a career.

Although the four-dimensional framework provides the most comprehensive account of local gender norms, we should hesitate before hastily rejecting previous approaches. Instead, there is some evidence that cultural frameworks are complementary, rather than competing. Although the unidimensional model provided only marginal model fit, it did surprisingly well considering the simplicity of the single factor it proposes. This suggests that the unidimensional model remains valuable in providing a broad overview of egalitarian cultural environments. Incremental improvements from the unidimensional model were also observed in the two-dimensional public/private sphere model. These findings confirm previous research in the United States showing that gender egalitarianism in the public and private spheres has advanced at different rates and constitutes distinct components of gender norms (Scarborough, Sin, and Risman 2019; Shu and Meagher 2018). Therefore, this two-dimensional public/private sphere model also remains useful in empirical research focusing specifically on differences between social realms. The vertical/horizontal model did not offer an improvement from the unidimensional model. Instead, vertical/horizontal concepts were better integrated in the public/private sphere model via the four-dimensional framework.

Collectively, these findings suggest that existing frameworks for describing gender norms can be ordered hierarchically based on level of detail. This conceptual map is illustrated in Figure 2.7. At the broadest level, a unidimensional understanding of local norms conceptualizing places as varying from traditional to egalitarian provides a clearly interpretable measure of local culture. At the next level of analytical detail, differentiating between norms in the public and private spheres makes it possible to identify contradictions between these two realms and investigate what these cleavages mean. At greatest detail, vertical and horizontal dimensions are identified within both public and private spheres. Here, it is possible to identify specific areas where commuting zones advance in egalitarianism as well as where they may be more traditional.

The benefit of this multilevel approach to understanding gendered environments is that it leverages the strengths of previous models at the same time that it pays attention to their limitations. If we lack detailed data, there is still some empirical usefulness to differentiating places along a simple unidimensional axis from traditional to egalitarian. While less than ideal, the findings presented in this chapter do suggest that this is, at the least, a marginal approach that can provide suggestive descriptions on local gender norms. With greater data availability, we can further impose a two-dimensional framework to see how local gender norms differ across the public sphere of work and the private sphere of the family. This approach gets us a little closer to recognizing the complexity of local norms and may be particularly useful for research focusing on work-family conflict where these social spheres are focal. Last, when fully comprehensive data are available, the most accurate depiction of local gender norms is provided by a four-dimensional model that further breaks down public and private spheres to identify vertical and horizontal components within. Here, we can differentiate between norms around women's advancement and gender essentialism in the public sphere, as well as intensive mothering norms and gender essentialism in the private sphere.

In short, the major takeaway from my analysis is that we can conceptualize local gender norms with varying levels of detail, from the most general unidimensional model to the most detailed four-dimensional framework. This conclusion may surprise some readers familiar with conventional practices in the social sciences. For all intents and purposes, the four-dimension-

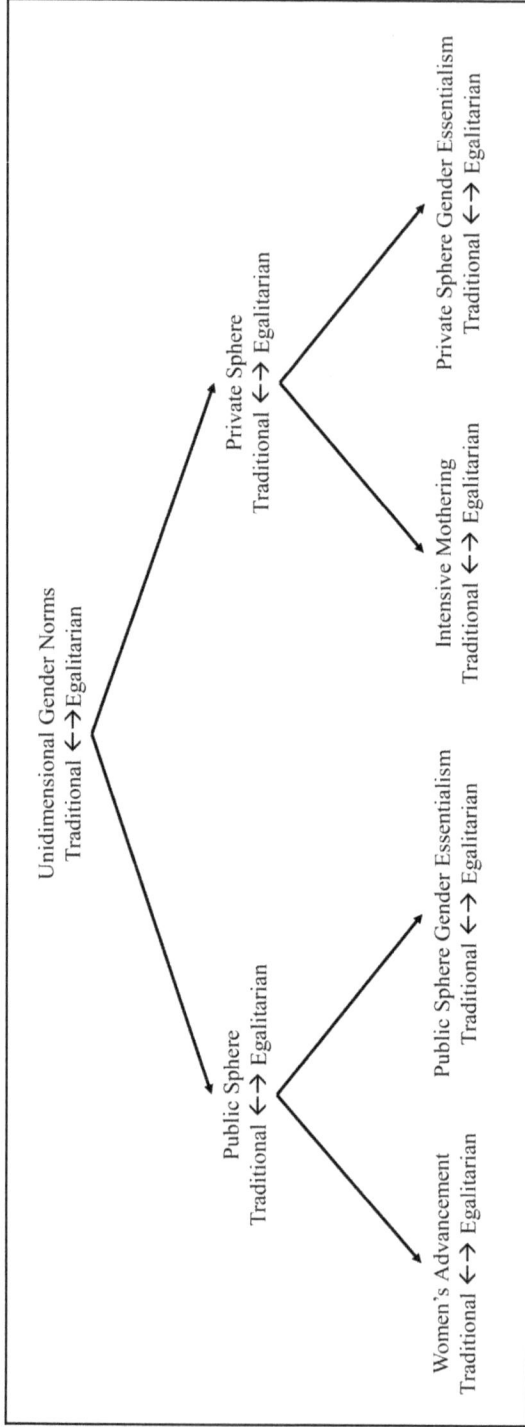

Figure 2.7 Multilevel Framework of Local Gender Norms

al model outperformed all other frameworks in its ability to describe local gender norms. Usually, social scientists would use this as evidence for rejecting previous frameworks as "not good enough" and endorsing the new model. This "warfare" model of science pits theories against each other as though they are competing (P. Collins 2008; Risman 2004). Yet, in reality, many theories, such as the ones tested here, are complementary. The four-dimensional model is developed directly from both the public/private and vertical/horizontal frameworks, which are themselves offshoots of a unidimensional concept. In other words, there is no competition or need to prove prior theories "false" but instead a collective effort to refine and advance our understanding of gender norms by incorporating and learning from what has already been done.

Furthermore, claiming that the four-dimensional model is the "best" misrepresents the primary task we perform in the social sciences. Phenomena like gender norms are tremendously complex and multifaceted. Social scientists reduce the complexity of the social world by using theoretical frameworks that allow us to make sense of social patterns and, in many cases, identify the causes of social inequality. Our aim is to develop frameworks that are accurate reflections of social reality while not being too complex or specific in ways that would render them useless. My contribution in this chapter is showing that the four-dimensional framework provides a more accurate representation of local gender norms than prior frameworks, but it does not mean that those prior frameworks are no longer helpful. Instead, it is possible that in certain applications, a more general conception differentiating unidimensionally egalitarian from traditional areas may shed some light on the role of gender norms. This is particularly true when data are not available to grasp further complexity but gender norms nonetheless should be considered. To the same extent, research focusing on differences between work and family dynamics may not need to use the four-dimensional framework uncovered here but instead could achieve the same ends with greater parsimony by adopting a framework of local norms that merely considers how they vary across public and private spheres.

The multilevel framework outlined in Figure 2.7 also leaves the door open for further inquiry. The work of social science and theoretical development is never done. Although the four-dimensional framework advances our current understanding of the complexity of local gender norms, future research may discover even further detail within these dimensions. Thus, Figure 2.7 could be further expanded on. Importantly, research may consider how gender norms intersect with norms related to other social structures. The relationship between race and gender norms is not a major focus of this text, but the theories and analytic frameworks proposed here may support future research incorporating this level of detail and complexity.

Conclusion

Each of us exists within a cultural environment associated with a particular location. The collection of these spatially bound cultural resources has been referred to by Ann Swidler (1986) as a "cultural tool kit." Although we have little choice with regard to the types of cultural tools in our tool kit, we do get to decide which to use and how to use them. One powerful aspect of these bounded cultural tool kits are gender norms—the set of expectations differentiating conduct between women and men (Pearse and Connell 2016). Studying gender norms, scholars have focused heavily on their cross-national variation. They have uncovered, for example, how gender norms in Italy are different from those in Germany, which are different from those in Great Britain.

Although cross-national research pays less attention to whether gender norms vary on a local level, it has established three frameworks for conceptualizing the structure of gender norms that we can use as a foundation for more local applications. First, a unidimensional framework theorizes that nations' gendered cultural environments range along a single axis from traditional to egalitarian. In traditional places, women are not expected to work or have leadership positions and are presumed to have full responsibility of home and family, while in egalitarian areas, women and men are held to similar expectations across all aspects of social life. A second framework proposes that gender norms vary between the public sphere of work and the private sphere of the family. This perspective accounts for instances where a nation's gender norms may support equality in the public sphere while continuing to exhibit traditional norms in the private sphere, where women are expected to do the majority of housework and childcare. A third perspective outlines two different dimensions: a vertical aspect privileging men's access to power and leadership and a horizontal component conveying norms of essential difference between women and men.

The three perspectives offered by cross-national research indicate that individuals' available cultural tool kit varies greatly depending on their geographical location. Gender-typical preferences are more likely to form in environments with strong horizontal norms of gender essentialism, while biases against women in the workforce are more prevalent in countries with traditional public sphere norms. Using these theoretical frameworks as a foundation to examine the structure of gender norms across U.S. commuting zones, this chapter introduced a fourth approach that integrated prior conceptions of gender norms. This integrated model outlines vertical and horizontal components of gender norms taking place in both the public and private spheres. In the public sphere, norms around women's advancement capture vertical aspects, while horizontal components are observed in norms of public sphere gender essentialism conveying beliefs that women and men are essentially suited for different types of jobs. In the private sphere, vertical aspects of culture are reflected in intensive mothering norms conveying expectations that motherhood is contradictory to employment. Horizontal norms of private sphere gender essentialism convey gendered expectations toward ideal family roles, such as men's breadwinning and women's home-making.

Using a set of eight cultural indicators capturing the many ways that gender norms shape various aspects of social life, this chapter presented the results of latent modeling (CFA), which allows us to examine the many impressions gender norms leave in society in order to define and triangulate their structure. Statistical diagnostics and the inspection of gender norms in twenty commuting zones revealed the strengths and limitations of each of the four frameworks used to describe the structure of gender norms. The unidimensional model provided only a marginal description of local gender norms, but it did surprisingly well given the simplicity of the framework. At greater detail, the public/private sphere approach highlighted how norms vary across different social spheres, but the results showed that this approach was also unable to capture important complexity in local gender norms. The vertical/horizontal framework did not perform well on its own and was better integrated into the four-dimensional model, which provided the most comprehensive account of local gender norms. Viewing gender norms as composed of four dimensions related to women's advancement, public sphere gender essentialism, intensive mothering, and private sphere gender essentialism provided the best framework for describing the complexity of local gender norms. Additionally, statistical diagnostics confirmed that the four-dimensional framework is ideal for describing how cultural indicators are related.

This chapter revealed that gender norms are multidimensional. As we observed with the opening vignette describing Elly May's transition from rural Missouri to the upper-class enclave of Beverly Hills, places can exhibit traditional norms in some respects (such as Elly May's overly feminine style) and egalitarian norms in others (Elly May's ability to overpower the school bully in a wrestling match). Those of us moving from place to place throughout the United States may experience complex forms of gender-based culture shock along the way. Moving to New Orleans, we would find that working mothers are culturally supported in employment but that there remain barriers to occupational gender integration as women and men are viewed as naturally suited for different jobs. Heading north to Chicago, we would find a more egalitarian environment in most respects except toward working mothers, as intensive mothering norms pose barriers to maternal employment. From Chicago we could go east to the liberal enclave of Burlington, only to find that the feminist ideals of gender egalitarianism do not extend to norms of women's advancement, as men are still viewed as more suitable for leadership and careers than women. An important lesson from this chapter is that we can expand our understanding of places' gender norms as not universally egalitarian or traditional but with dynamic, and often contradictory, dimensions pertaining to various aspects of social life.

Key findings from this chapter show that gender norms in U.S. commuting zones contain four dimensions. A typical hypothesis-testing interpretation of these findings would result in rejecting previous theories of gender norms (such as the unidimensional framework) and endorsing the new four-dimensional model. While this method of science has merit, sociologists have often noted how such "warfare" approaches of pitting theories against each other often limit inquiry by obscuring the way that theoretical frameworks can be complementary, rather than competing (P. Collins 2008; Risman 2004). Viewed from this epistemological standpoint, the results of this chapter point to a richer multilevel framework of gender norms (illustrated in Figure 2.7) that integrates previous theories while still advancing new innovations. From this perspective, we may recognize that the unidimensional model, while not providing the most comprehensive account of local norms, may still be valuable in contexts where data are unable to capture multidimensionality but gender norms should nonetheless be considered. We may similarly recognize that the public/private sphere framework also misses important detail but could be advantageous in certain circumstances, such as research focusing on work/family conflict. Although the vertical/horizontal framework did not perform well in describing local norms, it was crucial in formulating the four-dimensional framework that provided the most comprehensive and precise description of local gender norms. Using the four-dimensional framework, researchers can identify internal heterogeneity within commuting zones to understand where they exhibit egalitarianism and where they have stalled.

A multilevel theoretical framework for describing local gender norms recognizes that there are times when research requires a detailed analysis that would benefit from a four-dimensional model and other instances when a more simplified framework is needed. Researchers must balance nuance with relevance (Healy 2017). The theoretical tools, constructs, and models used in research are intended to simplify the complexity of social life to extract meaningful patterns and insight. In conceptualizing local environments, we must be cognizant of the level of abstraction used in our theoretical approach. The multilevel framework suggested here may help in this endeavor. Scholars using a unidimensional approach may position their research as simplifying more complex phenomena, while those adopting the four-dimensional model may remind readers that variation across the dimensions occurs within differentiation between broadly construed egalitarian and traditional areas.

Throughout the rest of this book, I focus on the four-dimensional framework of local gender norms because the extensive data applied here allows for this level of detail. In addition, examining local gender norms across these four dimensions adds important insight to our understanding of both geographical variation and the consequences of local culture on inequality. Moving forward, in the next chapter I map the terrain of gender norms, highlighting spatial variation across the country as well as providing a more detailed overview of gender norms in an illustrative set of commuting zones that represent the diverse array of cultural environments found within the United States.

TABLE 2.4   DETAILED RESULTS OF CONFIRMATORY FACTOR ANALYSIS EXAMINING DIMENSIONS OF LOCAL GENDER NORMS

Variables	One factor	Two factor		Three factor			Four factor		
	Gender egalitarianism	Public	Private	Vertical	Horizontal	Advancement	Public sphere gender essentialism	Intensive mothering	Private sphere gender essentialism
Proportion disagree, men better suited for politics than women	0.716***	0.801***		0.723***		0.869***			
Implicit attitudes toward women in careers	−0.270**	−0.338***		−0.268**		−0.335**			
Implicit attitudes toward women in science	−0.393***	−0.457***			−0.390***		−0.619***		
Gender segregation in field of bachelor's degree	−0.379***	−0.409***			−0.374***		−0.460***		
Proportion agree, working mothers can establish warm relationship with child	0.575***		0.563***	0.591***				0.735***	
Proportion disagree, preschool children suffer if mother works	0.534***		0.531***	0.548***				0.743***	
Proportion disagree, better if man works and woman tends home	0.928***		0.952***		0.950***				0.898***
Proportion of positive tweets toward feminism on Mother's Day/Father's Day	0.386***		0.382***		0.383***				0.404***

Correlations between latent variables

	Model 1	Model 2	Model 3	Model 4
Public, private		-0.958***		
Vertical, horizontal			0.850***	
Advancement, public sphere gender essentialism				-0.629***
Advancement, intensive mothering				0.488***
Advancement, private sphere gender essentialism				0.852***
Public sphere gender essentialism, intensive mothering				-0.175
Public sphere gender essentialism, private sphere gender essentialism				-0.679***
Intensive mothering, private sphere gender essentialism				0.742***

Goodness of fit

	Model 1	Model 2	Model 3	Model 4
χ^2	47.356	43.791	46.998	22.22
χ^2 model vs. saturated, p-value	0.000	0.001	0.000	0.052
$\Delta\chi^2$ (df) vs. gender egalitarianism	–	3.57 (1)	0.36 (1)	25.14*** (6)
$\Delta\chi^2$ (df) vs. public/private	–	–	non-nested	21.57*** (5)
$\Delta\chi^2$ (df) vs. vertical/horizontal	–	–	–	24.78*** (5)
RMSEA	0.092	0.090	0.095	0.063
CFI	0.846	0.860	0.843	0.950

Note: Latent variables scaled so that higher scores indicate gender egalitarianism. χ^2 = chi-squared statistic; $\Delta\chi^2$ = difference in chi-squared between models; df = degrees of freedom; RMSEA = root mean square error of approximation; CFI = comparative fit index. Significance levels: *p < 0.05, **p < 0.001, ***p < 0.001.

3

Mapping the Terrain of Local Gender Norms

Planning your next vacation any time soon? You might consider a tour of the state of Wisconsin. Sure, it gets less fanfare than the tourist hot-spots of Florida or California, but the "Badger State" has much to offer. Head to Milwaukee for a vibrant downtown and thriving brewery scene. Door County, a massive peninsula jutting into Lake Michigan, is known as the "Cape Cod of the Midwest" and is full of tranquil coastal towns, stunning beaches, and acres of wilderness. Move inland to discover rolling hills and striking sandstone formations along the state's western corridor. Those looking for more excitement could venture to the class IV rapids along the Wolf River or visit the theme parks in the Wisconsin Dells for a more family-friendly adventure. You might then consider a relaxing stay in the state capital of Madison—known for its bohemian atmosphere and laid-back vibes.

One thing you probably would not consider when planning your vacation is the local gender norms of the places you visit. After all, you cannot exactly use Google to find out whether the gender stereotypes in Appleton will be constraining or if norms of intensive mothering in Milwaukee will shape the way you are perceived with your child. Yet places already have reputations that can convey rather clear messages about local gender dynamics. Take, for example, the following descriptions of Milwaukee and Madison from Lonely Planet's online travel guide—one of the most widely used sources of travel information and a likely resource you may refer to when planning your Wisconsin vacation.

Here's the thing about Milwaukee: it's cool, but for some reason it slips under the radar. The city's reputation as a working man's town of brewskis, bowling alleys and polka halls persists. But attractions like the Calatrava-designed art museum, the badass Harley-Davidson Museum and stylish eating and shopping enclaves have turned Wisconsin's largest city into an unassumingly groovy place. (Lonely Planet entry for Milwaukee)

Madison reaps a lot of kudos—most walkable city, best road-biking city, most vegetarian-friendly, gay-friendly, environmentally friendly and just plain all-round friendliest city in the USA. Ensconced on a narrow isthmus between Mendota and Monona Lakes, it's a pretty combination of small, grassy state capital and liberal, bookish college town. (Lonely Planet entry for Madison)

It is hard to miss the gendered terms used by Lonely Planet to describe Milwaukee. Not only is the city known as a "working man's town," but even museums are described in masculine terms, such as being "badass." This gendered language is no coincidence. Considering the measures of local gender norms developed in the previous chapter (see Figure 3.1), we can see that

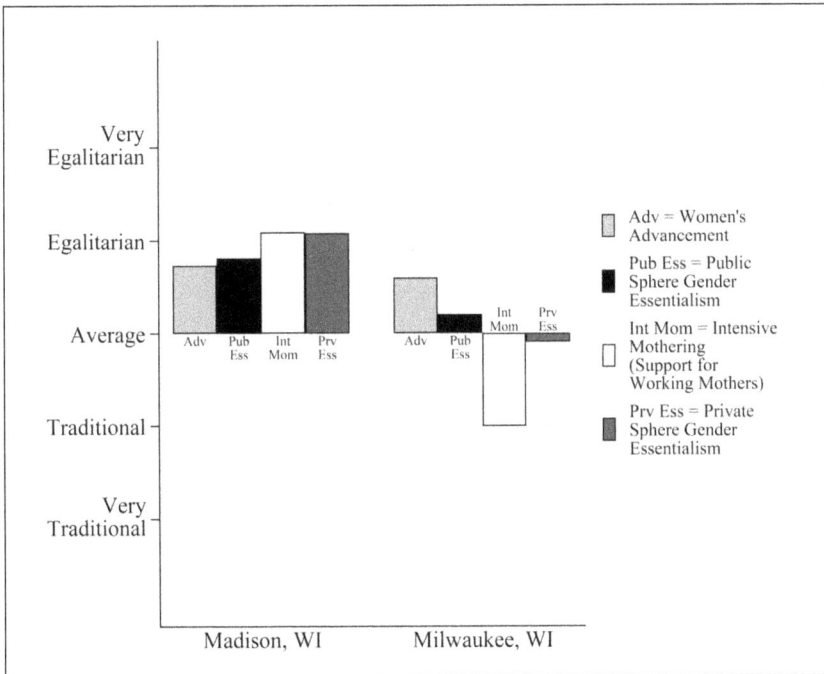

Figure 3.1 Local Gender Norms in Madison and Milwaukee

Milwaukee is very much a "working man's town" and not at all a town for working moms. More than any other area in Wisconsin, and more than the majority of places in the United States, Milwaukee has traditional gender norms toward intensive mothering—meaning that moms in this city are expected to leave their careers to focus entirely on childcare.

Contrast Milwaukee with neighboring Madison. Lonely Planet uses the word "friendly" four times in the first sentence of their description for this city. Vegetarian, gay friendly, environmental, liberal, small, bookish—Madison is portrayed as an easygoing, bohemian town. This narrative corresponds to Madison's scores on the four dimensions of gender norms developed in Chapter 2. Madison is not only the most egalitarian place in Wisconsin, but it is also much more egalitarian than most areas in the United States. Whereas careers are discouraged for mothers in Milwaukee, working moms are supported in Madison. Couples are expected to make equal contributions to the home, and women and men are viewed as generally suitable for the same types of jobs.

Only eighty miles away, Madison and Milwaukee appear a world apart. We might visit Milwaukee for the beer and baseball and Madison for the bookstores and eccentric coffee shops. But when traveling from one place to another, we also traverse different cultural environments that contain varying expectations toward women and men. In addition to the distinct gender norms in Madison and Milwaukee, your tour of Wisconsin would also reveal that women and men are viewed as having essentially different work-related skills in the area surrounding Appleton (see Figure 3.2). We would experience perceptions that men are more suited for leadership in La Crosse, but not so much in and around Wausau.

Variation in gender norms is not only unique to Wisconsin. Instead, gender norms vary on a local level across the country, with neighboring places often having very different gendered cultural environments. In this chapter, I provide the first-ever "travel guide" of local gender norms across the United States. First, I map nationwide variation in each of the four dimensions of local gender norms, illustrating some regional clustering while, at the same time, highlighting the ways neighboring commuting zones frequently have distinct gender norms. After reporting nationwide visualizations, I then zoom in to focus on an illustrative group of six commuting zones with different configurations of the four dimensions of gender norms. I highlight a set of commuting zones that are generally egalitarian across all dimensions of gender norms, a set that are universally traditional, and a third set that are egalitarian in some respects but traditional in others. To understand how these norms are reflected in individuals' experiences, I draw on qualitative research that has been conducted in each of these locations. Contextualizing findings from qualitative research with respect to the local gender norms

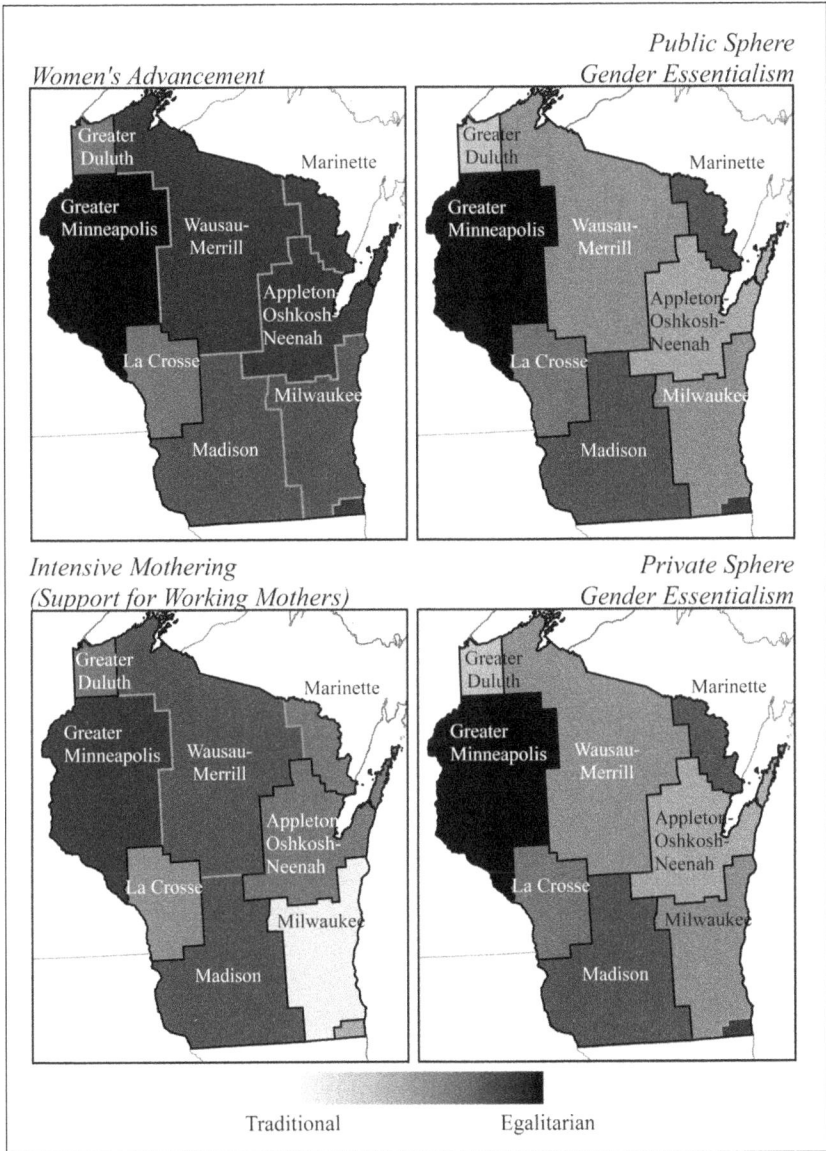

Figure 3.2 Local Gender Norms across Wisconsin Commuting Zones

identified in this book allows us to observe how individuals' behaviors and perspectives relate to their local cultural environment. In the last section of this chapter, I examine the factors associated with local gender norms. I compare three sets of commuting zones with similar economic conditions but very different gender norms, showing how gender norms are not reducible to the types of industries that predominate or the jobs available but instead constitute a central feature of places in their own right. This leads to the question of what causes gender norms to vary from place to place, a topic explored in Chapter 4.

Mapping the Terrain of Gender Norms across the United States

Figure 3.3 provides the first-ever map of local gender norms across U.S. commuting zones. At first glance, we can observe some regional clustering. In general, the most traditional areas are in the South and across the center of the country. The most egalitarian places, in contrast, are found along the West Coast and in the Northeast. Importantly, however, many West Coast commuting zones exhibit traditional norms with respect to intensive mothering, standing in contrast to places in the Northeast that are egalitarian on this dimension, as they are more generally across all dimensions of gender norms.

A closer look reveals greater complexity to regional clustering. First, traditionalism in the South is most pronounced with respect to norms of women's advancement. Places like Birmingham, Alabama; Memphis, Tennessee; Jackson, Mississippi; and Tallahassee, Florida, are all located in the South and have some of the most traditional norms toward women's advancement where women are viewed as less suitable for leadership positions than men. Second, norms of egalitarianism in the Northeast and along the West Coast are the strongest on the dimension pertaining to public sphere gender essentialism. In these coastal areas, women and men are viewed as equally capable across a variety of work-related tasks. The difference between the Northeast/West Coast and other regions is less pronounced with respect to norms toward private sphere gender essentialism while being virtually absent, particularly along the West Coast, when it comes to norms of intensive mothering. In fact, the West Coast is no better than the South when it comes to supporting mothers' employment. This confirms prior research examining state-level supports for maternal labor force participation that found that conditions in many Democratic-leaning states located along the West Coast are often no better at facilitating mothers' employment than the supports provided to mothers in Republican-leaning southern states (Ruppanner 2020).

Although there is some regional clustering, when we look within regions, we find that neighboring commuting zones often have very different gender norms. Austin, Texas, for example, is far more egalitarian than nearby Houston on all dimensions. Lexington, Kentucky, is more traditional than bordering Louisville. Meanwhile, Cleveland is generally more traditional than nearby Detroit while also being more egalitarian across the four dimensions

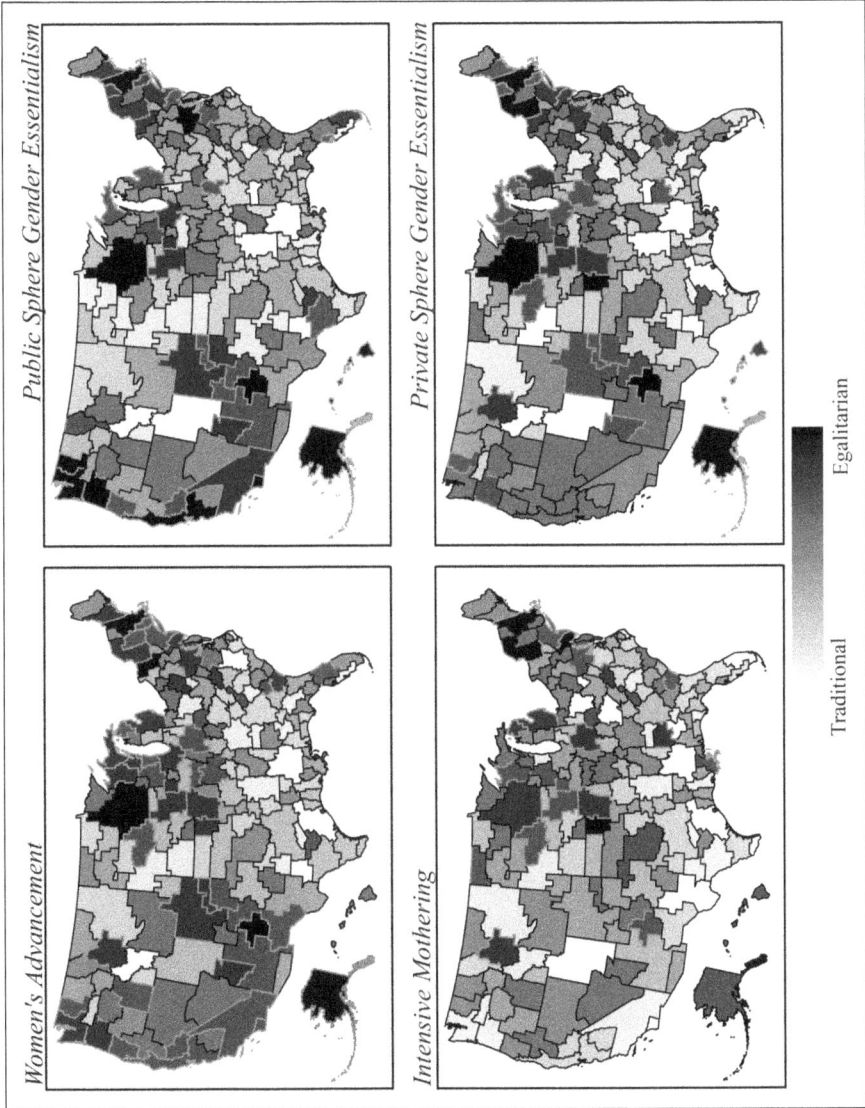

Figure 3.3 Mapping the Dimensions of Gender Norms across the United States

of gender norms than Columbus. In other words, we can often travel only a short distance to the nearest commuting zone and experience quite a different set of gender norms.

In other instances, differences between neighboring locales vary by specific dimensions of gender norms. New Orleans is more supportive of working mothers (egalitarian on intensive mothering norms) while exhibiting more traditional norms of women's and men's essential difference (public sphere gender essentialism) than nearby Baton Rouge. Las Vegas and Reno are both entertainment hubs known for casinos. These areas have similar gender norms with respect to women's advancement and private sphere gender essentialism, but Reno is more egalitarian than Las Vegas when it comes to public sphere gender essentialism, and Las Vegas reports greater cultural support for working mothers (egalitarian on intensive mothering) than Reno. There is also major variation in gender norms within Florida, where the most egalitarian commuting zone depends largely on which dimension of gender norms we examine. Orlando is the most egalitarian with respect to women's advancement. Norms toward public sphere gender essentialism are the most egalitarian in Miami. Support for working mothers (intensive mothering) and egalitarian norms of private sphere gender essentialism are most prevalent in Tampa.

The opening of this book started with a hypothetical road trip along the iconic Route 66. In Figure 3.3, we see that travelers along this highway not only experience an array of scenic landscapes and local flair but also very different gender norms. Starting in Chicago, we would enjoy mostly egalitarian gender norms, except when it comes to intensive mothering. Many in the Chicago area continue to hold the expectation that mothers should not be employed. Moving south toward St. Louis, we would find somewhat greater support for working mothers but less egalitarian norms on all other dimensions. In particular, women's occupational advancement is supported far less in and around St. Louis. We would likely encounter fewer women in management and political leadership during this stretch. Following Route 66 south, we would be pleasantly surprised to find that mothers' employment and equal divisions of household labor are highly valued in Oklahoma City, where we would likely see many engaged fathers. At the same time, however, it would be rare for us to find women and men working in the same occupations, or women in leadership, because gender norms toward women's advancement and public sphere gender essentialism are fairly traditional in Oklahoma City. Continuing our trip to the west, we would find that the most egalitarian gender norms along Route 66 are in Albuquerque. In this area, more than any other along Route 66, women's leadership is supported, women and men are viewed as equally suited for different jobs, maternal employment is embraced, and women and men are expected to contribute equally to family life. Finishing our trip along the sandy beaches outside Los Angeles, we might be surprised to end our journey in a place with gender norms that are not that different from where we started in Chicago. Like the Midwest metropolis, Los Angeles is mostly egalitarian except with respect to norms toward intensive mothering, where mothers continue to face cultural barriers to employment.

Mapping the terrain of gender norms across U.S. commuting zones, we find clear evidence that the United States is not a cultural monolith but instead is composed of a wide variety of different cultural environments related to gender that vary not only geographically but also across dimensions of gender norms within the same location. When traveling from place to place in the United States, we traverse an undulating terrain of gender norms. Considering this variety of cultural environments, we might be inclined to generate new monikers for the places we reside or visit. Minneapolis might be labeled as a "beacon of egalitarianism in the Midwest." In addition to the vibrant beaches and nightlife, a review of Miami might include a warning to mothers that they may be judged if they are not highly attentive to their children. In contrast, many commuting zones in Oklahoma, particularly Oklahoma City, might consider marketing their egalitarian gender norms on some dimensions: "Visit Oklahoma—come for the scenery, stay for the gender equal divisions of household labor."

The United States is both geographically large and highly diverse. Here, we have seen the varying landscape of gender norms across the United States. Taking a drive across the country, via Route 66 or otherwise, we would experience quite a variety of local gender norms. Yet, we need not travel very far to experience different gender norms; neighboring commuting zones often have distinct configurations of norms conveying expectations for women and men. Now that we have reviewed maps that illustrate this variation, we will zoom in to explore an illustrative set of commuting zones and get a better idea of what it is like to reside in places with a particular set of norms.

Zooming in on Six Illustrative Commuting Zones

In this section, I highlight six commuting zones with varying configurations of local norms. Two places, Boston and Minneapolis, are universally egalitarian across all dimensions of gender norms. Two other locations, Columbus and Salt Lake City, are universally traditional. Two additional commuting zones, San Francisco and New Orleans, have contradictory gender norms. They are egalitarian on some dimensions but traditional on others.

Boston and Minneapolis: Universally Egalitarian

Boston has a long-standing reputation as a center of feminist activism. During the height of feminist organizing in the 1960s and 1970s, Boston was home to some of the most active groups in the country (Spain 2016). Many of these groups ran or supported feminist bookstores and women's health centers—spaces that would be emulated in cities across the country. Perhaps one of the most influential feminist texts, the Combahee River Collective Statement, was authored by a feminist group of scholars and activists based in Boston. Given this history, it is unsurprising that the Boston commuting zone is found to have some of the most egalitarian gender norms in the country (see Figure 3.4). Across all four dimensions, gender norms in Boston are highly supportive of gender equality. Women are viewed as similarly qualified for leadership as men, women and men are seen as equally suited for different types of work, mothers' employment is supported, and equal divisions of family labor are highly encouraged.

On the aggregate, Boston is highly egalitarian. This not only resonates with its history of feminist activism, but it is also supported by qualitative research studying the experience of Boston residents. Allison Daminger (2020), for example, interviewed thirty-two different-gender Boston couples about their relationships and household divisions of labor. She finds that the vast majority felt strongly that household chores should be equally divided between women and men. Highlighting how one couple feels about gender norms, Daminger (2020: 806) writes:

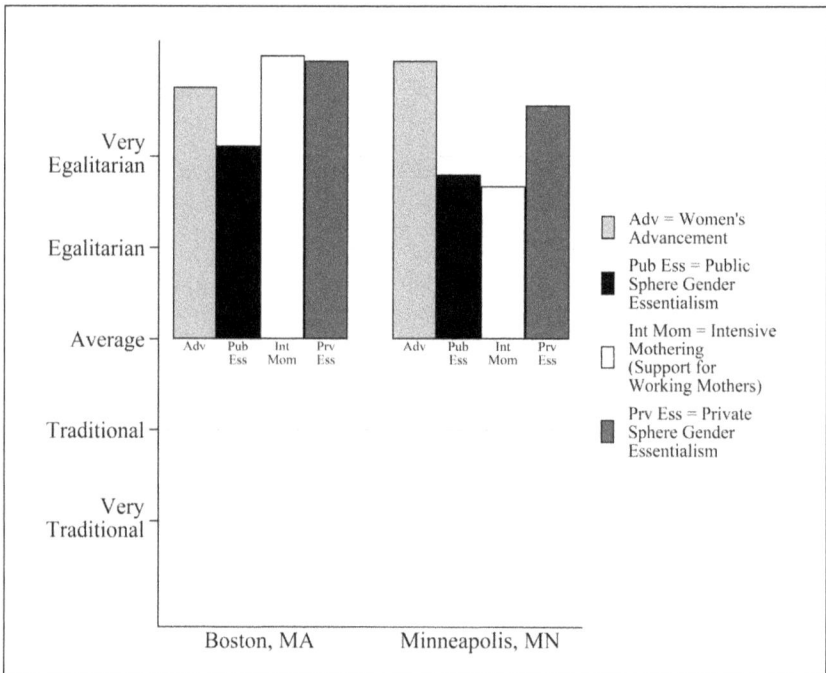

Figure 3.4 Illustrative Set of Universally Egalitarian Commuting Zones

> Heather and Jeremy, married parents of two toddlers, are a proudly egalitarian couple. In separate interviews, Jeremy reported that "[we] don't believe in a lot of traditional gender norms. . . . We think a lot of that stuff is nonsense," and Heather argued that "obviously ideally [our division of household labor] is 50/50."

Like Heather and Jeremy, the vast majority of couples interviewed by Daminger valued gender equality and supported egalitarian gender norms. Another of Daminger's (2020: 813) respondents stated that they "want it [division of labor] to be an equal partnership," and a third respondent is quoted as saying that, ideally, household labor "washes out to a good 50/50." Summarizing her full sample, Daminger (2020: 813) states, "Most respondents described their 'ideal world' division of labor as something close to a 50/50 split." Importantly, however, Daminger also found that few couples fulfilled these ideals. Logs of household tasks revealed that the majority nonetheless had unequal divisions of family labor, with women performing most of the domestic work. Her research shows that support for egalitarian norms does not necessarily translate to egalitarian behavior, a topic I explore in Chapter 4. Nonetheless, her research does illustrate that gender egalitarian ideals are normative in Boston, a major departure from other places in the United States, discussed in the following, where couples explicitly endorse more traditional norms.

Whereas egalitarian norms in Boston may be expected given the city's history of feminist activism, more surprising are the high levels of egalitarian gender norms across all four dimensions in the commuting zone of Minneapolis. Although the northern Midwest may be better known for cold winters than feminist activism, norms in Minneapolis are comparably egalitarian to those in Boston. For the most part, women's leadership is supported, they are perceived as equally capable of different jobs as men, women's employment is viewed as not in contradiction to motherhood, and equal divisions of family labor are valued. Support for mothers' employment is lower in Minneapolis than Boston but still much higher than the average commuting zone in the United States.

Confirming these patterns, Minneapolis is often cited as a beacon of egalitarianism and tolerance in the Midwest. In her book, *Men in Place*, Miriam Abelson drew from interviews with trans men residing throughout the United States to understand the areas where they felt safe and free to challenge conventional norms of masculinity in comparison to other locations where they perceived local environments as hostile to their personal expressions. Although the Midwest as a whole was described as being unwelcoming to trans men, Minneapolis was viewed as a safe and welcoming environment. One respondent quoted by Abelson (2019: 139) stated that the Twin Cities (Minneapolis and St. Paul) were "just a lovely little corridor" where "it's really open-minded and I feel perfectly safe." This was in contrast to other parts of the state where this individual did not feel safe or welcome—"west, closer to the Dakotas. Basically, that whole stretch of the side of the state I would avoid." Abelson's research highlights how local gender norms relate not only to relations between different gender couples but also to the experience of trans men and others whose identity may be viewed as violating gender norms in more traditional environments.

Egalitarian gender norms in Minneapolis are also reflected in the widely publicized family-friendly policies instituted by major employers in the city. About four thousand workers are employed at the corporate headquarters of Best Buy, located in a southern suburb of Minneapolis. This workplace was among the first in the country to pilot a Results-Only Work Environment (ROWE), where employees were evaluated not on the hours they worked but on the outcomes they produced. Under ROWE, workers have highly flexible schedules and are free to work remotely or in their office, so long as expectations are fulfilled. Research examining the effects of ROWE at Best Buy conducted by Phyllis Moen, Erin Kelly, and their research team (2007) found that the program reduced work-family conflict, lowered employee turnover, and improved worker satisfaction. ROWE and its associated benefits challenge conventional ideal worker norms that presume full-time employees have a partner (often a woman) to be fully responsible for housework and caregiving tasks while they perform forty or more hours of paid labor per week. It is no coincidence that this innovative and family-friendly program was first launched on such a large scale in the gender-egalitarian environment of Minneapolis.[1]

Salt Lake City and Columbus: Universally Traditional

A world apart from Boston and Minneapolis, Salt Lake City is the population center of the state of Utah and a cultural hub for the Mormon religion. Gender norms in Salt Lake City are traditional across all four dimensions (see Figure 3.5). In particular, there are strong beliefs that women and men are essentially suited for different work, that mothers should not be employed, and that men should work while women tend the home. Norms against women's leadership and advancement are also much more traditional than most places in the United States.

Salt Lake City's traditional gender norms reflect the place's reputation as a hub of religious conservatism and the center of the Church of Jesus Christ of Latter-day Saints (LDS) whose followers are commonly known as Mormons. Originally settled by Mormons in the mid-1800s, local culture and policies are deeply intertwined with the LDS church. To this day, religious leaders frequently double as local politicians. About 90 percent of state legis-

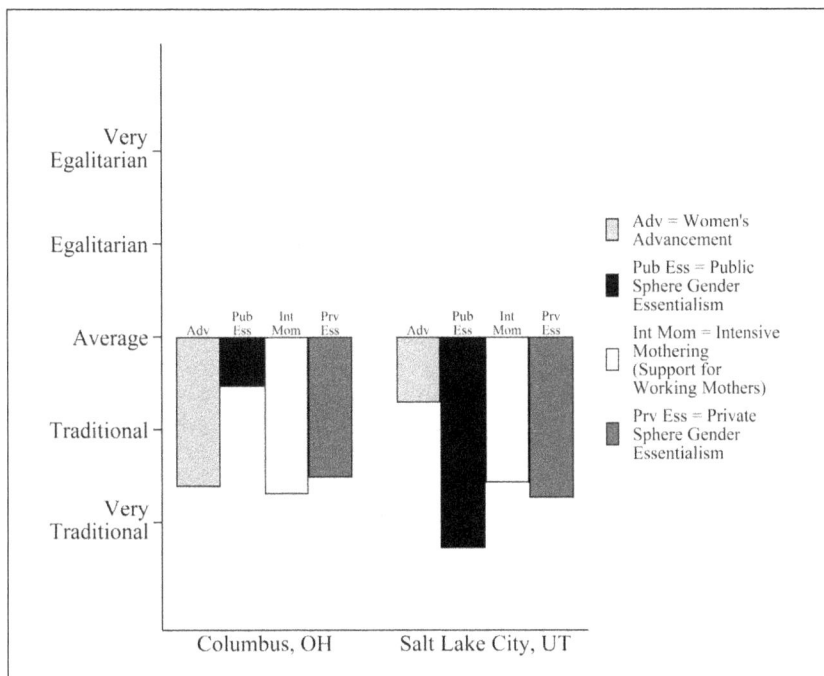

Figure 3.5 Illustrative Set of Universally Traditional Commuting Zones

lators in Utah are members of the LDS church, and it is not uncommon for these policy makers to cite religious scripture in arguing their political positions in Congress (Alexander 2020). Research from Reid Leamaster and Mangala Subramaniam (2016) shows just how much these religious ties shape local gender norms. They illustrate how leaders in the LDS church frequently endorse traditional gender norms emphasizing the expectation for women to marry and focus on childbearing. Leamaster and Subramaniam quote one leader speaking at a major religious conference in Salt Lake City who described contemporary feminism as:

> A pernicious philosophy that undermines women's moral influence is the devaluation of marriage and of motherhood and homemaking as a career. (Christofferson 2013: 30, quoted in Leamaster and Subramaniam 2016: 783)

These traditional values conveyed by the LDS church are also reflected in women's and men's ideals. In interviews with Mormon residents in and around Salt Lake City, Leamaster and Subramaniam found that the majority adhered closely to traditional gender norms endorsing men's role as primary decision makers, beliefs in essential differences between women and men, and strong views that women should be primarily responsible for home/ family while men should focus on generating family income. A common sentiment shared by respondents was the feeling that holding a career was in contradiction to motherhood. As stated by Leamaster and Subramaniam, many respondents felt that "mothering or achieving career success is an either/or proposition" (2016: 785). In fact, nearly all respondents felt there was no greater purpose than motherhood, as exemplified by an individual referred to by the authors as Nicole, who stated, "I think that's why it's so important that we as moms, in the gospel and in the LDS faith, help our daughters understand what a blessing it is to be a mom and to fulfill this role" (Leamaster and Subramaniam 2016: 785). Like many mothers in their study, Nicole was a college graduate but nonetheless did not plan to use her education in a career. Instead, she intended to stay at home once her children were born: "I just figured, get it [college degree] done and then I can be a mom and have my family and make that my main focus" (Leamaster and Subramaniam 2016: 792).

The views of Nicole and other individuals interviewed by Leamaster and Subramaniam illustrate the common endorsement of traditional gender norms in Salt Lake City, particularly those reflecting intensive mothering. Another interview by these researchers illustrates how traditionalism in the remaining dimensions of gender norms is also reflected in individuals' perceptions of family life and employment. Brian and his wife, Trish, were also college educated but, like Nicole, nonetheless planned to have a traditional household arrangement with Brian working and Trish staying home after they had children. As reported by Leamaster and Subramaniam (2016: 787), Brian stated,

> After Trish, my wife, finished her degree, she was basically staying at home at that point. . . . I worked for a temporary staffing agency, so every once in a while when there was a job I thought she would like, I would offer it to her. She would go out and do random jobs like that, but for the most part she was home. We decided we wanted to do that because we knew we were going to have a family at some point. We weren't ready at that time, but we didn't want to get used to two, having two, incomes.

Brian's quote exemplifies traditional norms of intensive mothering by framing Trish's employment in contradiction to their future goal of having children—they "didn't want to get used to two . . . incomes." Traditional norms against women's leadership are also reflected in the way Brian held control and decision-making power over the types of jobs Trish worked. Importantly, Brian reports that this arrangement was mutually agreed upon—"We decided we wanted to do that"—suggesting that it was normative for Brian to hold this type of authority. Although Brian and Trish did not have children at the time of the interview, it seems certain that once those plans were fulfilled, their household division of labor would be very traditional, with Brian working and Trish managing the home.

Although traditional gender norms in Salt Lake City are closely linked to the area's religious environment and the LDS church, Leamaster and Subramaniam also conducted a series of interviews with Mormons outside Utah and found that they were much less likely to adhere to traditional gender norms. In fact, some Mormon respondents in other parts of the country felt empowered by their religion to blend motherhood and careers, drawing different interpretations from religious scripture that challenged, rather than reinforced, conventional gender norms. As described by Leamaster and Subramaniam (2016: 790), "All of the women participants who felt enabled in their careers by Mormon religious schemas lived outside of Utah where Mormon culture is far from ubiquitous." These trends suggest that it is not Mormon affiliation alone that shapes the traditional gender norms in Salt Lake City. Instead, the area's traditional gender norms may influence the way religion is practiced.

Whereas Salt Lake City is among the most religious areas in the United States, Columbus is one of the least. A nationwide survey from Gallup (Newport 2013) reported that Salt Lake City is the forty-second most religious metro area in the United States. Nearby Provo, which is within the Salt Lake commuting zone, is ranked first. In contrast, Columbus is ranked as the 109th most religious metro area. Despite these differences, however, gender norms in Columbus are very similar to the traditional norms found in Salt Lake City. In Columbus, women are viewed as less suitable for leadership than men. Gender norms in the family are also highly traditional in Columbus, where motherhood is viewed in contradiction to employment and household labor is expected to be divided according to men's breadwinning and women's caregiving. Gender norms of public sphere gender essentialism are less traditional in Columbus than they are in Salt Lake City. Yet this dimension is still more traditional in Columbus than most places in the United States, with women and men viewed as possessing essentially different skills and suited for different types of employment.

Traditional norms in Columbus are clearly illustrated in research by Amanda Miller and Daniel Carlson (2016), who interviewed sixty-one different-gender couples residing in this city about their relationships and their division of household labor. According to these authors, the vast majority of couples endorsed traditional divisions of labor where women were responsible for cleaning, cooking, and childcare while men focused primarily on paid employment. This is despite the fact that many of the women in these couples were also employed. One respondent, referred to as Amy, clearly reflected local gender norms when she described her expectations for how housework would be divided between her and her partner:

> I knew he would not ever clean a bathroom and I knew I would be doing like most of the cleaning kind of things but I expected him to do his own laundry and take out the trash and help. (Miller and Carlson 2016: 353)

Amy's expectations illustrate how traditional norms of private sphere gender essentialism are reflected in couples' unequal divisions of household labor. In their relationship, Amy was responsible for cleaning. When her partner helped, he contributed to only minor tasks such as doing his own laundry or periodic chores like taking out the trash. Another respondent in Miller and Carlson's study, Robert, epitomized many men's contributions to housework:

> I don't do anything [housework]. She'll spend hours on it and I'll spend like half an hour. . . . When I was younger, my mom would just do all the dishes and clean everything. So, I've never really had to clean, you know. . . . So, it's hard for me now. (Miller and Carlson 2016: 354)

Like many men in Columbus interviewed by Miller and Carlson, Robert felt no obligation to contribute to housework. Instead, he was comfortable allowing his wife or girlfriend to do the work alone. Traditional norms are so entrenched in Columbus that respondents felt no shame sharing and justifying their gender-unequal household arrangements in an interview. This stands in stark contrast to the couples interviewed by Allison Daminger in Boston (discussed prior), who all expressed strong support for gender equality and equal divisions of household labor, even if their behaviors did not directly align with these ideals.

Miller and Carlson's study focused primarily on household divisions of labor, making it possible to clearly observe how norms of private sphere gender essentialism are reflected in Columbus couples' perceptions and behaviors. However, additional dimensions of gender norms also emerged in their interviews. One couple, Katherine and Evan, described themselves as having essentially different, and gender-stereotypical, traits that closely aligned with norms of public sphere gender essentialism. Katherine portrayed herself as a "perfectionist" whereas Evan stated, "I'm a guy: I'm sloppy to some extent. Having her around, [she's the] complete opposite" (Miller and Carlson 2016: 357). These differences, which the couple attributes to deep-seated characteristics of their genders—"I'm a guy . . . [she's the] complete opposite"—reflect conventional beliefs that women and men are essentially different and suited for separate types of work.

Other interviews by Miller and Carlson point to traditional norms toward women's leadership and intensive mothering. Dawn, who was frustrated with her partner at the time of the interview, stated:

> We're still kind of in that homemaker kind of phase of cleaning and taking care of the kids and stuff. So really in the long run, the women [are] working just as much as the men, getting paid less, doing all of the housework, taking care of the kids. So, the men are sitting on their butts, watching the football game. (Miller and Carlson 2016: 354)

Dawn's perspective that women work just as hard as men but are paid less reflects traditional norms toward women's leadership in Columbus. More than most places in the United States, women in Columbus are perceived as possessing fewer leadership qualities and decision-making skills than men. As a result, they are paid less, and Dawn is aware of it. Dawn's quote also illustrates the persistent expectation for mothers, more than fathers, to prioritize childcare. According to Dawn, it is normal for women to be the ones taking care of children in Columbus, while men's concerns center on the football game.

On first blush, Columbus might not strike many as a place we would expect to have very traditional gender norms. It is the state capital of Ohio, has a large population of nearly one million, votes steadily democratic, and is home to the state's flagship public university. Yet, interviews with local residents portray a very different setting that aligns closely with levels of traditionalism observed across the four dimensions of gender norms developed in this book.

San Francisco and New Orleans: Contradictory Gender Norms by Dimension

Before the rise of Silicon Valley and the tech giants, San Francisco and the Bay Area's greatest reputation was for its liberal politics, social activism, and environmental consciousness. It was in nearby Oakland that the Black Panther Party formed to challenge racial injustice and police violence against African Americans (Bloom and Martin 2016). The University of California, Berkeley has a global reputation for the feminist scholarship of its faculty and the activism of its student body. Although today the Bay Area is mostly known for Silicon Valley tech industries, values of equality remain central, even in the business environment. A recent study ranked San Francisco as the best place in the world for women entrepreneurs, citing the location's talent, cultural support for women, and women's access to venture capital (Gilchrist 2019).

For the most part, San Francisco's reputation is also observed in the four dimensions of gender norms developed here (see Figure 3.6). Norms toward women's advancement are egalitarian, indicating that support for women's leadership is greater here than most places in the United States. Indeed, the current mayors of both San Francisco (London Breed) and Oakland (Libby Schaaf) are women. Furthermore, the first woman vice president of the United States, Kamala Harris, was born in Oakland and raised in Berkeley. Yet support for women's leadership is lower in San Francisco than what we observed in Boston and Minneapolis, suggesting that barriers remain. One study by Shelley Correll and colleagues (2020) highlighted some of these remaining challenges. Analyzing over two hundred employee evaluations from a large Silicon Valley tech company, they found that men were more commonly praised as "visionaries" and "leaders," giving them an advantage over women for promotion and advancement.

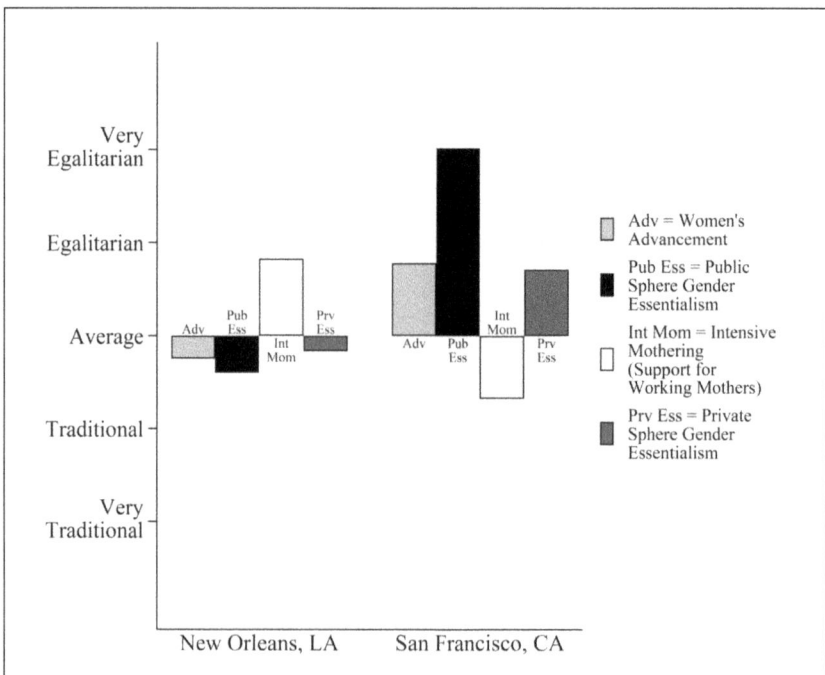

Figure 3.6 Illustrative Set of Commuting Zones with Contradictory Gender Norms across Dimensions

Although the Bay Area still has some way to go in supporting women's leadership, norms around public sphere gender essentialism here are some of the most egalitarian in the country. In places like Salt Lake City and Columbus, women are generally believed to be suited for jobs that emphasize care and interpersonal relations, whereas men are expected to be skilled in technical work. In the Bay Area, these differences are far less salient. Women and men in this commuting zone are viewed as possessing similar skill sets related to both technical and interpersonal expertise. These egalitarian norms toward public sphere gender essentialism were also reflected in the study by Correll and colleagues (2020) (mentioned prior) that examined gender differences in worker evaluations for a large Bay Area employer. Although men were more often described as "visionaries" and "leaders," there were no differences between women and men in how often they were praised for their technical expertise. Furthermore, women's technical skills were more commonly linked to positive overall performance assessments. In their study, Correll and coauthors highlight a positive evaluation of one woman employee who "learned planning code quickly and started delivering" (2020: 1036). While coding and other technical skills are commonly associated with men (Cech 2013), Correll's work illustrates that women's expertise in this domain is commonly observed and respected in the Bay Area, a pattern consistent with local egalitarian norms toward public sphere gender essentialism.

San Francisco and its surrounding area also report slightly egalitarian norms with respect to private sphere gender essentialism. This indicates that support for equal divisions of household labor is fairly common here, although less than areas like Boston or Minneapolis. Qualitative research with parents in the Bay Area confirms that many fathers have a strong desire to be equal caregivers to their children. In interviews with service workers in San Francisco, Sigrid Luhr (2020) found that fathers often made significant efforts to balance their work lives with childcare demands. Many of the fathers in Luhr's study commonly asked managers and supervisors for time off or flexible working arrangements when they needed to stay home with a sick child or when their childcare arrangements fell through. One respondent, referred to as Bill, described how he commonly took work off when needed to care for his child:

> I have to call my manager. Usually he'll give me a break if it involves my kids. There is no other excuse; it's only for my kids, then he's like, "Go ahead. Take time off." But I don't have any other excuse. It's only that one. (Luhr 2020: 269)

In a separate study interviewing fathers employed in Silicon Valley tech companies, Marianne Cooper (2000) also found that many sought careers that allowed them to be engaged fathers. One father, for example, chose to pull back from his fast-paced career in order to have better work-life balance. In describing his decision, this individual stated,

> I chose this job not because it's the one that is going to make us rich. It probably won't. On the other hand, it's a good living. I'm having a fun time and I get to be around the kids all the time. (Cooper 2000: 403)

Reflecting egalitarian norms of private sphere gender essentialism, the Bay Area fathers interviewed by Luhr and Cooper expressed a desire to be involved in their children's lives. This is in stark contrast to fathers residing in Columbus or Salt Lake and more similar to those in Boston or Minneapolis, where egalitarian norms prevail.

Although mothers and fathers value equal contributions to the family, norms of intensive mothering are fairly traditional in the Bay Area. This indicates that many San Francisco residents feel that motherhood stands in contradiction to careers. Although San Francisco's norms of intensive mothering are less pronounced than those in Salt Lake City or Columbus, they are still relatively traditional in comparison to all U.S. commuting zones and stand in stark contrast to the broader reputation of the Bay Area as a feminist enclave. However, multiple studies confirm that intensive mothering norms pose a major challenge for women in the Bay Area. Correll and colleagues' (2020) analysis of employee evaluations, cited previously, showed that women employees are actually given more positive ratings if their manager perceives them as having work/family conflict. This suggests that employers incentivize conflict between caregiving and paid employment rather than creating the conditions for a healthy balance. In addition, Luhr's qualitative study of San Francisco's service workers included a number of mothers whose experiences were very different from fathers. In contrast to the balance fathers were able to achieve between the expectations of their managers and their role as parents, mothers commonly felt that they would be penalized, or even lose their job, if they asked for time off or flexibility to take care of their children. One mother in Luhr's study explained that when her child's daycare was closed or when her child was home sick, she would tell her employer that she was personally sick and needed time off instead of saying that she was staying home for childcare. In fact, many of the mothers in Luhr's study intentionally kept their children a secret from their employer out of concern that it would be held against them in promotion decisions or evaluations. In direct contrast to the flexibility offered to fathers in Luhr's study, mothers reported feeling very constrained in balancing work and parenting responsibilities. For example, one mother recounted the challenges she faced in negotiating work-family demands with her employer:

They had my schedule up and down and now I have problems with my daughter. She has pre-diabetes so I asked if they can work with my schedule and they said because I have open availability they cannot do anything about it. (Laura, quoted in Luhr 2020: 273)

The stark contrast between the treatment of fathers and mothers in the Bay Area affirms that norms of intensive parenting are traditional in this location. They also point to a critical double standard. Fathers receive substantial benefits and understanding in requesting flexible arrangements for their employment. This is consistent with prior research on the fatherhood premium showing that fathers are often evaluated more favorably by employers and are advantaged in terms of employment, promotion, and pay (Glauber 2011). Yet, if fathers receive the benefit of the doubt in their employment, mothers continue to face significant prejudice. Mothers in Luhr's study felt they would be less likely to be hired if their employer knew they had children, an assumption backed up by decades of research highlighting cognitive biases that disadvantage mothers relative to fathers and nonmothers in hiring (Correll, Benard, and Paik 2007). When mothers had to request work flexibility to address childcare needs, employers were less likely to oblige and more likely to criticize working mothers for their lack of commitment or contribution. These patterns reflect traditional norms of intensive mothering that frame motherhood in contradiction to paid employment.

Whereas San Francisco trends egalitarian on all dimensions of gender norms besides intensive mothering, New Orleans shows the mirror-opposite pattern (see Figure 3.6). In the Big Easy, gender norms are somewhat traditional with respect to women's advancement, public sphere gender essentialism, and private sphere gender essentialism, but not intensive mothering, where we observe egalitarian norms indicating support for working mothers. Reflecting these egalitarian norms, many of the young women interviewed by Carl Kendall and colleagues (2005) felt that the ideal time to have children was when they were able to have a firmly established career and financial stability. One eighteen-year-old woman said she planned to "wait until I get established before I have children" (Kendall et al. 2005: 303). Another respondent stated more clearly how motherhood went hand in hand with women's independent economic stability, stating the ideal conditions for having children: "You should be financially stable, emotionally stable, able to take care of the kids" (Kendall et al. 2005: 304). These expectations for motherhood stand in stark contrast to what was reported by women in Salt Lake City, where motherhood was framed as a time to become economically dependent. Whereas the ideal mother in Salt Lake City may be a stay-at-home caregiver for her children, ideal motherhood in New Orleans is defined by reliable employment and financial independence.

Egalitarian norms supporting mothers' employment are the exception to more traditional gender norms in New Orleans across the three remaining dimensions. Although mothers' employment is normative, women still face barriers in access to leadership, they are expected to work in different jobs than men, and family gender norms still convey mothers as essentially better caregivers. These traditional components of New Orleans' local culture are apparent in interviews conducted by Lori Peek and Alice Fothergill (2008) with New Orleans families affected by Hurricane Katrina. In describing how families coped with the challenges posed by the disaster, these researchers found that many parents relied on traditional divisions of family labor to address childcare and household demands. One father interviewed in their study, for example, described the conventional way tasks were divided in his family:

> It seems like it's naturally the dads who just jump in and do the dirty work. We'll let moms try and take care of the kids, 'cause moms do that better because they can nurture 'em a little better. Most dads don't do a lot of nurturing. (Peek and Fothergill 2008: 87)

Although the respondent does not clarify what he means by the "dirty work" that fathers generally do, it is clear that their household followed traditional scripts where mothers are the primary caregivers and fathers manage nonroutine tasks, presumably such as taking the garbage out, yard work, and maintenance. These divisions clearly reflect traditional norms toward private sphere gender essentialism in New Orleans and highlight that support for maternal employment does not necessarily occur alongside egalitarian norms toward the division of family labor. Instead, we see that normative support for maternal employment has not translated to greater involvement of fathers in housework and childcare, creating a double shift for employed mothers who provide financial stability for their family and also do the vast majority of caregiving and housework.

Summary

In this section, I have highlighted six commuting zones with unique configurations of gender norms. Boston and Minneapolis are universally egalitarian, Salt Lake City and Columbus are universally traditional, and San Francisco and New Orleans have contradictory norms that are egalitarian on some dimensions but traditional on others. Drawing from qualitative research taking place in each of these locations, we can also see how individuals' perceptions, experiences, and behaviors differ in ways that relate to the gender norms where they reside. Bostonians readily embrace feminist ideals of gender equality and fairness—the opposite of Columbus residents, who hold no reservations about sharing their conventional expectations that women should do the majority of housework. For many residents in San Francisco, the local culture is supportive of gender equality. But mothers in this area have a very different experience characterized by limited support in balancing work and parenting. Mothers in New Orleans may not experience as many barriers to employment as those in San Francisco, but they also face cultural norms that excuse men from housework and childcare.

The undulating terrain of gender norms in the United States creates major differences in residents' experiences and the challenges they face in their daily lives. I further explore these consequences in Chapter 5. But first, it is important to consider the source of these gender norms. Where do they come from? How are they sustained? Importantly, do these differences in gender norms merely reflect economic differences between places? Perhaps the predominance of the service industry in New Orleans is driving support for mothers' employment, whereas the prevalence of manufacturing in Columbus relates to this area's traditionalism. To explore this possibility, I now explore a set of commuting zones with similar economic characteristics to descriptively examine whether differences in gender norms are reducible to local economic contexts.

Comparing Commuting Zones with Similar Economic Conditions

Just as places have local gender norms, they also have distinct economic characteristics commonly associated with specialization in a particular industry. Detroit is known as the Motor City because three of the largest car manufacturers are headquartered there (Chrysler, Ford, and General Motors). In Las Vegas, over eighty thousand people work in the major casinos along the main "strip," making this a major hub for service sector tourism (Schwartz and Rajnoor 2021). In Boston, over a third of workers are employed in information-based occupations, a concentration that is second only to San Francisco (Florida 2017). Economists have long observed the uneven concentration of industries across U.S. cities, labor markets, and commuting zones (Christopherson, Garretsen, and Martin 2008). Some have argued that this pattern facilitates innovation and improves productivity as companies in the same field are better able to exchange information and knowledge when in close proximity (Davis and Dingel 2019). Other scholars have identified a relationship between local culture and the types of industries that predominate in a particular location. Richard Florida argues that tech industries thrive in locations that embrace arts and creativity (Florida 2012). Empirically testing this theory, Rowena Crabbe and I (2021) found that places with a reputation for vibrancy and music had the largest growth in the tech industry from 2010 through 2016.

Although research has shown that local culture may relate to the concentration of tech industries, it is unclear whether economic composition is associated with local configurations of gender norms more broadly. Sociologists have shown, however, that industry concentration does have a consistent relationship to levels of gender inequality. This is because some industries offer greater opportunities for women's employment and advancement than others. Gordon Gauchat, Maura Kelly, and Michael Wallace (2012), for example, found that women's labor force participation is higher in metro areas with a larger service sector. This is because many service industry jobs are stereotyped as feminine and emphasize skills conventionally associated with women, such as caregiving and interpersonal relations. As a result, women face lower levels of bias in access to service sector jobs and are more likely to prefer employment in this industry when their personal outlooks reflect conventional gender expectations (England 2010). In contrast, numerous studies have identified the barriers facing women who work in male-dominated manufacturing sectors, where they experience higher rates of sexual harassment and pay discrimination (Crawley 2011; McCall 2001). In tech, studies have shown how stereotypes associating men with technical skills can bias managers against recognizing women's contributions (Alfrey and Twine 2017). However, other work has found that the tech sector has grown the most in areas with the lowest levels of occupational segregation (Scarborough, Sobering, et al. 2021), suggesting that the most productive tech sectors are also those where women have equal opportunities.

Economic settings are strongly related to patterns of inequality between women and men. It is therefore possible that the variation in gender norms we have observed thus far is related to the different types of industries that predominate across commuting zones. For example, egalitarianism in Boston may reflect the area's innovative tech scene, or the traditionalism in Columbus could be due to the large manufacturing sector there. To explore this possibility, I provide a descriptive comparison of how gender norms differ in places with similar economic conditions. Focusing on the prevalence of different industries, I explore whether places with similarly sized service, manufacturing, and tech sectors also share comparable configurations of local gender norms. This analysis forms the foundation for a deeper investigation of the factors driving spatial variation in local gender norms that I present in Chapter 4.

Service Sector Size

Las Vegas, Nashville, and Miami are three places renowned for vacation get-aways and vibrant nightlife. In fact, each city is named by *Real Simple* magazine (Seaver 2017) as one of the top five best locations for bachelorette parties. Further yet, Las Vegas and Miami rank number one and two for bachelor parties. Heavy tourism in these locations relates to larger service sectors more broadly. In Las Vegas and Miami, about nine in ten workers are employed in the service sector. Nashville's service sector is slightly smaller, but still nearly eight in ten workers are in the service sector in this location.

Despite their similar reputations and economic contexts, Las Vegas, Miami, and Nashville have very different gender norms (see Figure 3.7). Las Vegas trends egalitarian across all four dimensions of local norms, although norms toward public sphere gender essentialism are only slightly egalitarian, suggesting that women and men are still viewed as somewhat suited for different types of work, if only to a lesser extent than many other locations in the United States. In contrast to Las Vegas, Miami has contradictory gender norms. In this beachside metro area, traditional expectations prevail toward the family, particularly in norms of intensive mothering that convey employment as in conflict with motherhood. At the same time, Miami has egalitar-

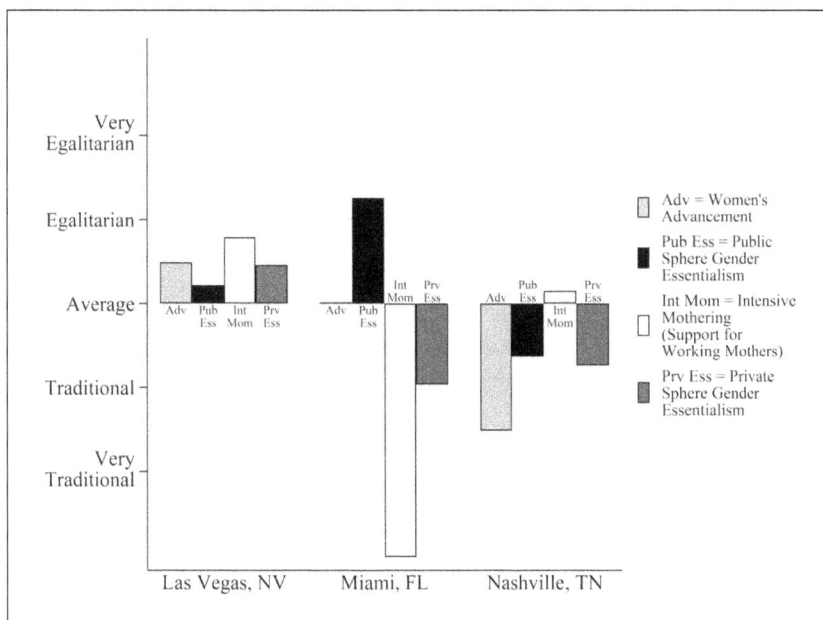

Figure 3.7 Comparing Gender Norms in Commuting Zones with Large Service Sectors

ian norms toward public sphere gender essentialism. In yet another unique configuration, gender norms in Nashville trend more traditional on all dimensions except intensive mothering, where support for mothers' employment is about average.

Las Vegas, Miami, and Nashville have similar reputations and economic conditions but very different gender norms. Although service sector size has been shown in prior research to be associated with patterns of gender inequality, the comparison of these three areas suggests that local gender norms may exist independently from service sector density.

Manufacturing Concentration

Nearly one in five workers in both the Cleveland and Detroit commuting zones work in manufacturing, about double the national average. These Rust Belt cities have long been known as manufacturing centers with significant employment in both automotive and steel companies. But do not tell locals that the two cities are similar. Sports rivalries between Cleveland and Detroit run deep and have existed for decades. Located only a three-hour drive from one another, visiting teams often arrive with their legions of fans for an afternoon of heckling and banter with the opposing side.

Examining the different cultural environments between Cleveland and Detroit (Figure 3.8), we find that the differences between these places extends far beyond sport loyalties. Across every dimension of gender norms, Detroit is more egalitarian than Cleveland. In the Motor City, women's leadership and working mothers are supported. Fathers are expected to contribute equally to childcare and housework. Norms of public sphere gender essentialism are only slightly above average in Detroit but nonetheless indicate that women and men are viewed as similarly suited for a wide variety of occupations. Whereas Detroit trends egalitarian across all dimensions, Cleveland is steadily average. Only with respect to support for women's leadership are gender norms in Cleveland slightly egalitarian, but still far below the levels observed in Detroit. Women face greater challenges overcoming gendered expectations at work and family in Cleveland than in Detroit, but less than highly traditional places like nearby Columbus. Despite both having a high concentration of manufacturing employment and their close proximity, Cleveland and Detroit have very different gender norms.

Tech Hubs

Boston and Seattle are two coastal metro areas where the tech industry has grown dramatically over the past several decades. Supported by a large proportion of residents with a college degree, the presence of several major tech

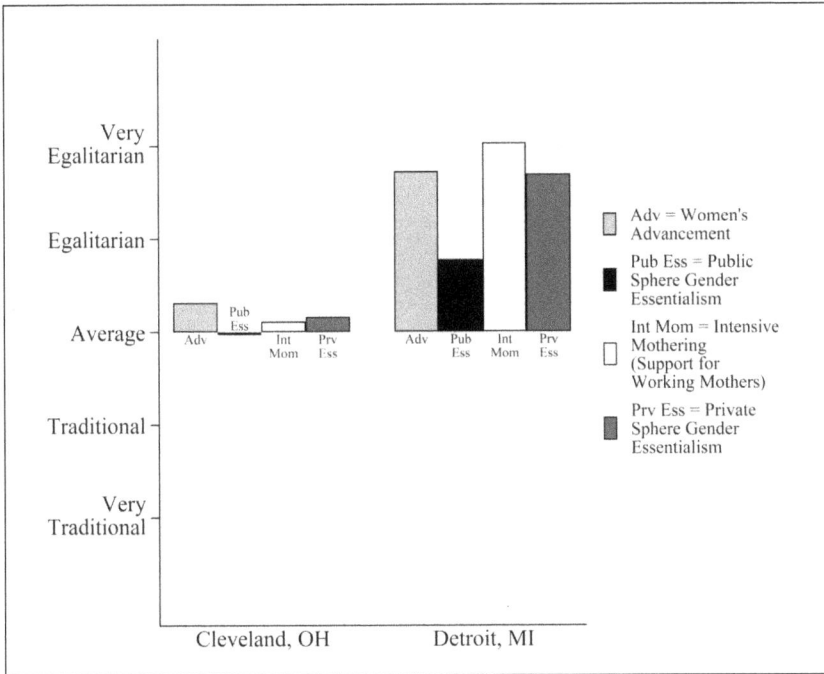

Figure 3.8 Comparing Gender Norms in Commuting Zones with Large Manufacturing Sectors

employers, and significant venture capital investments, Boston was recently ranked as the fourth-best, and Seattle the sixth-best, tech hub in the United States (Florida 2017). Scholars of economic growth often cite local cultural conditions as a major asset to sustained innovation and tech expansion (Scarborough and Crabbe 2021). The reputations of Boston and Seattle as liberal places where diversity is embraced and creativity is celebrated fit the mold for the prototypical setting where tech innovation thrives (Florida 2012).

For all their similarities, however, travelers visiting these two cities may notice important differences in local gender norms (see Figure 3.9). This is particularly true when it comes to the family. In Seattle, traditional intensive mothering norms exist that discourage mothers' employment. In contrast, support for working mothers in Boston is among the highest in the United States. Norms toward private sphere gender essentialism are slightly egalitarian in Seattle but nowhere near as egalitarian as they are in Boston. If you are a tech worker hoping to live in an environment that supports gender equality in the home, head to Boston over Seattle.

Despite different gender norms toward the family, Boston and Seattle are more similar with respect to norms toward women's leadership and pub-

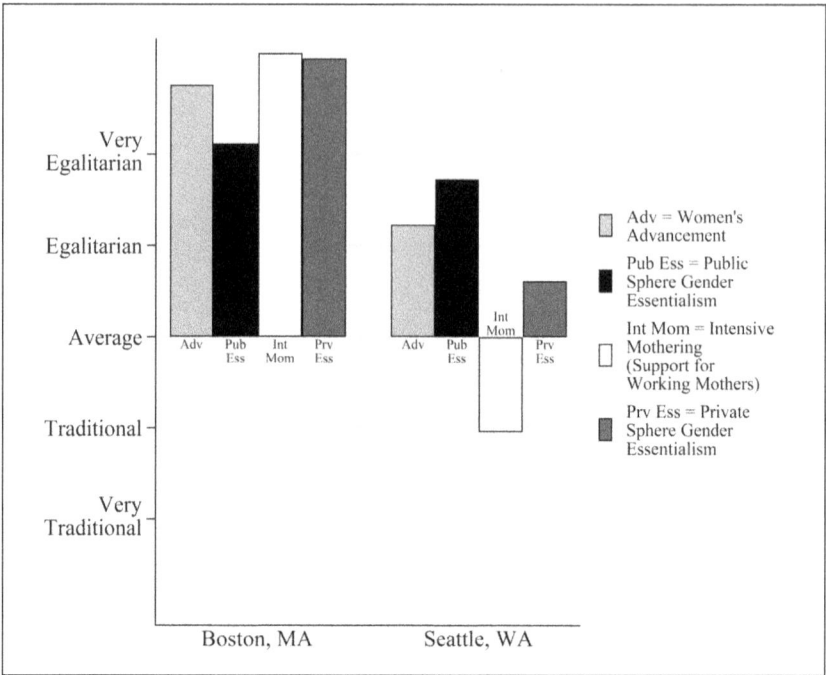

Figure 3.9 Comparing Gender Norms in Commuting Zones with Large Tech Sectors

lic sphere gender essentialism. Each location is egalitarian on these dimensions, although Boston remains much more egalitarian than Seattle in support for women's leadership. It is possible that gender egalitarianism in these two dimensions has supported recent tech growth in both Boston and Seattle. As stated previously, research has shown that local tech industries have greater growth and productivity when women and men more commonly work in similar occupations (Scarborough, Sobering, et al. 2021). Egalitarian norms toward women's leadership and public sphere gender essentialism may facilitate these interactions, leading to greater innovation and improved outcomes for local tech sectors.

Conclusion

In this chapter, I have mapped the spatial distribution of the four dimensions of gender norms. In some respects, their geographical variation was unsurprising. At the most general, gender norms tend to be egalitarian in the Northeast and West Coast and traditional in the South. This is consistent with popular stereotypes of the South as highly conservative and the coasts as more liberal. It also confirms prior research on regional differences in gender attitudes (Scarborough, Sin, and Risman 2019). Yet, closer examination revealed that neighboring commuting zones often have very different gender norms. Madison is far more egalitarian than Milwaukee (separated by only 80 miles), Houston is more traditional than Austin (162 miles), and the gender norms in Louisville are much more egalitarian than the norms in Lexington (78 miles). In other cases, differences between nearby commuting zones depend on the dimension of gender norms. Orlando is more egalitarian than Tampa with respect to norms toward women's leadership but more traditional when it comes to intensive mothering norms. These detailed patterns underscore a major point from this chapter: The United States is composed of a variety of cultural environments with distinct gender norms conveying expectations toward women and men.

To better understand how the measures of gender norms developed in this book correspond to residents' experiences, perceptions, and behaviors, I drew upon previous qualitative research in locations with different gender norms. Contextualizing findings from these studies with respect to their spatial environments revealed how individuals' perceptions of gender and gender relations often reflected local norms. Residents of Boston support gender equality at home and at work (Daminger 2020), whereas research conducted in Columbus revealed a number of people who openly embrace traditional gender roles of women's homemaking and men's breadwinning (Miller and Carlson 2016). It is likely that respondents in qualitative studies often respond to researcher questions in ways that are socially desirable rather than how they may truthfully feel. Even in these cases, however, the fact that what is considered to be socially desirable varies from place to place further reflects differences in local gender norms. Although locations with egalitarian gender norms, like Boston, still have a long way to go to achieve gender equality, the fact that most people express vocal support for equality puts them at an advantage over places where it is still socially acceptable to express old-fashioned beliefs that women should tend the home and men should be the primary earners and decision makers.

Gender norms vary from place to place and are reflected in the way people discuss relationships and their expectations for different-gender partnerships. But where do gender norms come from, and how are they sustained? One potential source is that commuting zones have distinct economic conditions, such as the type of industry concentrated in the area (McCall 2001). To examine this factor, I reviewed local gender norms for three sets of locations with similar economic conditions: Las Vegas, Miami, and Nashville each have large service sectors, Detroit and Cleveland are manufacturing hubs, and Boston and Seattle have a high concentration of tech companies. Despite similar economic conditions within each set, local gender norms varied widely.

Las Vegas is generally more egalitarian than Miami and Nashville, and Miami is more egalitarian than Nashville when it comes to women's advancement and public sphere gender essentialism but not in norms toward intensive mothering and private sphere gender essentialism. Across the two manufacturing centers, Detroit has much more egalitarian norms on all dimensions than nearby Cleveland. Comparing tech hubs, we found that Boston and Seattle are similar with respect to norms toward women's advancement and public sphere gender essentialism but diverge when it comes to norms pertaining to the family: Seattle is much more traditional than Boston with respect to both intensive mothering and private sphere gender essentialism.

Differences in gender norms between places with similar economic conditions provide initial evidence that gender norms are not reducible to local economic context but instead exist as a fundamental feature of commuting zones in their own right. Importantly, however, these initial conclusions are based on a set of only seven commuting zones and solely with respect to economic contexts. It remains to be tested whether other features of commuting zones, such as the sociodemographic composition of residents, may explain the spatial variation of gender norms observed in this chapter.

At this point, we have identified four dimensions of gender norms and mapped their variation across U.S. commuting zones. The purpose of this chapter is to describe spatial differences in gender norms to underscore how places in the United States have very different cultural environments related to gender. This was achieved through mapping the distribution of gender norms, as well as through contextualizing previously conducted qualitative research to illustrate the ways that gender norms are reflected in individuals' experiences, perceptions, and attitudes. Chapters 2 and 3 defined and described local gender norms. I now turn to understanding their sources and consequences. In Chapter 4, I provide a deeper examination into the mechanisms that sustain variation in local gender norms. Specifically, I ask the question: Are local gender norms shaped by the types of people who tend to live in a particular location, or does the experience of residing in a place influence the behaviors, attitudes, and perceptions of those residents?

4

What Sustains Local Gender Norms?

Family car trips were a staple of my childhood. Whether it was driving across the state for a vacation on Lake Michigan or making the twelve-hour trek to my grandparents in the East Coast, I always looked forward to seeing new places and exploring sections of the country, even if it was constrained to a car window while going seventy-five miles per hour down the turnpike. As you can imagine, those long trips required frequent bathroom breaks. Each family has its quirks, and mine was that we would always stop at a McDonald's to use the bathroom. We would hold it until those golden arches appeared in the distance, passing many other suitable options along the way. In retrospect, the bathrooms at McDonald's were not any cleaner than those found in other pit stops. What drew us was that we knew there would not be any surprises. Faded brown stalls, square tile flooring, push-metered faucets, and air hand dryers were the guaranteed features of bathrooms at McDonald's. The inside of these spaces was indistinguishable, no matter if you were in the rural community of Claire, Michigan, or the vibrant hub of Washington, D.C.

This is, of course, no coincidence. As a company, McDonald's goes to great lengths to standardize almost everything about the restaurant. Each franchise's menu, employee uniforms, furniture, decorations, and, of course, bathrooms closely follow corporate designs to create the same experience no matter the location. More than the Big Mac, conformity is part of the McDonald's brand. And it is not just McDonald's. Almost all large-scale restaurants and retailers offer standardized services and experiences. During my first trip to

Target after moving to Texas, I had no problem finding diapers because the store was laid out identically from the one I frequented in Chicago. And when my family and I made the long cross-country drive to our new home, we knew Starbucks would have the same options along our journey, whether we ordered coffee in Bloomington, Illinois; St. Louis, Missouri; Fayetteville, Arkansas; or Ada, Oklahoma. George Ritzer (2018) famously referred to this pattern as the "McDonaldization of society" to describe how companies and organizations discard local specialization in favor of rationalized uniformity that offers predictable experiences for customers while also increasing operating efficiency and stabilizing expenses.

The McDonaldization of society has been made even easier with advances in communications and distribution networks over the past thirty years. An Egg McMuffin ordered in Kansas City uses eggs from the same farm in Ionia County, Michigan, as an Egg McMuffin ordered in Portland, Maine. Despite being 1,500 miles apart, the staff prepping this breakfast sandwich were trained with the same online learning management system designed by an instructional designer at a corporate office in Chicago. It is these technological advances that make such standardization possible and facilitate the global reach of companies like McDonald's. They also enhance communication channels between individuals residing hundreds or thousands of miles apart. Email, video conferencing, and social media have made remote work increasingly common while also facilitating friendships regardless of physical distance.

In the face of McDonaldization and technological advances, it is remarkable that places retain their unique character. In this book, I have already documented the tremendous variety of gender norms from place to place, but numerous other works have also found distinct cultural environments within the United States. Richard Florida (2012) has examined how places have varying levels of "coolness" or "bohemianism" that make up the local culture. Sociologists such as Harvey Molotch, Krista Paulsen, and Japonica Brown-Saracino have argued that areas have unique "place characters" composed of the collection of cultural reputations, values, and community ideals associated with a particular location (Brown-Saracino 2017; Molotch, Freudenburg, and Paulsen 2000; Paulsen 2004). And while there are many forces driving homogenization from place to place, market researchers have focused on cities' unique reputations as forming a specific "place brand" that can attract investment, tourism, or new residents (Scarborough and Crabbe 2021).

Thirty years ago, many anticipated that technological advances and routinization would lead to a "flat earth" where economic productivity was evenly distributed and places shared a universal culture (Porter 1998). Yet places continue to specialize in certain industries, and they have retained distinct cultural environments. We may be able to order the same coffee in every city in the United States, but as we saw in the last chapter, this routine occurs in the context of very different types of local gender norms. The morning rush of commuters is likely to have more men than women in the traditional atmosphere of Columbus compared to the egalitarian context of Minneapolis. It might be rare to see a father in line with a stroller in Miami but a common sight in Boston. My local Starbucks in North Texas requires a large parking lot for customers (mostly men) to park their oversized trucks, a massive departure from the electric car charging stations commonly found at Starbucks in Los Angeles.

In this chapter, I explore what sustains these differences in gender norms between U.S. commuting zones. Despite so many forces toward uniformity and routinization, how do places maintain distinct gender norms? To answer this question, I investigate two possibilities. First, places' gender norms could be sustained by *compositional effects*. From this perspective, commuting zones could have distinct gender norms due to demographic differences in the types of people who reside there. College-educated individuals, for example, more commonly hold egalitarian attitudes that endorse gender-equal caregiving in families. It is possible that the concentration of these individuals (as well as others with more egalitarian outlooks) in some commuting zones over others helps maintain places' unique culture. A second possible factor sustaining gender norms is *contextual effects*. According to this perspective, the experience of residing in a particular location makes individuals hold perspectives that are in alignment with the norms where they live. For example, someone with a college degree might hold much more egalitarian views in Boston, where such perspectives are encouraged, than in Columbus, where more traditional outlooks are supported.

To examine the factors sustaining local gender norms, I first review the relationship between individuals' attitudes and local cultural environments. Considering the reflexivity between individual-level characteristics and macro-level contexts provides an opportunity to test for compositional and contextual effects by examining the factors driving the relationship between commuting zone gender norms and individuals' attitudes. With this understanding, I proceed to test the role of compositional effects by examining whether the social and demographic characteristics of places can explain the relationship between commuting zone gender norms and individual-level attitudes. Next, I test the role of contextual effects to explore whether individuals with the same characteristics, such as the college educated or the highly religious, have different attitudes depending on the context of gender norms where they reside. Comparing the role of compositional and contextual effects reveals that both contribute to places' distinct gender norms but that contextual effects play a larger role. In other words, places shape us much more than we shape the places where we reside. Yet important nuance is also un-covered. Contextual effects are prominent among the college educated for norms directed toward the public sphere of employment (women's advancement and public sphere gender essentialism). Here, the experience of living in an egalitarian context has a very strong influence on the attitudes of the college educated. However, those with college degrees were less influenced by local norms toward the private sphere of the family (intensive mothering and private sphere gender essentialism). On these dimensions, religious affiliation plays a much larger role. Respondents associated with moderate and liberal religions were much more supportive of gender equality in families when they resided in places with egalitarian norms toward intensive mothering and private sphere gender essentialism. In short, local gender norms shape individuals' attitudes, but the mechanisms driving this relationship vary by dimension.

The Relationship between Macro-Level Gender Norms and Individual-Level Attitudes

Norms are the collective expectations of attitudes and behaviors associated with a particular context (Horne and Mollborn 2020). Gender norms pertain to the set of expectations differentiating conduct between women and men (Pearse and Connell 2016). These standards emerge in feelings of approval or disapproval toward gender relations and the way women and men act. This was discussed at length in Chapter 2 and is captured in the variables reflecting local gender norms: Do people approve of women in politics? Should mothers work or devote themselves fully to childcare? Are women suited for careers in the sciences? Importantly, these items were not originally measured at the level of commuting zones. Instead, they were responses by individuals that were aggregated to understand the typical expectations held toward women and men. This connection between individual attitudes and macro-level commuting zone norms is crucial. Norms are widespread expectations (Coleman 1994). For any individual, norms do not determine attitudes, behaviors, or perceptions. After all, many of us intentionally reject the norms we find constraining. But in the aggregate, norms are comprised by the most common and widespread attitudes. This is because norms are impossible to sustain, or at least highly unstable, if they are not commonly supported.

The relationship between norms and individuals' attitudes is reciprocal. Norms are reinforced by prevailing attitudes that are themselves supported by overarching norms (Horne and Mollborn 2020). In this sense, individual-level attitudes are the lifeblood of macro-level norms. Individuals reinforce norms through expressed attitudes and the sanctioning of others for breaking norms. Only through ongoing attitudinal and behavioral patterns are norms sustained. This means that norms are also subject to change when prevailing attitudes shift. Today, it is very common and widely acceptable for women to wear pantsuits. In fact, they have become the iconic style associated with 2016 presidential candidate Hillary Clinton. But this style was not always viewed acceptably. In 1938, a Los Angeles woman was arrested for wearing slacks in court (Harrison 2014), and up until 1993, it was forbidden for women to wear pants in the U.S. Senate (Givhan 2007). As more women challenged constraining norms toward formal wear, often led by notable celebrities or leaders, public sentiment slowly shifted and norms against women's pantsuits dissipated.

Although clothing norms have changed dramatically over the past several decades, other gender norms remain quite prevalent. As shown in prior chapters, these gender norms relate to women's advancement, public sphere gender essentialism, intensive mothering, and private sphere gender essentialism. To examine what sustains distinct configurations of these norms across U.S. commuting zones, we can draw on the dynamic relationship between individual-level attitudes and macro-level norms. Specifically, we can investigate the underlying mechanisms driving spatial variation in norms by focusing on the link between individuals' attitudes and the gender norms where they reside.

First, we must establish whether patterns in individuals' attitudes correspond to variation in local gender norms. In Chapter 2 I measured gender norms by focusing on aggregate patterns of attitudes and behaviors across commuting zones. Therefore, commuting zone measures of gender norms should have a strong relationship to individual-level attitudes. To test this, I performed a series of hierarchical regression models predicting an individual-level attitude that corresponded to each dimension of commuting zone gender norms. The results (see Figure 4.1) confirm our expectations. Individuals residing in commuting zones with more egalitarian attitudes toward women's advancement were more likely to disagree with a statement that men are better suited for politics than women. Those living in more egalitarian contexts with respect to public sphere gender essentialism held lower levels of cognitive bias against women in science. Commuting zone intensive mothering norms also predicted the way individuals felt about working mothers. Those residing in areas with traditional norms of intensive mothering were the most likely to feel that a working mother harms her child when she sends her child to preschool. Last, individuals living in places with more egalitarian norms toward private sphere gender essentialism were the most likely to disagree that it is best if men work and women tend the home.

If we break down these trends by individuals' race, we continue to see the same pattern where commuting zone gender norms strongly predict individ-

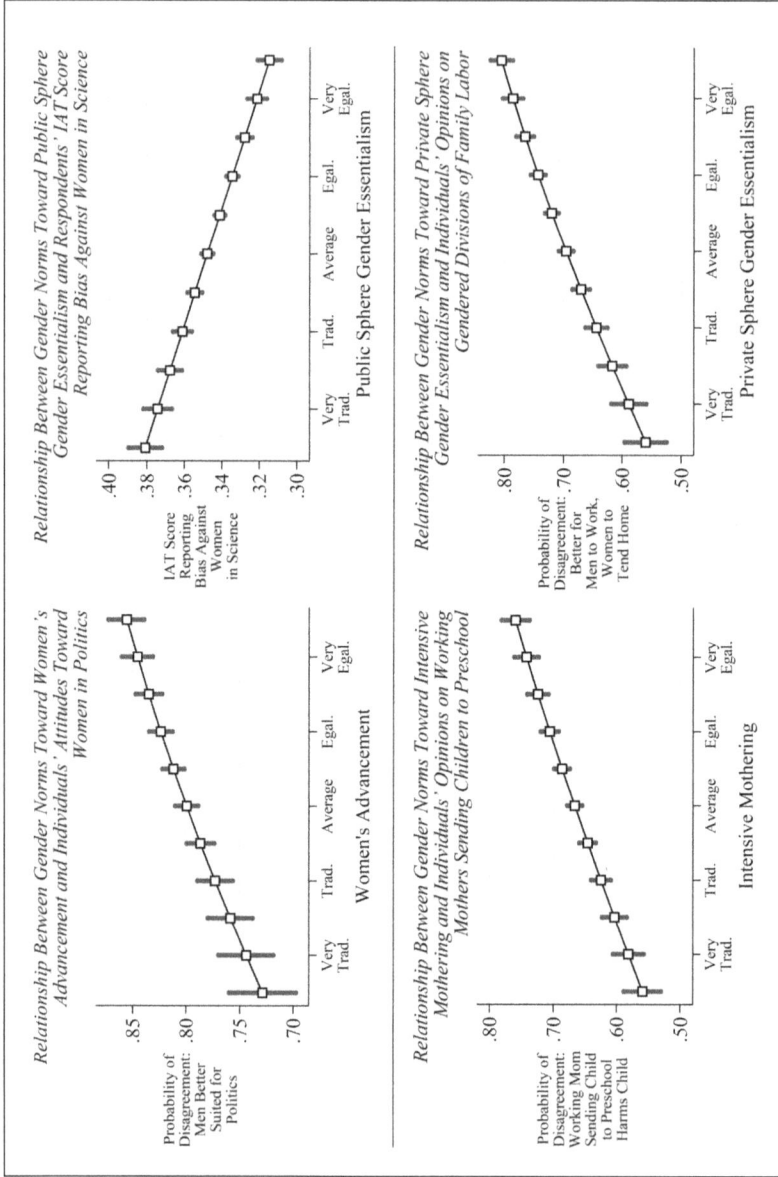

Relationship Between Gender Norms Toward Women's Advancement and Individuals' Attitudes Toward Women in Politics

Probability of Disagreement: Men Better Suited for Politics

.85 — .80 — .75 — .70

Very Trad. — Trad. — Average — Egal. — Very Egal.

Women's Advancement

Relationship Between Gender Norms Toward Public Sphere Gender Essentialism and Respondents' IAT Score Reporting Bias Against Women in Science

IAT Score Reporting Bias Against Women in Science

.40 — .38 — .36 — .34 — .32 — .30

Very Trad. — Trad. — Average — Egal. — Very Egal.

Public Sphere Gender Essentialism

Relationship Between Gender Norms Toward Intensive Mothering and Individuals' Opinions on Working Mothers Sending Children to Preschool

Probability of Disagreement: Working Mom Sending Child to Preschool Harms Child

.80 — .70 — .60 — .50

Very Trad. — Trad. — Average — Egal. — Very Egal.

Intensive Mothering

Relationship Between Gender Norms Toward Private Sphere Gender Essentialism and Individuals' Opinions on Gendered Divisions of Family Labor

Probability of Disagreement: Better for Men to Work, Women to Tend Home

.80 — .70 — .60 — .50

Very Trad. — Trad. — Average — Egal. — Very Egal.

Private Sphere Gender Essentialism

Figure 4.1 Relationship between Commuting Zone Gender Norms and Individual-Level Attitudes

Note: Each figure represents predicted outcome (on vertical axis) calculated from hierarchical regression models with a varying intercept (by commuting zone) including only a control for survey year. Hierarchical logistic models were used to predict attitudes toward women in politics, opinions toward working mothers sending children to preschool, and opinions on gendered divisions of family labor. Hierarchical linear models were used to predict IAT score.

ual-level attitudes (see Figure 4.2). One exception is Black individuals' implicit bias toward women in science. Regardless of local gender norms toward public sphere gender essentialism, African Americans express low levels of implicit bias. This contrasts with White and Hispanic respondents, whose implicit attitudes are highly sensitive to local gender norms. White and Hispanic people residing in places with egalitarian norms on public sphere gender essentialism have lower implicit bias against women in science. This racial difference between Black and White/Hispanic respondents is likely driven by historically high rates of labor force participation among Black women that have normalized occupational integration across fields of work for this group (Davis 1983). Considering this difference, it is possible that some commuting zones have more egalitarian norms on this dimension because they have a larger population of Black residents. I explore this in the following as one component of compositional effects sustaining gender norms. Other than this exception, the relationship of commuting zone gender norms to individuals' attitudes was consistent across all four dimensions and for White, Black, and Hispanic respondents.

Local gender norms correspond to individual-level attitudes across commuting zones. This is consistent with our understanding that norms are sustained by widespread attitudes. Differences in gender norms between Madison and Milwaukee, for example, are maintained by the fact that each place has different patterns in individuals' attitudes about gender. This relationship presents a valuable opportunity to explore the factors sustaining local gender norms by identifying the sources of the association between individual-level attitudes and commuting zone-level norms. Two mechanisms may underlie differences in average attitudes between places with different norms. First, attitudinal variation could be the result of demographic differences in the type of people who live in each commuting zone. If highly religious individuals, for example, tend to hold more traditional gender attitudes and also more commonly reside in some commuting zones than others, attitudinal patterns may simply be the result of religious people clustering in the same locations. This mechanism was introduced earlier and is known as *compositional effects* because spatial differences in attitudes are due to the composition of individuals residing in various locations. The second mechanism occurs when the experience of residing in a particular location makes people adopt attitudes and behaviors consistent with local norms (Maxwell 2019). If highly religious people express more egalitarian views in a commuting zone with egalitarian norms but more traditional outlooks in a commuting zone with traditional norms, it is not their individual-level characteristic driving spatial patterns in attitudes; rather, their experience in different cultural environments influences how they express their views. This mechanism is known as *contextual effects* and focuses on the way exposure to par-

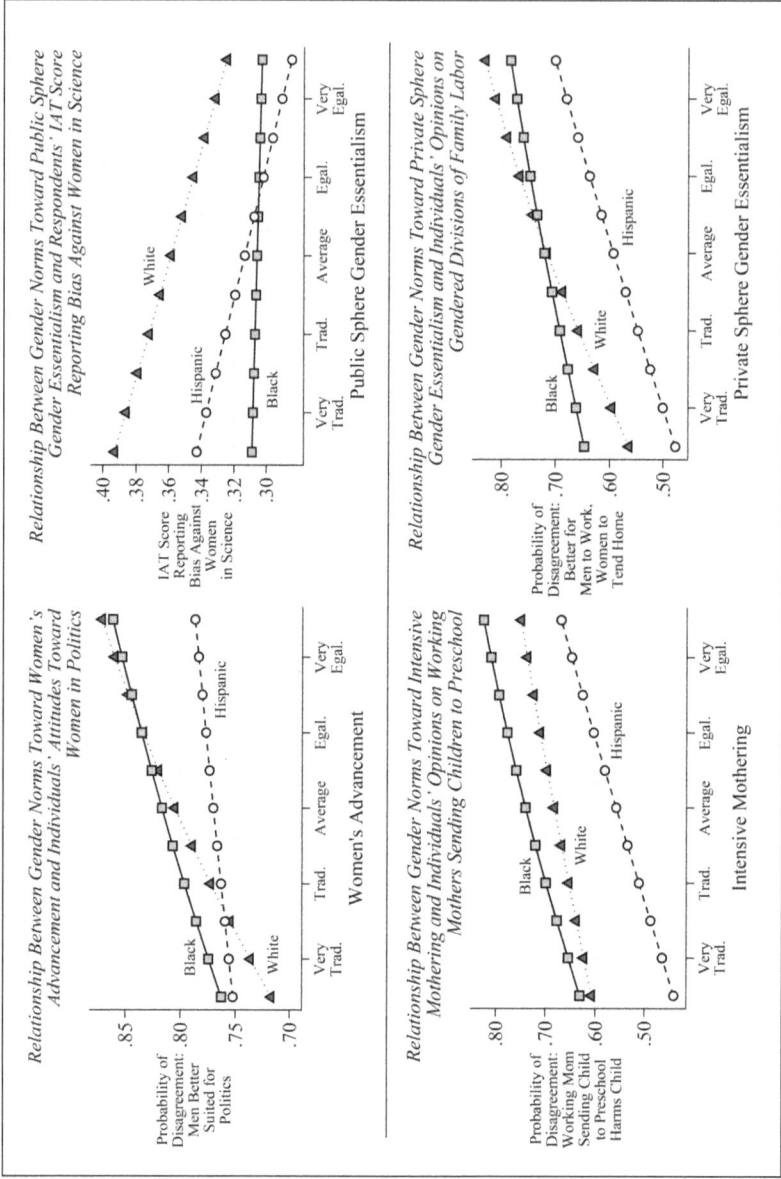

Figure 4.2 Relationship between Commuting Zone Gender Norms and Individual-Level Attitudes by Race

Note: Each figure represents predicted outcome (on vertical axis) calculated from hierarchical regression models with a varying intercept (by commuting zone) including only a control for survey year. Hierarchical logistic models were used to predict attitudes toward women in politics, opinions toward working mothers sending children to preschool, and opinions on gendered divisions of family labor. Hierarchical linear models were used to predict IAT score.

ticular contexts shapes individuals' attitudes and behaviors to align with local norms. In the following two sections of this chapter, I further expand on each of these mechanisms. Drawing on the relationship between individual-level attitudes and commuting zone gender norms, I also test the merits of each mechanism in explaining how variation in local gender norms is sustained.

Compositional Effects: How People Shape Places

Every four years, millions of Americans wait in anticipation, watching as states on a U.S. map turn either blue or red depending on which presidential candidate won the state's Electoral College votes. During the long periods between outcomes, analysts zoom in on the map to highlight metro areas, counties, or even voting precincts that could swing the state in either direction. In these segments, we see a much more complex national map. Within Republican states that often turn red on election nights, there are the liberal enclaves of Austin, New Orleans, and Indianapolis, whereas strongly Democratic-leaning states also have Republican strongholds in places like Bakersfield, California; St. Cloud, Minnesota; and Springfield, Illinois. In swing states, the outcomes often come down to whether conservative or liberal regions have higher turnout.

These election maps underscore a long-standing feature of the United States that political attitudes are unevenly distributed across the country. As a result, political divides often turn into animosities between places and their residents. Since moving to Texas in 2019, I have seen several neighbors with stickers on the back of their cars that state, "Don't California my Texas." One or two have expressed concern that their state was becoming increasingly liberal as a result of the influx of people moving from California. Indeed, Donald Trump's margin in Texas during the 2020 presidential election was the smallest for a Republican candidate in over twenty years.

My neighbors' concerns are based on the assumption that the state's voting trends are a result of compositional effects driven by changing demographics among the electorate. As more liberal-minded people move to Texas (presumably from California), the culture of the state will become more liberal. Apparently, they have little confidence in their ability to sway newcomers to their views or that new residents' experience in the state will make them more conservative (contextual effects). Perhaps their anxieties are well placed. Research by political scientists has generally found that compositional effects play a prominent role in driving spatial differences in political attitudes (Maxwell 2020).

Although compositional effects have been found to be prominent with respect to local politics, we do not yet know if they are a major driver of gender norms. Nonetheless, there is good reason to believe that compositional effects play an important role. Prior research has uncovered several demographic, economic, and cultural characteristics that predict individuals' gender attitudes. If the people holding these characteristics are clustered in some areas over others, this may drive aggregate patterns in egalitarian attitudes that help sustain local gender norms.

Demographic characteristics are some of the strongest predictors of individuals' gender attitudes. In general, women, African Americans, those who are foreign born, the college educated, and those younger in age have each been shown to hold more egalitarian attitudes (Scarborough, Sin, and Risman 2019). Women are more commonly disadvantaged by traditional gender attitudes that pose barriers to their employment and equal treatment. They are therefore more likely to oppose these viewpoints in favor of more egalitarian arrangements. As stated earlier, African Americans have historically held greater support for gender equality at home and in the workplace, corresponding to Black women's higher rates of employment (Davis 1983). In addition, Black fathers more commonly endorse equal childcare arrangements and take a greater role in children's lives than White fathers (Kane 2000). One reason for Black fathers' greater engagement in childcare is that they often express a desire to prepare their children for experiences of racism in the United States (Scarborough 2019). In addition, research has shown that areas with a higher density of immigrant residents tend to have lower levels of gender inequality and more liberal attitudes toward social issues (Florida 2012; Gauchat, Kelly, and Wallace 2012). One reason for this is that immigrants often have egalitarian gender attitudes; however, these views often depend on where they are migrating from (Pessin and Arpino 2018). Alternatively, immigration density often increases residents' exposure to people with different backgrounds, perspectives, and ways of life. This, in turn, can influence individuals' attitudes to be more tolerant of difference and embracing of equality.

One of the most consistent findings from research on gender attitudes is that those with higher levels of education, particularly the college educated, more commonly support efforts to advance gender equality (Mason, Czajka, and Arber 1976; Scarborough, Sin, and Risman 2019). A major reason for this trend is that individuals may embrace egalitarianism after being exposed to feminist ideals in university settings (Crossley 2017; Mason, Czajka, and Arber 1976). Another common trend in existing research is that younger individuals tend to hold more egalitarian attitudes than those who are older (Shu and Meagher 2018). Researchers focusing on cohort effects argue that common exposure to cultural ideas, events, and discourse during individuals' childhood can influence their long-standing attitudes on issues like gender relations (Kiley and Vaisey 2020). Because those born in more recent decades received greater exposure to feminism and women's empowerment than those in older birth cohorts, younger individuals more commonly endorse gender-equal arrangements.

Demographic characteristics are a major predictor of individuals' attitudes. However, economic circumstances have also been found to influence the degree to which people endorse egalitarian or traditional gender relations. Studies on the effects of job loss have shown that many men react to economic precarity by seeking to compensate for their loss of breadwinner status (Cha and Thébaud 2009; Legerski and Cornwall 2010). Rather than supporting their families through contributing more to unpaid labor, many unemployed men continue to disregard caregiving and housework. Mirroring these trends, women experiencing job loss or those who are voluntarily out of the labor force often express more traditional gender attitudes that justify their primary responsibility for housework and childcare (Rao 2021). Among those who are employed, individuals holding middle- or upper-class occupations more commonly possess gender egalitarian views, whereas those in blue-collar jobs are often more traditional in their outlooks (Scarborough, Pepin, et al. 2021). One reason for this is that upper- and middle-class white-collar occupations have become more gender integrated in recent decades, whereas blue-collar manufacturing occupations remain mostly dominated by men (England 2010). Therefore, opportunities for women and men to work alongside one another can reduce traditional expectations that women should primarily focus on family and childcare. Similar to these occupational dynamics, the type of industries where individuals work has also been shown to shape gender attitudes and relationships between women and men. Service sector growth since the 1980s has corresponded to a major increase in women's employment, as this part of the economy provided numerous jobs for women entering the labor market (Stainback and Tomaskovic-Devey 2012). Therefore, individuals working in the service sector may be more likely to support women's and mothers' employment because they more commonly have women as colleagues. Consequently, the growth of the service sector has corresponded to greater support for gender equality (Inglehart and Norris 2003).

In addition to demographic and economic characteristics, individuals' cultural identities have also been found to be highly related to their gender attitudes. In particular, religious affiliation and political ideology are two of the most consistent and strongest predictors of individuals' expectations toward women and men (Whitehead and Perry 2019). People who belong to more fundamentalist religions, such as Southern Baptists, endorse conventional arrangements of women's homemaking and men's breadwinning to a much greater extent than individuals who belong to liberal religions, such as United Methodists, or those who report having no religion (Bolzendahl and Myers 2004). Fundamentalist religions are characterized by the direct and literal interpretation of the Bible or religious texts (Smith 1987). For followers of these religions, Bible passages such as "The women are to keep silent in the churches for they are not permitted to speak" (1 Corinthians 14:34, quoted in Adams 2007) are taken as literal mandates barring women from leadership positions and authority. In contrast, liberal religions view the Bible and religious texts as metaphorical; they are less likely to interpret scriptures as explicit directives and instead view them as written with the values and norms of an ancient, and often troublesome, history. As a result, liberal religions have a higher proportion of women in leadership and more commonly endorse gender equality in family caregiving (Adams 2007). Scholars have argued that these differences in biblical interpretation and conservative gender attitudes stem from the efforts of some religions to differentiate themselves from the values of a "lay" public. Adherence to fundamentalist traditional values, particularly with respect to gender in the family, can enhance a congregation's visibility and attract individuals who embrace those beliefs while at the same time reinforcing them (Perry and Whitehead 2015). Andrew Whitehead and Samuel Perry (2019) argue that religious fundamentalism, particularly when coupled with a belief that the United States should be a Christian nation, is the most powerful predictor of traditional gender attitudes.

Although religious fundamentalism is strongly related to gender attitudes, political ideology has also been found to influence the way individuals feel about gender relations and their support for equality between women and men. Liberals express greater support for women's leadership and gender-equal divisions of caregiving than conservatives (Cotter, Hermsen, and Vanneman 2011; Scarborough, Sin, and Risman 2019). Driving this trend is the way liberal political ideologies have incorporated rights-based frameworks in recent decades that emphasize social equality and equal opportunity across groups (Brooks and Bolzendahl 2004). Support for women's advancement and gender equality in the home is part of a broader political agenda for those who identify as liberal, whereas political conservatives advocate for conventional gender arrangements in the name of supporting family values.

In summary, there is a well-established set of demographic, economic, and cultural individual-level characteristics that have been found to be powerful and consistent predictors of gender attitudes in prior research. These attributes and their relationships to gender attitudes are summarized in Table 4.1 and illustrate clear patterns between social groups and expectations toward women and men. To the extent that these social groups are unevenly distributed across commuting zones, the differences documented in Table 4.1 may contribute to spatial variation in gender norms because widespread attitudes sustain prevailing norms. For example, Minneapolis may have more egalitarian gender norms because it has a higher percentage of college-educated and politically liberal residents who more commonly endorse gender equality and women's leadership. From this perspective, the composition of places with respect to the key characteristics listed in Table 4.1 could be a major force sustaining variation in local gender norms.

TABLE 4.1 INDIVIDUAL-LEVEL PREDICTORS OF GENDER ATTITUDES	
Individual-level characteristic	*Relationship to gender attitudes*
Demographic characteristics	
Gender	Women generally hold more egalitarian attitudes than men.
Race	African Americans generally hold more egalitarian attitudes than Whites.
Foreign-born status	Immigrants often hold more egalitarian attitudes. Areas with a greater share of immigrants also tend to have more egalitarian gender attitudes.
Education	Individuals with a college degree are generally more likely to support gender egalitarianism than those with less education.
Age	Younger individuals more commonly hold gender egalitarian attitudes.
Economic characteristics	
Employment status	Unemployed individuals often hold more conventional gender attitudes than those who are employed.
Occupation	Those working in managerial/professional occupations generally have more egalitarian gender attitudes than those in blue-collar occupations.
Industry	Those employed in the service sector generally have more egalitarian gender attitudes than those in male-dominated industries such as manufacturing.
Cultural characteristics	
Religious fundamentalism	Those belonging to fundamentalist religions commonly hold more traditional gender attitudes than those affiliated with a moderate or liberal religion or those with no religious affiliation.
Political ideology	Liberals generally hold more egalitarian gender attitudes than conservatives.

Examining the Role of Compositional Effects
in Sustaining Local Gender Norms

To test for the role of compositional effects, I examine the extent to which the relationship between commuting zone-level gender norms and individual-level attitudes is explained by the composition of residents with different demographic, economic, and cultural characteristics. I start by establishing the baseline relationship of commuting zone norms to individuals' attitudes. Specifically, I examine how a difference in one unit of egalitarianism in each dimension of commuting zone gender norms predicts individuals' attitudes. I standardize commuting zone gender norms so that a score of zero reflects the average commuting zone, negative scores indicate traditional environments, and positive scores reflect egalitarian places. A difference in one unit in this standardized measure relates to the difference between a very traditional and traditional, traditional and average, average and egalitarian, or egalitarian and very egalitarian environment. Using this measurement, I examine how gender norms predict four different types of attitudes that each sustain a corresponding dimension of norms. To examine the effects of norms toward women's advancement on individuals' attitudes, I use a question from the GSS (Smith et al. 2018) measuring respondents' disagreement with the statement that women are unsuited for politics. In analysis of gender norms toward public sphere gender essentialism, I examine individuals' IAT score, derived from Project Implicit (Xu et al. 2018; details discussed in Chapter 2), which measures their cognitive bias against women in science. To test the relationship between norms toward intensive mothering and individuals' attitudes, I use a question from the GSS that measures support for working mothers by asking respondents' opinions of whether children suffer if their mother works and sends them to preschool. Last, I examine the relationship between norms of private sphere gender essentialism and individuals' attitudes by using an additional item from the GSS measuring respondents' disagreement with the statement that the best family arrangement is where a man works and a woman tends the home. Each of these variables and data sources were described at length in Chapter 2.

Earlier in this chapter, Figure 4.1 illustrated a strong relationship of commuting zone gender norms to each of the corresponding individual-level attitudes listed in the preceding paragraph. These patterns were expected because gender norms are sustained by widespread patterns in attitudes. To test whether this relationship is driven by compositional effects, I add controls for each of the demographic, economic, and cultural individual-level variables listed in Table 4.1 to the hierarchical regression model used to identify the relationship of gender norms to individual attitudes. If the relationship of commuting zone norms to individuals' attitudes disappears, this means that gender norms are driven entirely by compositional effects because the association of norms to attitudes is fully accounted for by differences in the characteristics of residents living in egalitarian versus traditional places. If the relationship of gender norms to individuals' attitudes changes little or not at all, this indicates that there are other factors besides compositional effects sustaining local gender norms. If the relationship of gender norms to individuals' attitudes weakens somewhat but does not disappear, we can calculate the percentage of the relationship due to compositional effects by determining just how much the effect of norms on attitudes decreases when individual-level controls are added relative to when no control variables are included.

In the following sections, I report results of these analyses designed to test for the role of compositional effects in the relationship between the four dimensions of gender norms and their constituent individual-level attitudinal patterns. These results are visualized in Figures 4.3 through 4.6.

Women's Advancement

Figure 4.3 reports the degree to which commuting zone composition sustains gender norms toward women's advancement. The first bar, labeled "Full effect," reports the full relationship between local gender norms toward women's advancement to individuals' probability of disagreeing with a statement that women are not suited for politics. This is calculated without any control variables that would account for the composition of commuting zone residents.[1] The coefficient, 0.0244, indicates that a difference of one unit in local egalitarianism toward women's advancement is associated with a 2.44 percentage point increase in the probability of supporting women in politics. In other words, a respondent living in a commuting zone with very egalitarian norms toward women's advancement (two units above the mean) is 2.44 percentage points more likely to support women in politics than someone living in a commuting zone with egalitarian norms (one unit above the mean). This corresponds to levels of agreement illustrated earlier in Figure 4.1, where only about 75 percent of individuals in very traditional commuting zones, 77.4 percent of those in traditional commuting zones, 79.9 percent of those in average commuting zones, 82.3 percent of those in egalitarian commuting zones, and 84.8 percent of those in very egalitarian commuting zones felt women were suited for politics. Hence, with each level of egalitarianism, the probability of supporting women in politics increases by about 2.44 percentage points—corresponding to the full-effect coefficient in Figure 4.3.

The second bar in Figure 4.3 reports the effect of local gender norms toward women's advancement after controlling for demographic, economic, and cultural composition. Here, we see that the effect size decreases by about 23 percent (illustrated in the third bar in Figure 4.3) but remains significant

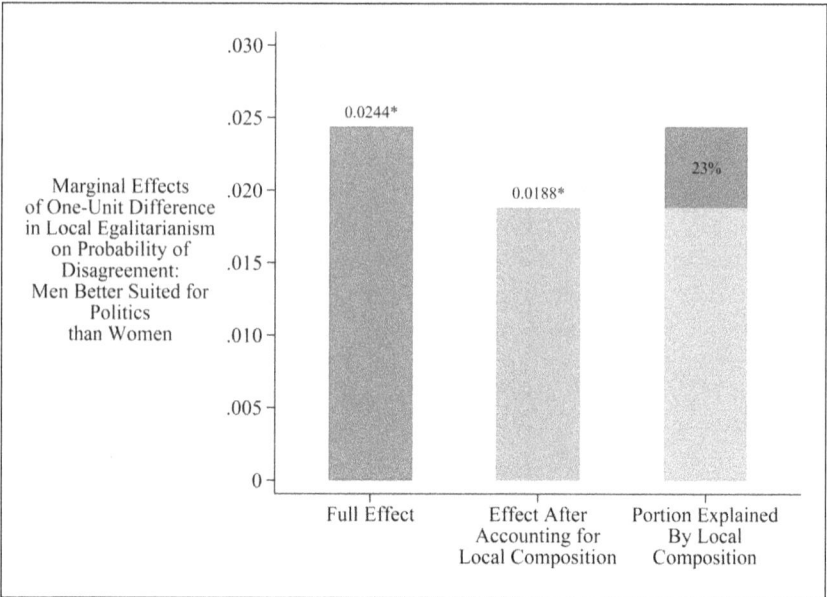

Figure 4.3 Compositional Effects on the Relationship of Gender Norms toward Women's Advancement to Individual-Level Attitudes toward Women in Politics

Note: Portion explained by local composition calculated with a series of hierarchical logistic regression models. The first model identified the effect of gender norms on individuals' attitudes with fixed effects for survey year. Average marginal effects of gender norms on the probability of supporting women in politics were calculated from this model and reported under "Full effect." The second model added controls for gender, race, foreign-born status, education, age, employment status, occupation (managerial/professional status), service sector employment, religious affiliation, and political ideology. Average marginal effects were again calculated from the second model and reported as "Effect after accounting for local composition." The difference in the average marginal effects of the two models was used to estimate the portion explained by local composition. Varying intercepts (by commuting zones) were specified in all models. * indicates significance of marginal effect at $p < 0.05$ level.

and meaningful. Even after controlling for local composition, a difference in one unit of egalitarianism (e.g., between very traditional and traditional) in local norms toward women's advancement relates to a 1.9 percentage point increase in the probability of supporting women in politics.

These results indicate that local composition explains some, but not a substantial portion, of the relationship between individual-level attitudes and commuting zone gender norms toward women's advancement. In general, less than a quarter of the relationship between norms and individuals' attitudes is due to the fact that the types of people who generally support women in politics, such as those who are college educated, tend to live in some commuting zones over others. This indicates that other factors, potentially related to contextual effects, play a more prominent role in the relationship between local gender norms and individuals' attitudes.

Public Sphere Gender Essentialism

Turning to the relationship of public sphere gender essentialism to individuals' attitudes, Figure 4.4 reports that the full effect, before including compositional controls, indicates that a difference of one unit in local egalitarianism on this dimension (e.g., comparing very traditional to traditional or egalitarian to very egalitarian) is associated with a reduction of 0.0133 in individuals' IAT score measuring cognitive bias against women in science. This corresponds to the predicted levels of cognitive bias across commuting

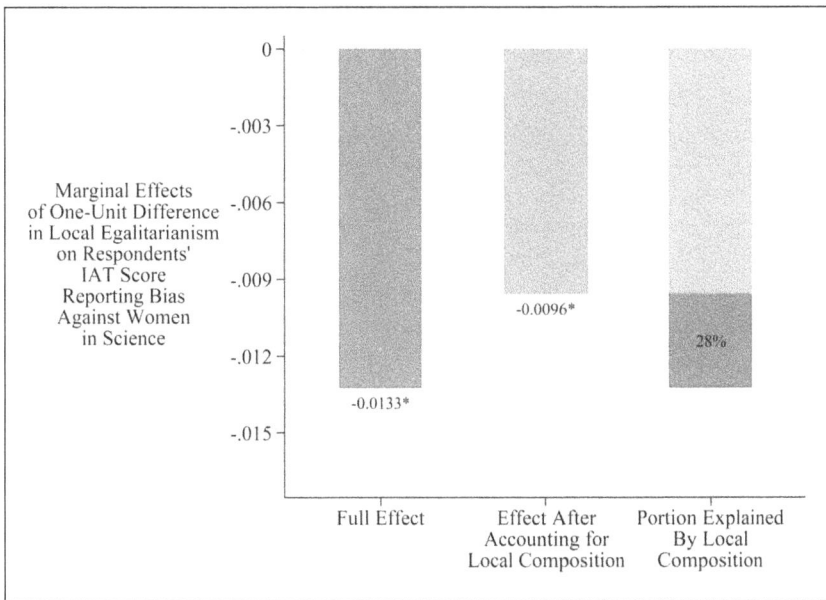

Figure 4.4 Compositional Effects on the Relationship of Gender Norms toward Public Sphere Gender Essentialism to Respondents' IAT Score Reporting Bias against Women in Science

Note: Portion explained by local composition calculated with a series of hierarchical linear regression models. The first model identified the effect of gender norms on respondents' Gender-Science IAT score with fixed effects for year. The coefficient for the predicted effect of one unit in local egalitarianism on respondents' Gender-Science IAT was calculated from this model and reported under "Full effect." The second model added controls for gender, race, foreign-born status, education, age, employment status, occupation (managerial/professional status), service sector employment, religious affiliation, and political ideology. The coefficient for local gender norms was again calculated from the second model and reported as "Effect after accounting for local composition." The difference in the marginal effects of gender norms between the two models was used to estimate the portion explained by local composition. Varying intercepts (by commuting zone) were specified in all models. * indicates significance of marginal effect at p < 0.05 level.

zones reported earlier in Figure 4.1. Those residing in more egalitarian areas toward public sphere gender essentialism report lower levels of cognitive bias than those in traditional locales.

After accounting for demographic, economic, and cultural composition, the effect of norms toward public sphere gender essentialism on individuals' IAT score reduces to −0.0096, a difference of about 28 percent from the full effect. Despite this reduction, the relationship of local gender norms to individuals' IATs remains significant and substantial.

Like norms toward women's advancement, we find that the relationship of commuting zone public sphere gender essentialism to individuals' IAT score is only partially related to differences in the types of people who live in places with egalitarian norms toward public sphere gender essentialism versus the types residing in areas with traditional norms on this dimension. This indicates that composition plays a small role in sustaining local norms toward public sphere gender essentialism and that there are other mechanisms that may be more prominent.

Intensive Mothering

Respondents residing in areas with more egalitarian norms toward intensive mothering—that is, places where norms support maternal employment—are more likely to disagree with a statement that working mothers harm children by sending them to preschool. The full effect reported in Figure 4.5 shows that a difference of one unit in egalitarianism toward intensive mothering relates to a four percentage point increase in the probability that an individual will disagree with this statement opposing working mothers. Comparing very traditional to very egalitarian commuting zones, this means that only about 59 percent of individuals residing in the most traditional areas toward intensive mothering disagree with this statement, compared to 75 percent in the most egalitarian locales.

Just under a third of this relationship, however, is due to local demographic, economic, and cultural composition. After accounting for these characteristics, the effect of norms toward intensive mothering decreases from 0.04 to 0.0271, a change of 32 percent. Nonetheless, the relationship remains significant and substantial, indicating that norms toward intensive mothering are associated with individuals' attitudes regardless of local composition.

Commuting zone gender norms toward intensive mothering are strong predictors of individuals' attitudes toward working mothers. About a third of this relationship is due to differences in the types of people who tend to reside in places with egalitarian versus traditional norms on this dimension. This leaves a substantial portion of the relationship between individual attitudes and commuting zone norms toward intensive mothering that may be explained by additional factors unrelated to local composition.

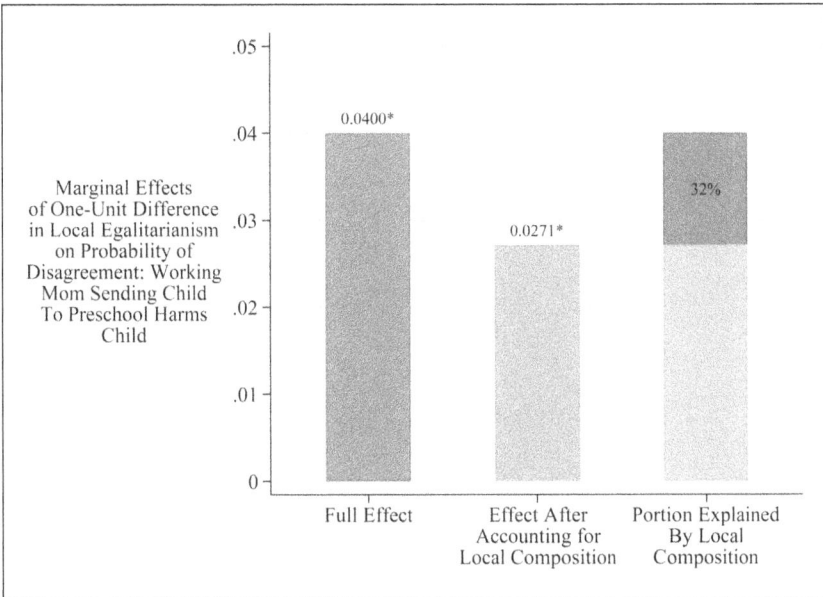

Figure 4.5 Compositional Effects on the Relationship of Gender Norms toward Intensive Mothering to Individuals' Attitudes toward Working Mothers Sending Children to Preschool

Note: Portion explained by local composition calculated with a series of hierarchical logistic regression models. The first model identified the effect of gender norms on individuals' attitudes with fixed effects for survey year. Average marginal effects of gender norms on the probability of supporting working mothers were calculated from this model and reported under "Full effect." The second model added controls for gender, race, foreign-born status, education, age, employment status, occupation (managerial/professional status), service sector employment, religious affiliation, and political ideology. Average marginal effects were again calculated from the second model and reported as "Effect after accounting for local composition." The difference in the average marginal effects of the two models was used to estimate the portion explained by local composition. Varying intercepts (by commuting zone) were specified in all models. * indicates significance of marginal effect at p < 0.05 level.

Private Sphere Gender Essentialism

Figure 4.6 reports the full effect, the effect after accounting for local composition, and the portion explained by local composition for the relationship between local norms of public sphere gender essentialism and individuals' probability of disagreeing with the statement that it is better for men to work and women to tend the home. The full effects report that, before accounting for local composition, individuals residing in more egalitarian commuting zones on this dimension of gender norms are much more likely to disagree with conventional family arrangements. Those in very egalitarian commuting zones are 4.75 percentage points more likely oppose conventional family arrangements than those in egalitarian places, 9.5 percentage points more

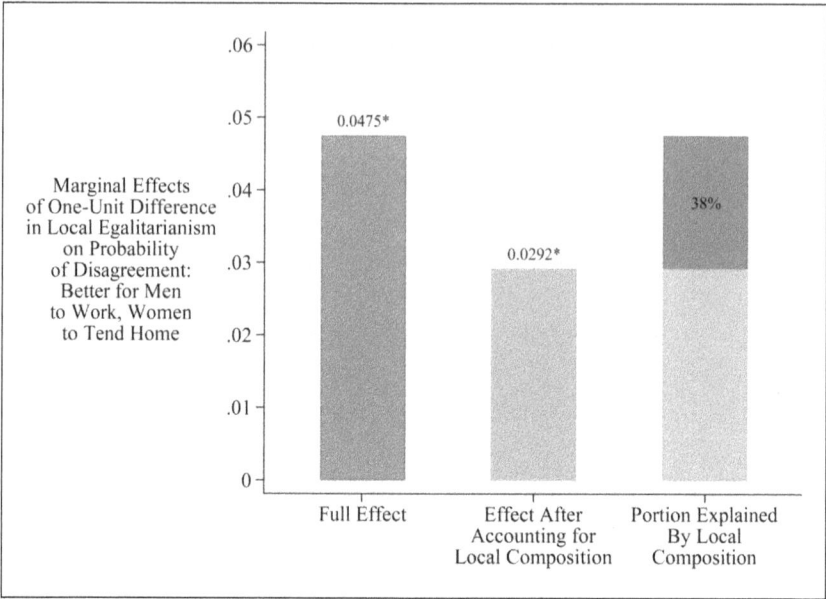

Figure 4.6 Compositional Effects on the Relationship of Gender Norms toward Private Sphere Gender Essentialism and Individuals' Attitudes toward Gendered Divisions of Family Labor

Note: Portion explained by local composition calculated with a series of hierarchical logistic regression models. The first model identified the effect of gender norms on individuals' attitudes with fixed effects for survey year. Average marginal effects of gender norms on the probability of disagreeing with traditional gendered divisions of family labor were calculated from this model and reported under "Full effect." The second model added controls for gender, race, foreign-born status, education, age, employment status, occupation (managerial/professional status), service sector employment, religious affiliation, and political ideology. Average marginal effects were again calculated from the second model and reported as "Effect after accounting for local composition." The difference in the average marginal effects of the two models was used to estimate the portion explained by local composition. Varying intercepts (by commuting zone) were specified in all models. * indicates significance of marginal effect at p < 0.05 level.

likely than residents of areas with average norms, 14.25 percent points more likely than those in traditional areas, and 19 percentage points more likely than individuals residing in very traditional locations. Overall, for every unit difference in local egalitarianism on this dimension, the probability of disagreeing with conventional family arrangements increases by 4.75 percentage points.

Nearly 40 percent of this full effect is due to local demographic, economic, and cultural composition. When adding compositional controls, the relationship of local gender norms to individuals' attitudes reduces from 0.0475 to 0.0292, a difference of 38 percent. Yet, there remain substantial and significant effects of norms on individuals' attitudes even after accounting for demographic, economic, and cultural characteristics. Whereas the difference in attitudes between individuals residing in a very traditional versus a very egalitarian commuting zone was predicted to be 19 percentage points in the full model without controls, it is 11.7 percentage points after accounting for local composition—a smaller, but still substantively large, effect.

Local gender norms toward private sphere gender essentialism are related to individuals' views toward conventional family arrangements. About 40 percent of this effect is driven by the fact that individuals with characteristics that predispose them to disagreeing with traditional family dynamics are more likely to reside in areas with egalitarian norms toward private sphere gender essentialism. Yet, even after accounting for these compositional dynamics, local norms continue to be associated with individuals' attitudes.

Summary of Findings: Compositional Effects

To test whether local gender norms are sustained by differences in the types of people who live in each commuting zone, I focused on whether the relationship of gender norms to the attitudinal patterns that maintain them can be explained by the spatial variation of individuals with characteristics shown to predict gender attitudes. Across each of the four dimensions of gender norms, local composition accounts for only a portion of this relationship. This indicates that compositional effects play a minor role in sustaining variation in local gender norms. Interestingly, composition appears to be more influential with respect to the two dimensions of gender norms related to the family (intensive mothering and private sphere gender essentialism) than the two dimensions pertaining to work (women's advancement and public sphere gender essentialism). Local composition accounted for about a quarter of the relationship between attitudes and the two dimensions of norms related to work. In contrast, compositional effects explained about a third of the relationship between attitudes and the two dimensions of norms toward the family.

Overall, compositional effects do not fully explain how variation in local gender norms is sustained. This leaves the remaining possibility that gender norms are driven by contextual effects whereby the experience of residing in a particular location and being exposed to certain norms influences individuals' attitudes. I explore this mechanism in the following section.

Contextual Effects: How Places Shape People

The 1990 single "In the Ghetto," by hip-hop duo Eric B. and Rakim, is known for containing thoughtful observations on social life and inequality. Yet the song is best remembered for a phrase occurring at the end of each verse: "It ain't where you're from, it's where you're at." Reflecting on this lyric years later, Rakim shared that it was motivated from his observation that when he visited new places, his music was shaped by the local culture and the type of music made by local artists (Rakim 2014). Although Eric B. and Rakim's style was originally influenced by the type of rap performed in their hometown of New York City, the eclectic style of their later albums was attributed, in part, to their experience visiting regions across the United States.

Perhaps Eric B. and Rakim's lyrics resonated so broadly because they reflected the common experience of personal change that occurs when moving to a new place. Not long after my brother-in-law moved to Minneapolis from Detroit, he started to speak with a heavy emphasis on the letter r in words and commonly ended sentences with "eh?" My sister's wardrobe suddenly included an endless number of black leather jackets after moving to Chicago. And my cousin's relocation to Los Angeles was soon followed by a new, much longer, hair style. Perhaps their new locales were simply allowing these individuals to express parts of themselves that were stifled when they resided in other places. Or perhaps it was the experience of residing in the new environments that eventually rubbed off on them as they slowly came to acquire the local style. Scholars refer to this dynamic as "contextual effects"—the process through which exposure to a local cultural environment influences individuals' attitudes, perceptions, sense of identity, and personal style (Maxwell 2019).

Although compositional effects have been found to play a large role in political attitudes, research on gender expression and gender attitudes reveals greater support for the role of contextual effects. Studying the migration of women workers from rural to urban areas in Cambodia, Alice Evans (2019) found strong evidence that their experience living in a city made them more perceptive of, and resistant to, gender inequality in their rural hometowns. While residing in major cities such as Phnom Penh, urban migrant women had greater exposure to other women who commonly broke conventional gender norms and regularly demonstrated independence and agency. It was far more common for women to be educated, fully employed, and financially independent in Phnom Penh than in the rural villages where Evans's respondents originated. With greater exposure and interaction, these new urban migrants came to embrace independence, with many seeking further education and financial freedom from their husbands.

In Cambodia, rural/urban divides have clear differences in gender norms shaping the experience of women who traverse these spatial boundaries (Evans 2019). In other circumstances, cities of similar size can nonetheless have very different contexts that shape the attitudes of residents. Katja Guenther (2010), for example, compared local views toward feminism in two German cities that were similar in most demographic and economic indicators but had very different local histories and cultural reputations. In one city, values and norms around personal independence fostered an environment where feminist values were supported and mainstreamed into local politics. In the other, socially conservative traditions presented challenges for local feminists who met resistance when pursuing agendas that contradicted essentialist notions of gender difference. Despite each city being located in East Germany and containing similar demographic characteristics, their varying cultural environments fostered two very different contexts shaping local views toward feminism. In one city, feminism was highly regarded and mainstreamed into local politics, while in the other city, feminism was viewed with much more skepticism.

Guenther describes the different cultural environments of each city in her study as their "place character." As discussed in prior chapters, place character refers to the collection of cultural reputations, values, and community identities that shape how residents perceive a place and the type of people who live there. These images exist in our collective imagination of places' reputations but also manifest in cultural products that emerge from specific locations, such as art, music, billboards, tourism materials, and literature (Paulsen 2004). Wendy Griswold (2008), for example, studied how popular books emerging from different cities reflect each area's local reputations, a major draw for readers who find it intriguing to imagine life in different contexts.

The influence of local cultural settings has even been found to shape some of the most intimate aspects of our identity. In interviews with LBQ women in Ithaca, New York; San Luis Obispo, California; Portland, Maine; and Greenfield, Massachusetts, Japonica Brown-Saracino (2017) found that individuals' expression of sexual identity greatly depended on local place character. LBQ residents in Portland more commonly rejected conventional forms of women's dress, used nonbinary pronouns, and outwardly challenged binary conceptions of gender. This reflects Portland's "rebel" culture and embrace of creative expressions. In contrast, LBQ residents in Ithaca more commonly integrated into the local scene. Their sexual identity was not outwardly apparent. This reflected the culture of Ithaca, which is known as a small, close-knit town where collectivist sentiment outweighs individual freedoms.

Brown-Saracino's work reaches similar conclusions as other studies examining how local culture shapes individuals' sense of identity. Mariam Abelson (2019), for example, found that trans men expressed less traditional forms of masculinity in places with liberal reputations like San Francisco than areas with more conservative leanings located in the U.S. South. Studying racial identity, Zandria Robinson (2014) examined how residents of Memphis, known as the cultural "heart of the South," constructed distinct ideals of Black authenticity that were rooted in southern culture and reflected in food, hairstyles, and fashion.

Each of these studies point to the presence of contextual effects where the local set of norms where we reside influences individual characteristics related to our identities and our attitudes. Across studies, contextual effects operate by encouraging some behaviors while discouraging others. The LBQ residents in Ithaca studied by Brown-Saracino (2017), for example, had little choice but to adopt an integrationist identity because their city did not have the infrastructure, such as gay or LBQ-friendly bars, to allow LBQ residents to form a separate community. In other instances, longtime residents pose models of behavior for those new to the area. Women in New York City, for example, may be more comfortable balancing full-time employment with parenting because it is so common, whereas those in Columbus would feel greater pressure to leave their careers in this context where fewer mothers sustain both full-time work and parenting. In other instances, contextual effects operate when some behaviors or attitudes are discouraged. The trans men interviewed by Abelson (2019) reported that they intentionally behaved in more traditional ways when in conservative areas like western Minnesota because they feared violence from men who uncovered they were trans or who felt threatened by nonconventional expressions of masculinity.

Through multiple mechanisms, prior research has shown how local cultural environments associated with places can shape individuals' identities and personal attitudes. It is therefore possible that the four dimensions of local gender norms identified in this book are sustained by contextual effects whereby residents' exposure to these norms influences their attitudes in ways that generate distinct spatial patterns. From this perspective, commuting zone norms and individuals' attitudes are reflexive and self-sustaining. Individuals' attitudes are influenced to align with local norms; in turn, these aggregate attitudinal patterns help sustain those very norms.

Examining the Role of Contextual Effects in Sustaining Local Gender Norms

To test for the role of contextual effects, we again take advantage of the empirical relationship between commuting zone gender norms and individuals' attitudes, but instead of determining whether the demographic composition of places accounts for this relationship (the approach used to test for compositional effects), we can examine whether individuals with the same personal characteristics have varying attitudes depending on the local cultural environment where they live. This method is established in research testing for the presence of contextual effects (Maxwell 2019; Scarborough and Sin 2020). The basic premise is that we can isolate the role of local context by comparing individuals who hold the same personal characteristics but differ only in that they live in places with different norms. Therefore, any observed differences in their attitudes are due to the influence of the place where they live, rather than demographic characteristics.

In the previous analysis of compositional effects, I used a series of hierarchical regression models that predicted individuals' attitudes with commuting zone gender norms and an extensive set of demographic, economic, and cultural control variables that accounted for the distribution of individuals with different characteristics across commuting zones. To test for the presence of contextual effects, I build from those analyses. I use the same regression models but add an interaction term between commuting zone gender norms and two individual-level characteristics identified in prior research as being highly related to attitudes: level of education, measured by whether the respondent holds a college degree or not, and religious affiliation, measured by whether respondents belong to a liberal/no religion, a moderate religion, or a fundamentalist religion. These analyses effectively test for contextual effects by determining whether the size of the gap in attitudes by education and religious affiliation differs by local commuting zone gender norms.

As noted previously, prior research has found consistent and long-lasting gaps in gender attitudes between the college educated and those whose highest level of education is less than college (Mason, Czajka, and Arber 1976; Scarborough, Sin, and Risman 2019). Analyzing survey data spanning 1977 through 2016, my prior research with Ray Sin and Barbara Risman (2019) found that the college educated were about ten percentage points more likely to support gender equality at work and in the home than those with a high school or less education and five percentage points more likely to hold these views than those with some college education. Other research confirms these patterns and finds that they hold even when controlling for family background characteristics such as social class (Campbell and Horowitz 2016). This education gap in attitudes is well established. However, it has not yet been examined whether this gap varies spatially and if such variation is due to distinct configurations of gender norms across commuting zones. It is possible that local norms amplify or diminish the impact of education on individuals' gender attitudes. Mary Jackman (1994), for example, argues that the college educated are more perceptive of cultural values and commonly adopt perspectives that allow them to "fit in" to local settings. Although the college educated tend to hold greater support for gender equality and feminist ideals, in highly traditional contexts, it is possible that these individuals shift their attitudes to align with local norms. This would result in a closing of the gap in gender attitudes between college- and less-than-college-educated residents in places with traditional norms. From this perspective, contextual effects may be observed if the relationship of local norms to attitudes is stronger among the college educated.

In addition to education, religious affiliation has been found to be a consistent individual-level predictor of gender attitudes (Schnabel 2016). In fact, Andrew Whitehead and Samuel Perry (2019) argue that differences between individuals holding fundamentalist, moderate, and liberal religions are among the most powerful factors contributing to views toward gender equality and gender relations. Religious texts, leaders, and institutions convey a direct set of moral virtues and values that often incorporate prescriptive expectations for women and men. In fundamentalist religions, women rarely hold leadership positions, and gender relations in the family are often expected to follow conventional patterns of women's caregiving and men's breadwinning. In contrast, liberal religions tend to have more women in leadership and commonly embrace feminist values of gender equality. These differences drive major variation in gender attitudes by religious affiliation. Yet it is possible that the types of values conveyed by one's religious community vary according to the local cultural environment. Catholic churches in Dallas may be more likely to convey the belief that mothers should not work than a Catholic church in Minneapolis where prevailing norms support maternal employment. Lutheranism is known as a more moderate religion where women are officially allowed to hold leadership positions such as pastors or bishops, yet it may be more common for women to lead congregations in the egalitarian context of Boston than the traditional setting of Columbus. Comparing whether attitudes vary among individuals with the same religious affiliation but residing in areas with different gender norms can shed light on whether contextual effects shape individuals' attitudes over and above demographic composition.

In the following four sections, I report the results of my analysis testing for the role of contextual effects. I compare whether the education and religion gap in gender attitudes varies depending on the cultural context in the commuting zone where individuals reside. If the gap varies across local contexts, this provides evidence that exposure to particular cultural norms influences individuals' gender attitudes to be different from what we would expect given their demographic characteristics alone. The results of these analyses are reported in Table 4.2, where coefficients representing the size of the relationship between norms and attitudes are reported by respondents' level of education and religious affiliation. Each coefficient in Table 4.2 represents the predicted difference in gender attitudes when comparing individuals residing in commuting zones with local gender norms that differ by one unit of egalitarianism, equivalent to the difference between very traditional and traditional, traditional and average, average and egalitarian, and egalitarian and very egalitarian locales. Evidence for contextual effects is observed if coefficients between comparison groups (e.g., the college and less than college educated) are substantially different in size. To ease interpret-

TABLE 4.2 CONTEXTUAL EFFECTS IN THE RELATIONSHIP OF GENDER NORMS TO INDIVIDUAL ATTITUDES

	Column 1	Column 2	Column 3	Column 4
	Marginal effects of norms toward women's advancement on probability of disagreement: Men better suited for politics than women	Marginal effects of norms toward public sphere gender essentialism on respondents' IAT score (bias against women in science)	Marginal effects of egalitarian intensive mothering norms on probability of disagreement: Working mom sending child to preschool harms child	Marginal effects of norms toward private sphere gender essentialism on probability of disagreement: Better for men to work, women to tend home
By education				
Less than college	0.016**	−0.004	0.029***	0.032***
College degree or more	0.024***	−0.012***	0.025**	0.026**
By religious affiliation				
Fundamentalist religion	0.015**	−0.010***	0.012	0.023**
Moderate religion	0.025***	−0.007***	0.036***	0.041***
Liberal religion/ no religion	0.016**	−0.011***	0.031***	0.023**

Note: Coefficients calculated from independent hierarchical regression models with varying intercept (by commuting zone). Coefficients from columns 1, 3, and 4 represent average marginal effects of one-unit difference in local egalitarianism on the probability of each outcome, calculated from logistic regression equations. Coefficients from column 2 represent marginal effects of one-unit difference in local gender norms on predicted IAT score, calculated from linear regression models. All models included controls for gender, race, foreign-born status, education, age, employment status, occupation (managerial/professional status), service sector employment, religious affiliation, political ideology, and survey year. Significance levels: $^*p < 0.05$; $^{**}p < 0.01$; $^{***}p < 0.001$.

ation and provide further insight on these contextual effects, I also visualize these patterns in Figures 4.7 through 4.14, which I discuss in the following.

Women's Advancement

Figure 4.7 illustrates the predicted probability of college- and less-than-college-educated respondents disagreeing with the statement that men are better suited for politics than women across levels of commuting zone gender norms toward women's advancement. As previously established, there is a general trend for individuals residing in commuting zones with egalitar-

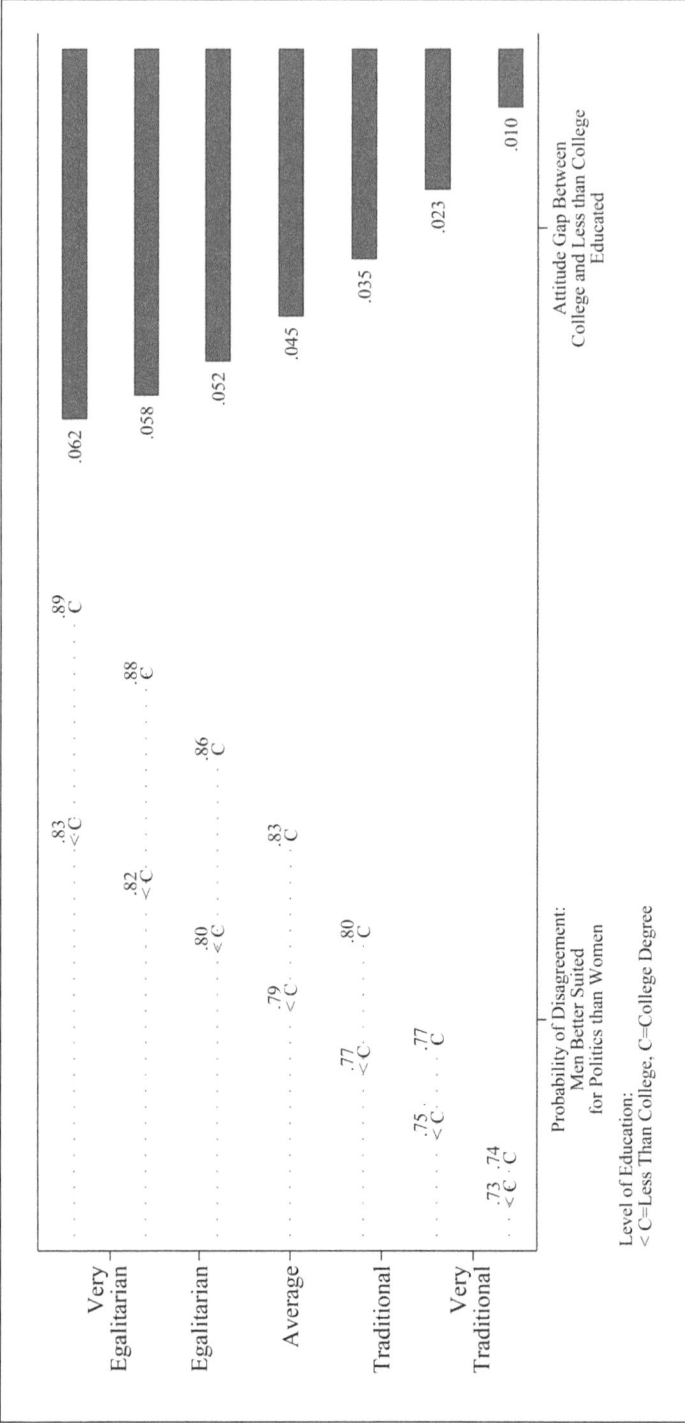

Figure 4.7 Contextual Effects of Norms toward Women's Advancement: Within-Commuting Zone Differences in Attitudes toward Women in Politics by Level of Education

Note: Estimates calculated from a hierarchical logistic regression model predicting support for women in politics with an interaction between local gender norms toward women's advancement and an indicator of whether respondents held a college degree. The model includes controls for gender, race, foreign-born status, age, employment status, occupation (managerial/professional status), service sector employment, religious affiliation, political ideology, a fixed effect for survey year, and a varying intercept (by commuting zone).

ian norms toward women's advancement to be more likely to disagree that men are better suited for politics than women. Confirming previous research, Figure 4.7 also shows that, for the most part, individuals with a college degree hold greater support for women in politics than those whose education is less than a college degree. However, the size of this difference varies greatly depending on the local cultural context. In commuting zones with very egalitarian norms toward women's advancement, college-educated respondents are about six percentage points more likely to support women in politics than those with less education. This gap shrinks to four percentage points in commuting zones with average norms on this dimension and nearly disappears, reducing to only one percentage point, in the most traditional areas.

The varying education gap in attitudes illustrated in Figure 4.7 occurs because local norms toward women's advancement have a stronger relationship with individuals' attitudes among the college educated than those with lower levels of education. A difference of one unit in local egalitarianism (e.g., between an egalitarian and a very egalitarian commuting zone) predicts a difference of 2.4 percentage points in college-educated respondents' probability of supporting women in politics, compared to a difference of 1.6 percentage points for those with less than a college degree. In other words, the effect of local norms is 50 percent greater for the college educated.

These findings show that context plays a large role in sustaining local gender norms. Individuals with a college degree hold similar gender attitudes as those with less education in areas with traditional gender norms, indicating that local norms that convey women as less suitable for leadership have a pronounced effect on the college educated who would otherwise espouse greater support for women in leadership.

Figure 4.8 examines support for women in politics by individuals' religious affiliation and by levels of local gender norms toward women's advancement. Across cultural environments, overall support for women in politics increases for all religious groups. The size of this relationship is similar for both religious fundamentalists and liberals, even while liberals consistently hold greater support. Among individuals affiliated with moderate religions, however, the effect of local gender norms is over 50 percent larger than it is for fundamentalist or liberal religious adherents. In very traditional contexts, adherents to moderate religions hold the least support for women in politics, while in very egalitarian commuting zones, their levels of support are virtually the same as those affiliated with liberal religions. This provides additional evidence for contextual effects, particularly among those affiliated with moderate religions. It is likely that these religions are less dogmatic and uniform in their gospel, making them more open to the influence of local gender norms. Importantly, those affiliated with moderate religions make up the

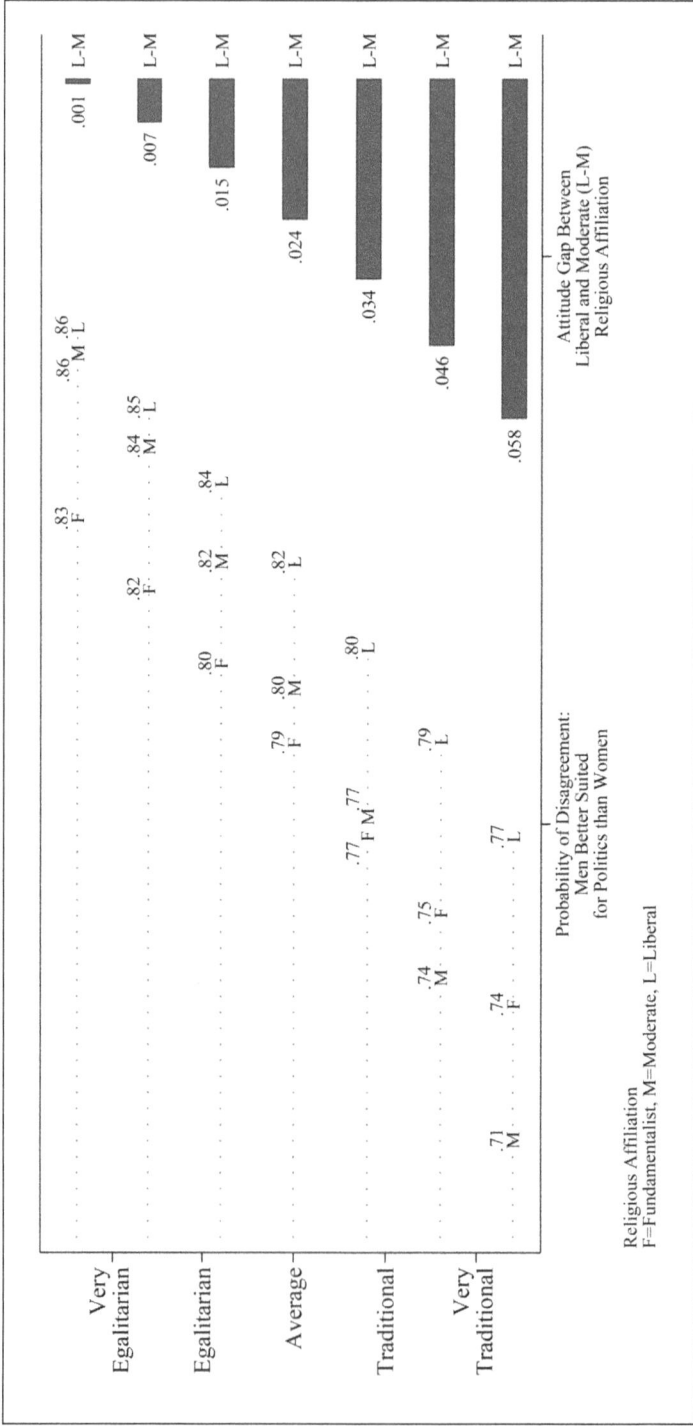

Figure 4.8 Contextual Effects of Norms toward Women's Advancement: Within-Commuting Zone Differences in Attitudes toward Women in Politics by Religious Affiliation

Note: Estimates calculated from a hierarchical logistic regression model predicting support for women in politics with an interaction between local gender norms toward women's advancement and religious affiliation (fundamentalist, moderate, liberal/no religion). The model includes controls for gender, race, foreign-born status, education, age, employment status, occupation (managerial/professional status), service sector employment, political ideology, a fixed effect for survey year, and a varying intercept (by commuting zone).

majority of respondents. In the sample used for these analyses, 42 percent of respondents were affiliated with moderate religions, compared to 31 percent who were adherents to liberal religions (or held no religion) and 26 percent who were fundamentalists.

Overall, these results show that contextual effects play a large role in sustaining local gender norms toward women's advancement. Although the college educated generally hold more support for women in politics than those with less education, this gap is nearly absent in very traditional contexts—meaning that it is the experience of living in these places, rather than the population of college degree holders, that maintains consistent patterns in gender attitudes sustaining local norms. Comparing religious affiliations, all groups tend to be more supportive of women in politics when in egalitarian normative contexts. But moderates were particularly influenced by local culture: They held the least support for women in politics in very traditional commuting zones and the most support, alongside liberal religious adherents, in very egalitarian environments, suggesting that their attitudes are significantly swayed by local norms toward women's advancement.

Public Sphere Gender Essentialism

To examine the role of contextual effects sustaining gender norms toward public sphere gender essentialism, I tested whether the relationship of education and religious affiliation to individuals' implicit attitudes toward women in science (measured as their IAT score) differed across commuting zones with varying gender norms on this dimension. The results are illustrated in Figures 4.9 and 4.10. Overall, the findings are consistent with what was found with norms toward women's advancement and point to the important role of contextual effects in sustaining gender norms toward public sphere gender essentialism. Implicit bias against women in science is smallest in very egalitarian versus very traditional environments. But the relationship of these commuting zone norms to implicit attitudes is three times larger among the college educated than those with less than a college education. In very egalitarian commuting zones, those with less than a college education report IAT scores that are 15 percent higher than the college educated. This gap reduces in egalitarian, average, and traditional commuting zones and disappears in places with very traditional norms toward public sphere gender essentialism. This finding indicates that it is not the distribution of college graduates across commuting zones that makes some areas more egalitarian on this dimension than others. Instead, local gender norms are sustained by contextual effects whereby the college educated in traditional commuting zones hold much more conventional views, such as bias toward women in science, than the college educated in egalitarian areas.

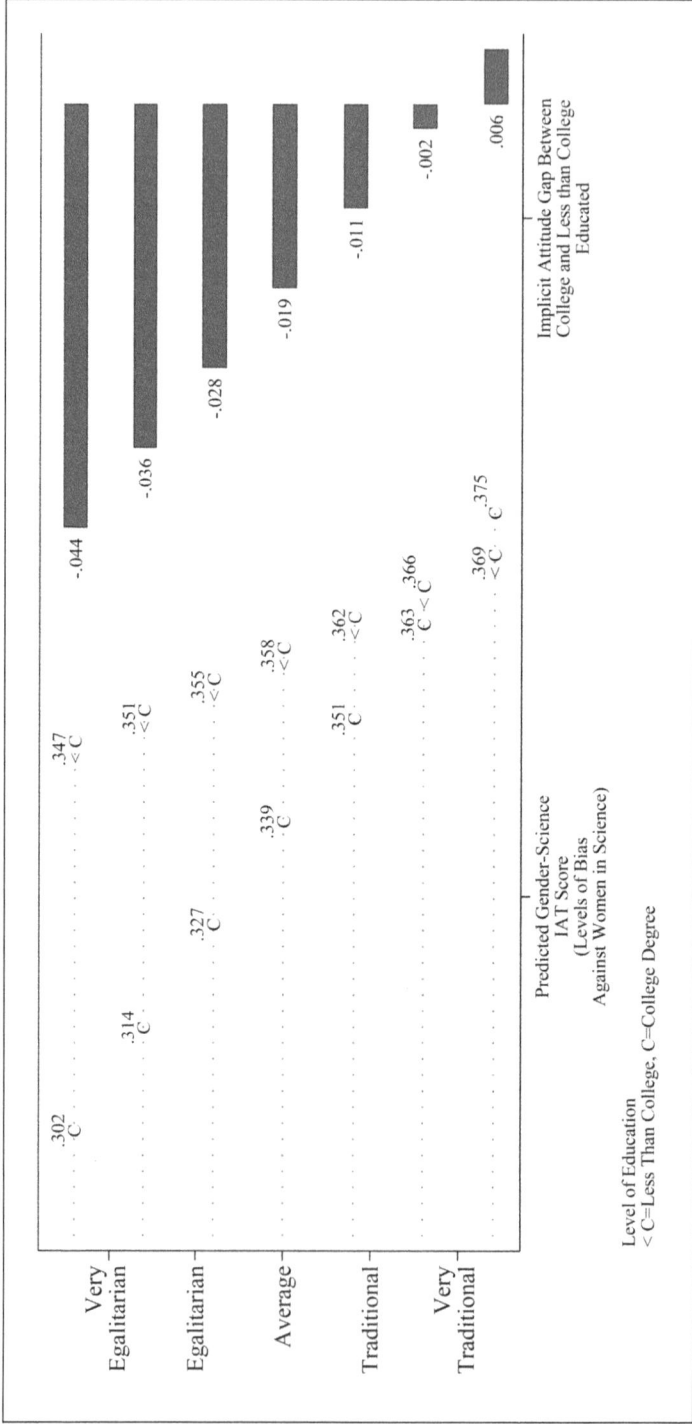

Figure 4.9 Contextual Effects of Norms toward Public Sphere Gender Essentialism: Within-Commuting Zone Differences in Implicit Attitudes toward Women in Science by Level of Education

Note: Estimates calculated from a hierarchical linear regression model predicting Gender-Science IAT scores with an interaction between local gender norms toward public sphere gender essentialism and an indicator of whether respondents held a college degree. The model includes controls for gender, race, foreign-born status, age, employment status, occupation (managerial/professional status), service sector employment, religious affiliation, political ideology, a fixed effect for survey year, and a varying intercept (by commuting zone).

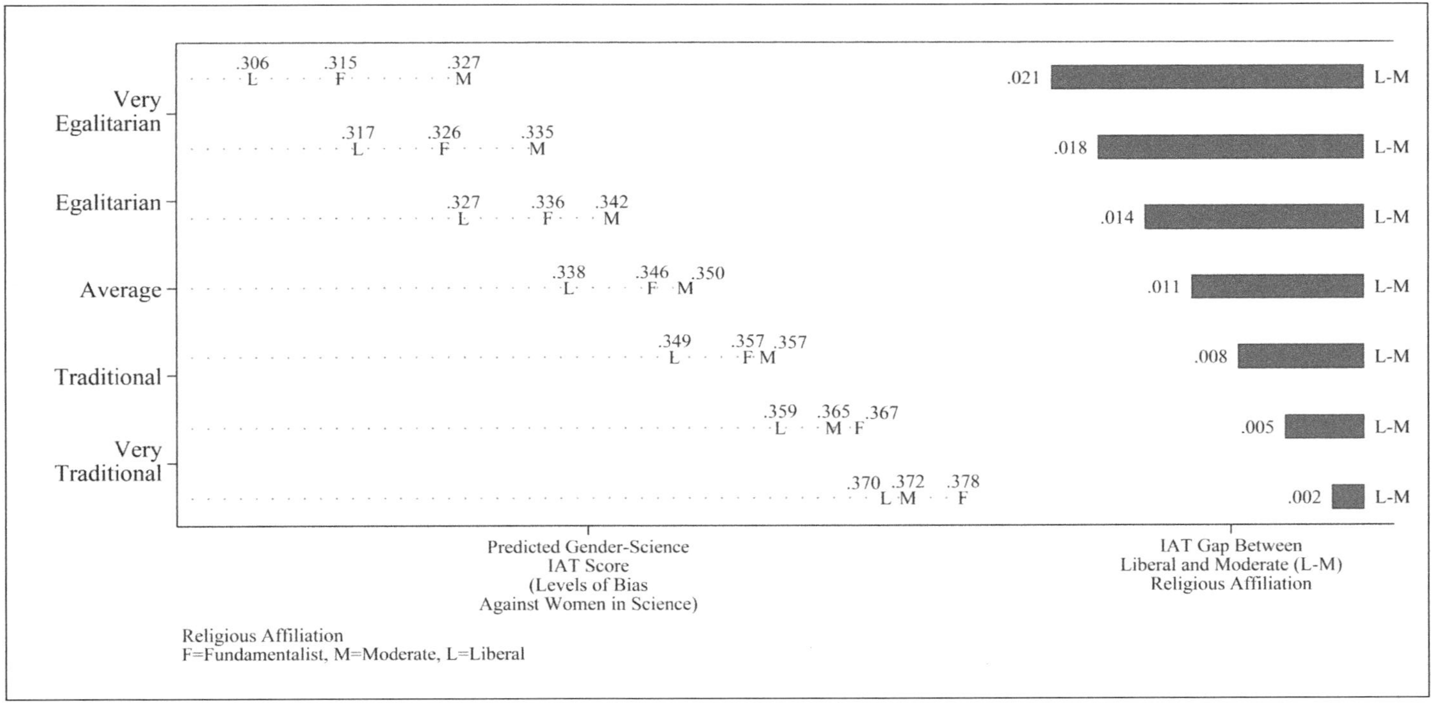

Figure 4.10 Contextual Effects of Norms toward Public Sphere Gender Essentialism: Within-Commuting Zone Differences in Implicit Attitudes toward Women in Science by Religious Affiliation

Note: Estimates calculated from a hierarchical linear regression model predicting Gender-Science IAT scores with an interaction between local gender norms toward public sphere gender essentialism and religious affiliation (fundamentalist, moderate, liberal/no religion). The model includes controls for gender, race, foreign-born status, education, age, employment status, occupation (managerial/professional status), service sector employment, political ideology, a fixed effect for survey year, and a varying intercept (by commuting zone).

Contextual effects are also observed with respect to differences by religious affiliation. However, the dynamics between these groups are slightly different from what was observed when focusing on norms toward women's advancement. Commuting zone gender norms toward public sphere gender essentialism have a stronger effect on individuals affiliated with liberal and fundamentalist religions than those belonging to moderate religions. This indicates that it is not the distribution of liberal, moderate, and fundamentalist adherents across commuting zones that drives differences in local norms but instead suggests that those belonging to liberal and fundamentalist religions are more heavily influenced by their local cultural context. For example, in very egalitarian environments, those affiliated with liberal religions have IAT scores that are 7 percent lower than those affiliated with moderate religions. In very traditional contexts, this gap reduces to less than 1 percent.

Like norms toward women's advancement, the evidence presented in Figures 4.9 and 4.10 indicates that contextual effects play a major role in sustaining gender norms toward public sphere gender essentialism. To examine whether this pattern persists across the two dimensions of norms pertaining to the private sphere of the family, I now examine the role of contextual effects in sustaining norms toward intensive mothering and private sphere gender essentialism.

Intensive Mothering

Respondents who reside in commuting zones with more egalitarian norms toward intensive mothering are more likely to support working mothers. In addition, those with a college degree also report greater support for working mothers, a finding that confirms prior research (Scarborough, Sin, and Risman 2019). The education gap in support for working mothers does not vary to a large degree by commuting zone gender norms, even while both college- and less-than-college-educated individuals report uniformly higher levels of support in egalitarian locales (see Figure 4.11). Put differently, the difference between the college educated and those with less than a college degree is consistent across commuting zones regardless of local norms toward intensive mothering. This confirms earlier findings showing that compositional effects account for a larger portion of the relationship between gender norms toward intensive mothering and individuals' attitudes. Because the education gap in attitudes toward working mothers is consistent across varying levels of intensive mothering norms, commuting zones with a larger share of residents with a college degree will have more people who support working mothers.

Comparing the religion gap in support for working mothers across commuting zone gender norms toward intensive mothering, we find much stronger evidence for contextual effects (see Figure 4.12). In particular, the rela-

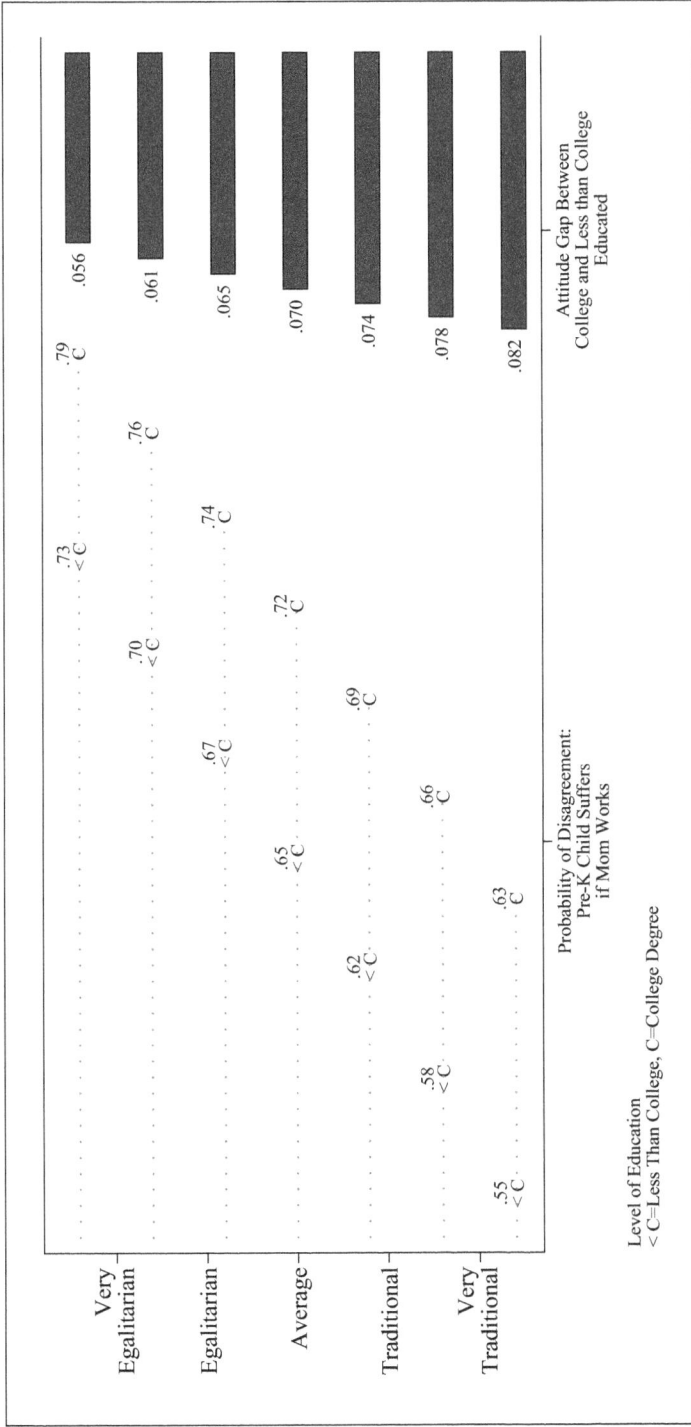

Figure 4.11 Contextual Effects of Norms toward Intensive Mothering: Within-Commuting Zone Differences in Attitudes toward Working Mothers by Education

Note: Estimates calculated from a hierarchical logistic regression model predicting support for working mothers with an interaction between local gender norms toward intensive mothering and an indicator of whether the respondent had a college degree. The model includes controls for gender, race, foreign-born status, age, employment status, occupation (managerial/professional status), service sector employment, religious affiliation, political ideology, a fixed effect for survey year, and a varying intercept (by commuting zone).

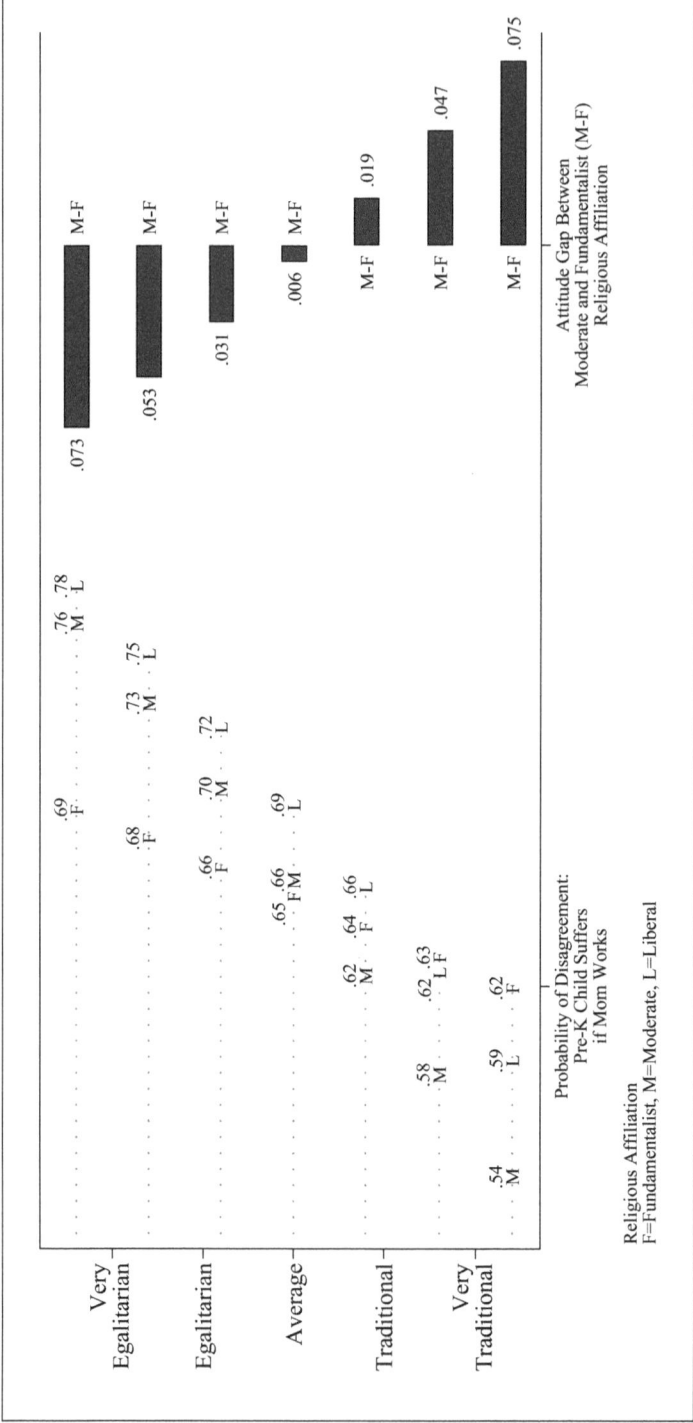

Figure 4.12 Contextual Effects of Norms toward Intensive Mothering: Within-Commuting Zone Differences in Attitudes toward Working Mothers by Religious Affiliation

Note: Estimates calculated from a hierarchical logistic regression model predicting support for working mothers with an interaction between local gender norms toward intensive mothering and religious affiliation (fundamentalist, moderate, liberal/no religion). The model includes controls for gender, race, foreign-born status, education, age, employment status, occupation (managerial/professional status), service sector employment, political ideology, a fixed effect for survey year, and a varying intercept (by commuting zone).

tionship of local gender norms toward intensive mothering to individuals' support for working mothers is three times larger for those affiliated with moderate religions, and over two and a half times larger for those belonging to liberal religions, compared to individuals adhering to fundamentalist religions. In very egalitarian contexts, liberal and moderate religious adherents are nearly ten percentage points more likely than fundamentalists to believe it is fine for a working mother to send her child to preschool. This gap shrinks in more traditional commuting zones and reverses in the most traditional areas, where moderates are predicted to be about eight percentage points less likely than fundamentalists to support working mothers. These patterns indicate that it is not the distribution of individuals holding different religions across commuting zones that sustains gender norms toward intensive mothering. Instead, the views of moderate and liberal religious adherents are influenced by the local context where they reside: They hold more opposition to working mothers in traditional contexts but are much more supportive in egalitarian environments. As a result, the religion gap in support for working mothers varies by local gender norms.

Collectively, these findings suggest that norms toward intensive mothering may be driven both by the composition of residents with a college degree as well as contextual effects across those with different religious affiliations. The education gap in attitudes toward working mothers was consistent across commuting zones with varying gender norms on this dimension, suggesting that the distribution of college-educated residents across commuting zones helps sustain distinct patterns in attitudes that sustain local norms. In contrast, differences by religious affiliation point to the important role of contextual effects. The experience of residing within a certain cultural context shapes individuals' attitudes to align with local norms, particularly for individuals adhering to moderate or liberal religions.

Private Sphere Gender Essentialism

Examining the role of contextual effects in sustaining norms of private sphere gender essentialism, we find similar patterns observed earlier with respect to norms of intensive mothering. In general, the education gap in individuals' support for gender-equal contributions to the family is consistent across commuting zones with different norms toward private sphere gender essentialism (see Figure 4.13). Although overall levels of support for gender equality in families are greater in places with egalitarian norms on this dimension, the difference between the college educated and those with less than a college education remains stable. This suggests that some of the compositional effects observed earlier on this dimension are due to the concentration of college degree holders in places with more egalitarian norms.

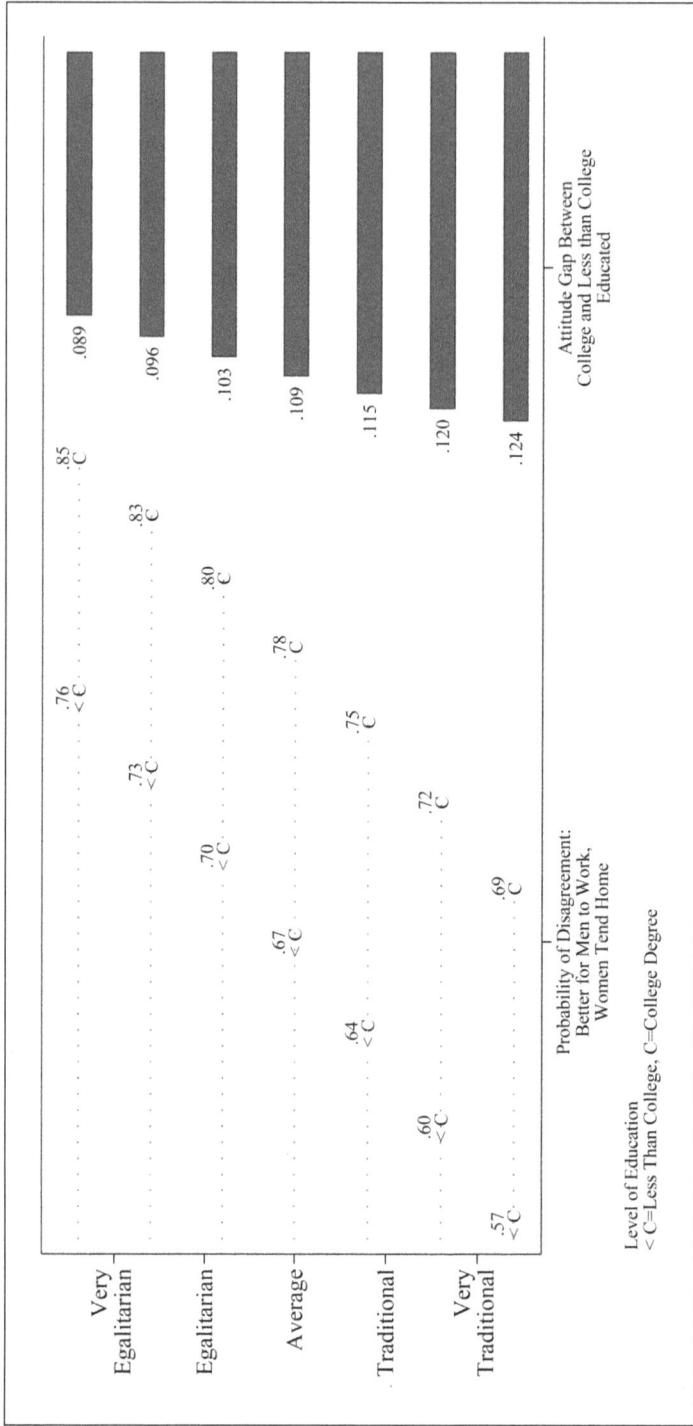

Figure 4.13 Contextual Effects of Norms toward Private Sphere Gender Essentialism: Within-Commuting Zone Differences in Attitudes toward Gendered Divisions of Family Labor by Education

Note: Estimates calculated from a hierarchical logistic regression model predicting support for gender-equal arrangements of family labor with an interaction between local gender norms toward private sphere gender essentialism and an indicator of whether the respondent had a college degree. The model includes controls for gender, race, foreign-born status, age, employment status, occupation (managerial/professional status), service sector employment, religious affiliation, political ideology, a fixed effect for survey year, and a varying intercept (by commuting zone).

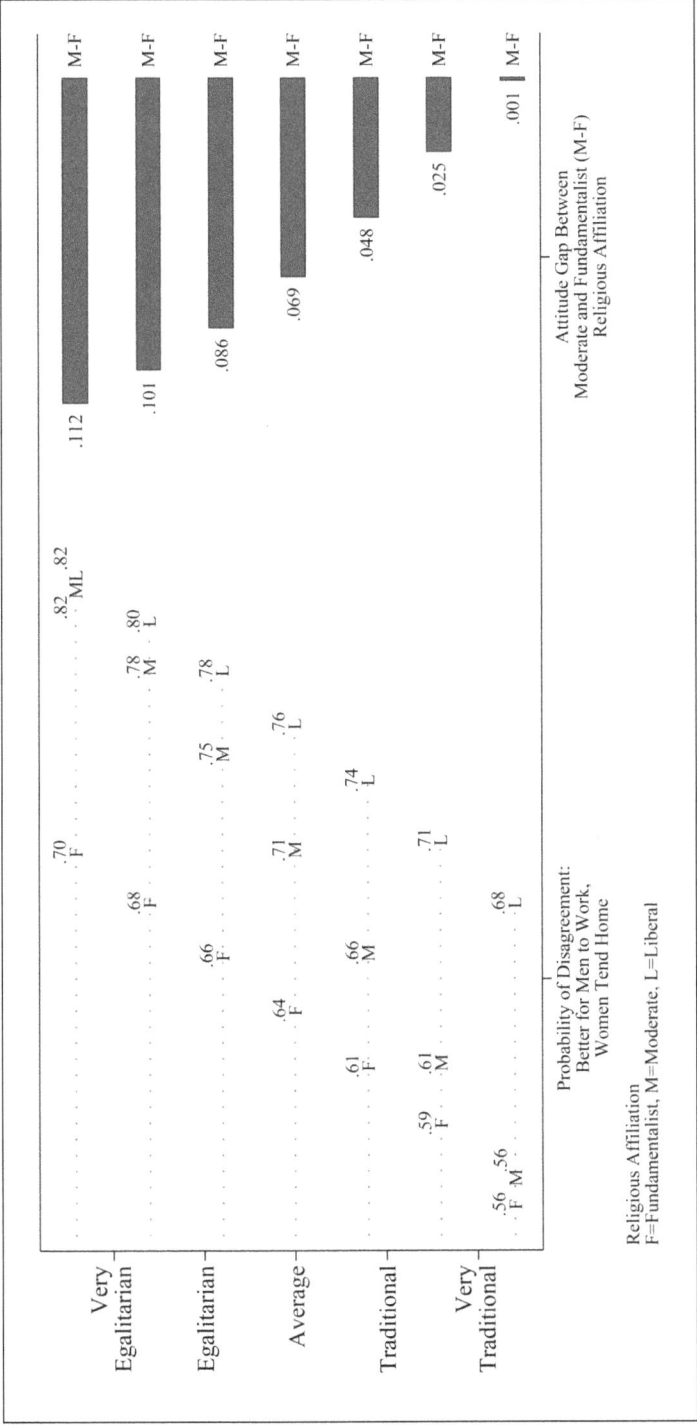

Figure 4.14 Contextual Effects of Norms toward Private Sphere Gender Essentialism: Within-Commuting Zone Differences in Attitudes toward Gendered Divisions of Family Labor by Religious Affiliation

Note: Estimates calculated from a hierarchical logistic regression model predicting views toward gender-equal arrangements of family labor with an interaction between local gender norms toward private sphere gender essentialism and religious affiliation (fundamentalist, moderate, liberal/no religion). The model includes controls for gender, race, foreign-born status, education, age, employment status, occupation (managerial/professional status), service sector employment, political ideology, a fixed effect for survey year, and a varying intercept (by commuting zone).

Although composition helps sustain gender norms toward private sphere gender essentialism, we also find strong evidence that contextual effects play a large role when we examine differences by religious affiliation in Figure 4.14. In commuting zones with very traditional norms toward private sphere gender essentialism, individuals adhering to moderate religions have similar views about the household division of labor as those belonging to fundamentalist religions. In these contexts, both moderates and fundamentalists are about twelve percentage points less likely to endorse gender-equal family arrangements than those adhering to liberal religions. Comparing differences between these groups in more egalitarian contexts, moderates become increasingly more supportive of gender equality than fundamentalists, closing the gap between themselves and those adhering to liberal religions. Whereas the gap between moderates and liberals was twelve percentage points in places with very traditional norms, it was nonexistent in places with very egalitarian norms toward private sphere gender essentialism. This indicates that the experience of residing in a place with certain norms shapes individuals' personal attitudes to align with those norms, particularly for individuals belonging to moderate religions.

Together, the patterns illustrated in Figures 4.13 and 4.14 indicate that both compositional and contextual effects help sustain local gender norms toward private sphere gender essentialism. The college educated are more likely to hold personal attitudes that align with egalitarian norms on this dimension regardless of the local context. Therefore, a greater concentration of these individuals in some commuting zones over others helps sustain these areas' greater levels of egalitarianism on this dimension via compositional effects. Contextual effects, however, come into play among religious moderates, who hold similar gender attitudes as religious fundamentalists in traditional contexts while being closer to religious liberals in egalitarian environments. This indicates that exposure to local norms shapes the attitudes of religious moderates, rather than their uneven spatial distribution.

Summary: Compositional and Contextual Effects Sustaining Local Gender Norms

Commuting zones across the United States contain distinct configurations of gender norms. In this chapter, I explored whether these norms are sustained by compositional or contextual effects. To do this, I took advantage of the inherent relationship between commuting zone gender norms and individual-level attitudes. Because gender norms are sustained by spatial patterns in individuals' attitudes, I tested whether these spatial patterns can be explained by the types of people who live in some commuting zones rather than others (compositional effects) or if individuals with the same characteristics have different attitudes as a result of exposure to the norms in the place where they reside (contextual effects).

Overall, the weight of the findings show that contextual effects play a larger role in sustaining local gender norms than compositional effects. The demographic, economic, and cultural composition of commuting zones accounted for only between 20 and 40 percent of the relationship between local gender norms and individuals' attitudes that sustain them. Even after accounting for a host of compositional characteristics, local gender norms continued to have a substantial and significant effect on individuals' attitudes. Nonetheless, compositional effects play an important role, even if they cannot fully account for the factors sustaining local gender norms. This is particularly true for dimensions of norms related to the private sphere of the family (intensive mothering and private sphere gender essentialism), where compositional effects accounted for upward of 40 percent of the relationship between norms and attitudes. Further analysis revealed that one driving factor behind these compositional effects is the distribution of college degree holders. Regardless of local gender norms, those with a college degree espouse greater support for working mothers and equal family responsibilities than those without a college degree. This means that the concentration of college degree holders is a contributing factor to places' egalitarian norms toward the dimensions of intensive mothering and private sphere gender essentialism.

Nonetheless, even after accounting for an expansive set of compositional characteristics, individuals' attitudes remain strongly linked to local gender norms. This remaining relationship is driven by contextual effects where the experience of residing in a particular location shapes individuals' attitudes in ways consistent with local norms. Contextual effects were highly pronounced in the two dimensions of local norms related to the public sphere: women's advancement and public sphere gender essentialism. Here, college-educated individuals held similar attitudes toward women in politics and possessed similar levels of implicit bias against women in science as those without a college degree when they resided in places with traditional gender norms. In other words, the experience of living in a place with traditional norms toward women's advancement and public sphere gender essentialism causes college-educated individuals to become more conventional in their outlook in ways similar to those with lower levels of education.

Contextual effects were also observed by comparing religious groups. Across each dimension of norms, the relationship of religious affiliation to individuals' attitudes depended on the prevailing gender norms in the local commuting zone. Gaps between those affiliated with liberal, moderate, and fundamentalist religions were generally largest in egalitarian contexts, driven by a greater effect of local norms on adherents to liberal religions and, particularly, those adhering to moderate religions. The religion gap in attitudes was smallest in commuting zones with traditional norms. Moderates held views more similar to religious fundamentalists in these traditional contexts, whereas their attitudes were more aligned with religious liberals in egalitarian environments. Collectively, these findings suggest that differences in gender attitudes among religious liberals, moderates, and fundamentalists are not fixed but depend on local cultural settings and contextual effects.

Contextual effects were observed across education and religion with respect to gender norms toward women's advancement and public sphere gender essentialism. In contrast, contextual effects were only observed across religion and not education in analyses of norms toward intensive mothering and private sphere gender essentialism. One reason for this pattern is that norms related to the public sphere may be more relevant to educational divides because education translates to labor market opportunities and outcomes. Therefore, expectations toward women's leadership and beliefs about suitable fields for women and men may have greater relevance in cultural differences between the college educated and those with less than a college degree. In contrast, family dynamics may be less salient to educational divides but more prominent in religious communities where sermons and faith-based groups often explicitly convey values about ideal family structures and responsibilities. The larger role of family norms in religion may foster pathways for local culture to influence both the expectations conveyed by religious groups and the corresponding attitudes held by adherents.

Conclusion: Pockets of Gender Traditionalism in the United States

When examining contextual effects, the education and religion gaps in gender attitudes was largest in commuting zones with the most egalitarian norms and smallest in the places where traditional norms prevailed. The only exception was the religion gap in attitudes toward women in politics. Otherwise, when contextual effects were observed, they were driven by a pattern where those we expect to have more liberal gender attitudes, such as the college educated or adherents to moderate/liberal religions, held much more conservative views in commuting zones with traditional norms. This indicates that contextual effects are particularly strong in traditional environments, where they influence individuals who would otherwise support gender equality to adopt more conventional perspectives.

These findings add crucial insight to our understanding of cultural variation and change in the United States. Scholars have devoted significant attention to the factors driving long-standing adherence to conventional attitudes, particularly views toward the gendered division of labor in the family (Cotter, Hermsen, and Vanneman 2011; Pepin and Cotter 2018). By uncovering the role of contextual effects in the relationship between commuting zone gender norms and individuals' attitudes, this chapter shows that remaining traditionalism in the United States has a strong geographic component. One reason for ongoing endorsement of conventional gendered arrangements is that people reside in places where these dynamics are supported by predominant norms. As a result of exposure to these norms, individuals adopt personal attitudes that align with conventional perspectives. This is true across populations but particularly for the college educated and those with moderate and liberal religious affiliations, who would otherwise hold more liberal attitudes in places with egalitarian gender norms.

Individuals' attitudes are the lifeblood of local gender norms. The most common attitudes in a particular context reinforce predominant norms in that setting that convey how people should behave and interact. These norms then feed back into attitudes, as individuals adopt personal viewpoints that align with prevailing norms. This contextual feedback loop is particularly strong in places with traditional gender norms. In these settings, individuals frequently encounter others who hold conventional outlooks on gender relations. They may be held accountable for breaking traditional gender norms and encouraged to adopt behaviors and attitudes that align with conventional arrangements between women and men. In these pockets of traditionalism, individuals who would otherwise support the feminist ideals of equal caregiving and women's leadership are more likely to reject those principles in favor of traditional perspectives more commonly endorsed and encouraged.

Thus far, we have identified the dimensions of local gender norms in Chapter 2, examined their spatial distribution in Chapter 3, and investigated the factors that sustain them in this chapter. The primary contribution of this chapter is highlighting two mechanisms, compositional and contextual effects, that help sustain spatial variation in local gender norms. Both mechanisms contribute to local norms, but contextual effects play a larger role by shaping the attitudes of individuals to align with local gender norms. In the next chapter, I examine the consequences of gender norms on local patterns of inequality.

5

Culture's Consequences

The Relationship of Local Gender Norms to Inequality

n 1994, the U.S. Department of Housing and Urban Development (HUD) launched the Moving to Opportunity project in five major cities: Baltimore, Boston, Chicago, Los Angeles, and New York City. The project was designed to test whether helping low-income families move from poverty-stricken neighborhoods to areas with less poverty would improve their well-being and their children's outcomes. Under Moving to Opportunity (MTO), 4,600 families with children living in public housing were randomly assigned to one of three conditions. One group received housing vouchers that could only be used to move to a low-poverty neighborhood. Another received vouchers with no parameters on where they could move. A third group did not receive vouchers. Because the conditions were randomly assigned, researchers were able to identify the causal impact of moving to a low-poverty neighborhood by studying how families fared in the first condition (those given a voucher for a low-poverty neighborhood) compared to the other two. This allowed researchers to determine whether neighborhood contexts influence family outcomes.

Early studies on MTO found short-term benefits to families' mental health for those moving to a low-poverty neighborhood (Kling, Liebman, and Katz 2007). Major benefits were also observed over the long run. Families who moved to low-poverty neighborhoods had more stable employment and higher earnings (Clampet-Lundquist and Massey 2008). Other studies have shown that benefits are particularly pronounced for children who moved prior to their teenage years. Raj Chetty, Nathaniel Hendren, and Lawrence Katz

(2016) uncovered that, by their midtwenties, children who moved to a low-poverty neighborhood as part of MTO earned wages that were 31 percent higher than those who were assigned to other conditions in the program. They were also more likely to attend college.

These results from the MTO program illustrate a key concept in studies of social stratification and family outcomes: Place matters. Where you grow up and where you live have a tremendous impact on the types of opportunities available, the barriers encountered, and even the adaptive characteristics developed. The importance of place is well established in the study of social mobility. In contrast, little attention has been directed toward examining how place impacts relationships between women and men and patterns of gender inequality. Instead, we tend to presume that the factors shaping gender inequality are more intimate, taking place in our families, homes, relationships, and workplaces. Certainly, many key contributors to gender inequality do occur in these settings. But the previous chapters have shown that the expectations characterizing gender relations within homes and workplaces can be very different across commuting zones depending on local gender norms. It is possible that spatial contexts play an important role in shaping levels of inequality between women and men. Just as place matters for social mobility, it may also matter for gender equality.

The purpose of this chapter is to explore the relationship between local norms and patterns of gender inequality across U.S. commuting zones. I ask the question: Does place matter for gender inequality? Specifically, I focus on whether the four dimensions of local gender norms can help us understand spatial variation in the gender wage gap across the United States. Research on the contributors to wage inequality between women and men has found that individual-level factors, such as differences in work hours, education, and experience, play an important role in sustaining gender wage gaps (Cha and Weeden 2014). Yet, even after accounting for these and other human capital characteristics, women's wages remain substantially lower than men's (Scarborough and Moeder 2022). Economists have argued that this unexplained portion of the wage gap represents discrimination: When all reasonable factors have been accounted for, any remaining differences in the wages between women and men reflect cultural beliefs (implicit or explicit) that women deserve lower pay than men (Darity and Mason 1998).

Recent studies report that women earn approximately 20 percent less than men in the United States (Hegewisch and Barsi 2020). But these nationwide estimates hide substantial local variation. Figure 5.1 visualizes gender wage gaps across thirty illustrative commuting zones. These wage gaps were calculated with equations that account for observed individual-level human capital characteristics, such as education, work experience, age, and work hours, and therefore report gender wage gaps stemming from the dif-

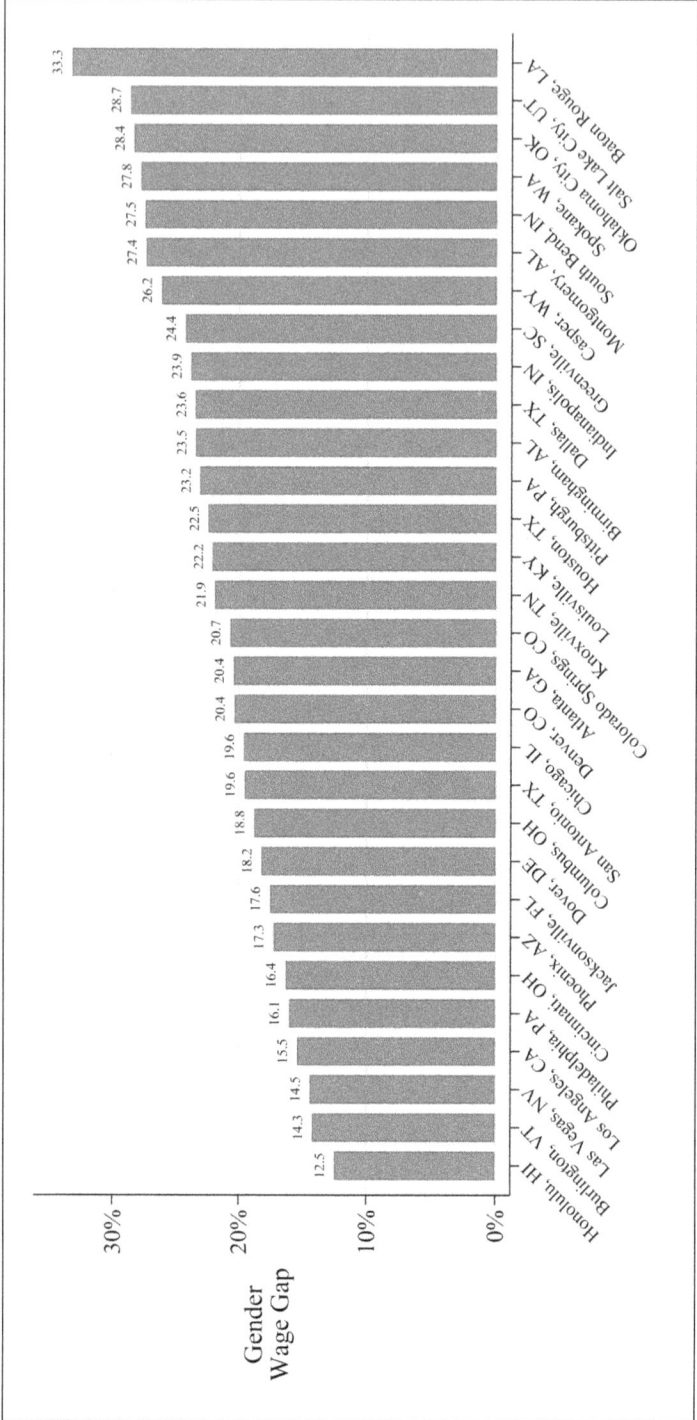

Figure 5.1 Gender Wage Gaps across Thirty Illustrative Commuting Zones

Note: Wage gaps calculated with independent regression models for each commuting zone predicting logged hourly wage with gender and controls for race, age, age squared, education, marital status, work experience, work experience squared, and hours worked. Data are from the 2018 American Community Survey (Ruggles et al. 2020). Sample includes employed persons aged twenty-five to fifty-four.

ferent experiences of women and men in the labor market rather than differences in skills or qualifications. Although no place in the United States has erased the gender wage gap, Honolulu comes the closest, where women are paid 12.5 percent less than men. In contrast, the gender wage gap is almost three times as large in Baton Rouge, where women are paid about a third less than their men counterparts. The remaining commuting zones fill the range between Honolulu and Baton Rouge. The wage gap is over 15 percent in Los Angeles, 19.6 percent in Chicago, and 28.4 percent in Oklahoma City. In many cases, commuting zones in the same state have very different wage gaps. In Pennsylvania, the wage gap is over seven percentage points lower in Philadelphia (16.1 percent) than Pittsburg (23.2 percent). Wage gaps in Texas are highest in Dallas (23.6 percent), followed by Houston (22.5 percent), with San Antonio reporting the lowest gender wage gap of these three Texas cities, where women are paid 19.6 percent less than men.

Wage gaps vary across U.S. commuting zones. So do gender norms. But do they vary together? Do places with more egalitarian gender norms have lower gender wage gaps? Establishing a relationship between gender wage gaps and local norms is a first step to understanding how norms pattern inequality between women and men. I tested this association using a series of hierarchical linear regression models that independently tested whether the size of local gender wage gaps depended on the types of norms that prevailed in a particular commuting zone. Each equation included individual- and commuting zone-level controls to ensure the relationship between local norms and wage gaps was not confounded by observed variables. Figure 5.2 shows that, with one exception, places with more egalitarian gender norms have lower gender wage gaps. The strongest relationship is observed with respect to norms toward public sphere gender essentialism, where a difference of one unit in local gender norms (e.g., going from very traditional to traditional or egalitarian to very egalitarian) predicts a reduction in local gender wage gaps by 2.29 percentage points. This is a very large effect considering that the gender wage gap for the United States as a whole has improved by only 0.4 percentage points in the last decade (Hegewisch and Barsi 2020). Comparing extremes, the gender wage gap is predicted to be 9 percentage points worse in commuting zones with very traditional norms toward public sphere gender essentialism than those with very egalitarian norms on this dimension.

Egalitarian norms toward women's advancement and private sphere gender essentialism also relate to lower gender wage gaps. The relationship is not as strong as observed for public sphere gender essentialism but still very substantial. For every one-unit increase in egalitarian norms on these two dimensions, gender wage gaps tend to reduce by about 1.3 percentage points. This means that the gender wage gap is predicted to be over 5 percentage points

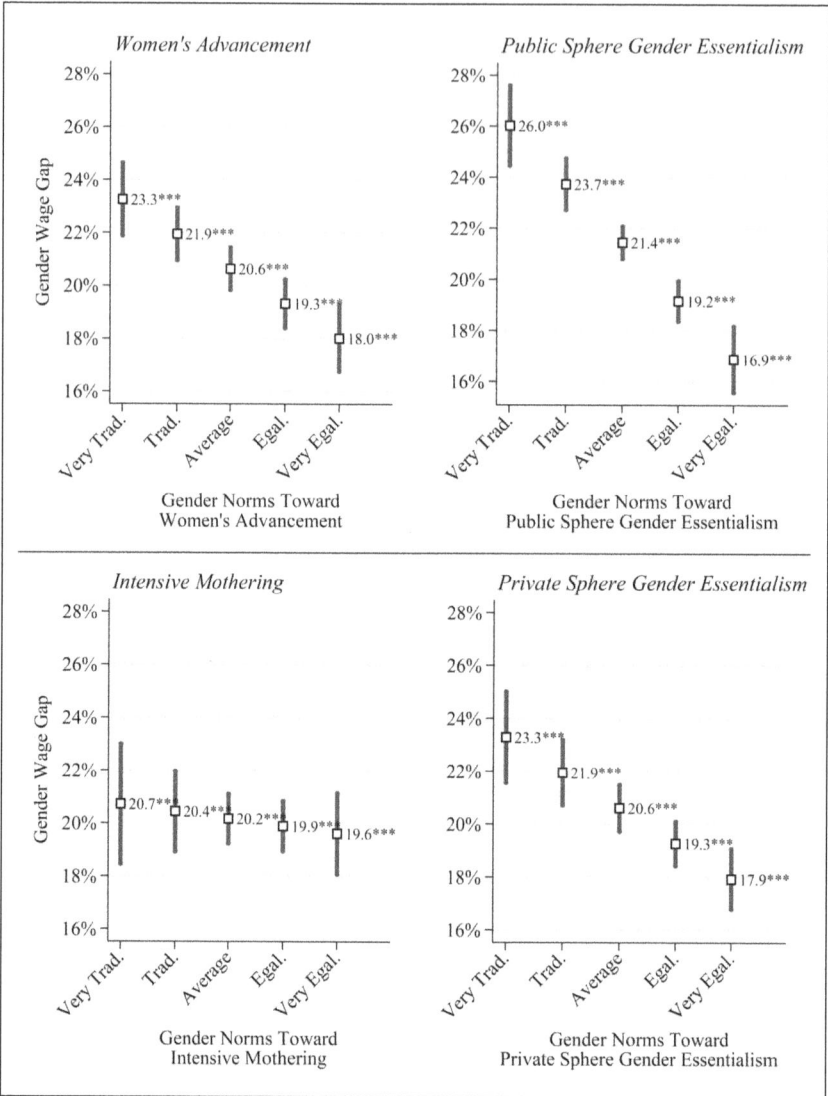

Figure 5.2 Relationship of Local Gender Norms to Gender Wage Gaps

Note: Results calculated with hierarchical linear regression models predicting logged hourly wages with individual-level (race, age, age squared, education, marital status, work experience, work experience squared, and hours worked) and commuting zone (service sector size, percent employed in management or professional occupations, unemployment rate, share of population with college degree, percent foreign born, and racial composition) variables and an interaction between gender and local norms. Intercepts varied by commuting zone. Data are from the 2018 American Community Survey (Ruggles et al. 2020). *** indicates significance of wage gap at p < 0.001 level.

worse in places with very traditional norms on these dimensions than areas that are very egalitarian.

Local gender norms generally relate to lower wage gaps, but one exception is gender norms toward intensive mothering. Here, there is very little difference in local wage gaps between places with egalitarian or traditional norms. Previous research has shown that traditional norms toward intensive mothering predict lower rates of maternal employment (Ruppanner et al. 2021). Therefore, it is possible that norms of intensive mothering primarily limit opportunities for mothers' employment and have a smaller effect on wage gaps for women who overcome these barriers to remain employed—likely a selective, highly skilled, and motivated group.

Besides norms toward intensive mothering, local gender norms have a strong relationship to gender wage gaps across commuting zones. This relationship even persists across diverse populations. Focusing on wage gaps for Black, Hispanic, and White residents, Figure 5.3 shows that the positive relationship of local egalitarian norms across dimensions of women's advancement, public sphere gender essentialism, and private sphere gender essentialism consistently predict lower gender wage gaps for each group. Similarities are also observed between college graduates and those with less than a college education. Although gender norms have a slightly stronger relationship to wage gaps for the less educated, the difference is not significant. It is notable that intensive mothering norms are significantly related to wage gaps for White workers when analyzed separately. Among Hispanic residents, the coefficient for intensive mothering norms is larger than that observed for White residents, but it is not significant because the standard error is larger due to the smaller sample of Hispanic respondents in the data and variability in the relationship between norms and wage gaps for this group. Together, this suggests that the association of intensive mothering norms to wage gaps is tenuous, whereas the relationship of wage gaps and egalitarian norms across the three remaining dimensions is strong and a consistent predictor of lower wage gaps across subpopulations.

By and large, gender norms have a strong relationship to local wage gaps. This relationship exists over and above individual-level factors as well as additional commuting zone characteristics—meaning that the relationship of egalitarian norms to lower wage gaps is not due to the types of individuals who reside in egalitarian versus traditional places or the ways that egalitarian commuting zones differ from traditional ones in terms of economic or demographic composition. Beyond establishing a relationship between norms and wage gaps, however, the patterns illustrated in Figures 5.2 and 5.3 tell us little about *how* gender norms relate to wage gaps. We are yet unable to determine the underlying mechanisms driving the relationship between norms and wage gaps, only that there is some relationship occurring that causes

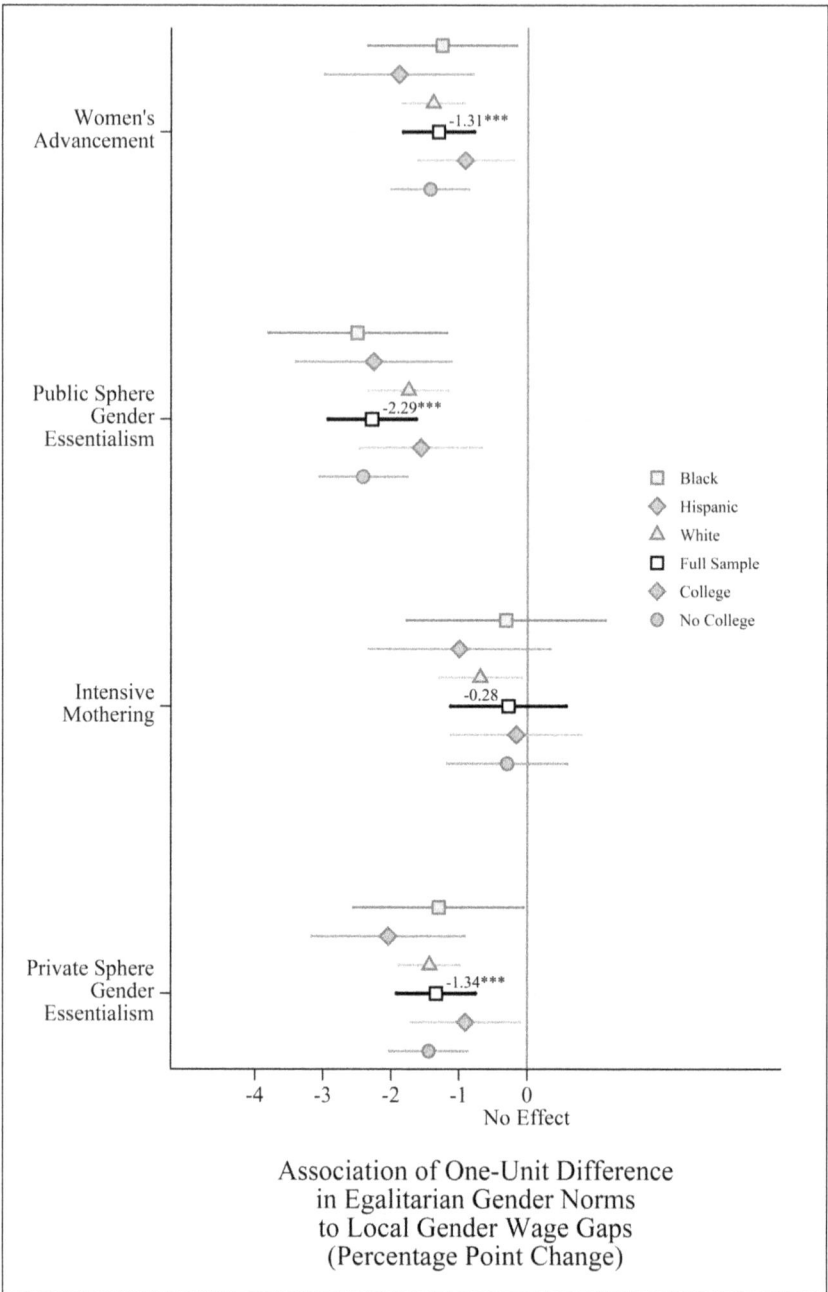

Figure 5.3 Relationship of Gender Norms to Gender Wage Gap for Full
Sample, by Education, and by Race

Note: Results calculated with the same equation used for Figure 5.2 applied independently
by race and education. Horizontal lines represent confidence intervals surrounding
estimated coefficients. Confidence intervals overlapping the vertical line at 0 represent a
nonsignificant relationship of norms to wage gaps. *** indicates significant effect of norms
on wage gaps for full sample at $p < 0.001$ level.

gender norms to be so strongly associated with varying levels of gender inequality. We can, however, look to previous literature to consider how gender norms may operate through two mechanisms found to be primary contributors to wage disparities between women and men.

The first of these mechanisms relates to the *sorting* of women and men into different occupations with unequal levels of compensation. Economists and sociologists have emphasized the role of sorting mechanisms in research showing that occupational gender segregation is one of the largest contributors to the gender wage gap because women more commonly work in lower-paying jobs than men (Blau and Kahn 2017; Petersen and Morgan 1995). Recent studies also show that occupational gender segregation remains high. Documenting patterns of segregation in the United States, Paula England, Andrew Levine, and Emma Mishel (2020) find that approximately 42 percent of women and men workers would have to switch jobs in order for them to be evenly distributed across occupations. This level of segregation has changed very little in recent decades because much of the gains in women's employment and occupational advancement have occurred in different fields than men. For example, women predominate in care and service sectors, whereas men make up the majority of workers in technical and blue-collar roles (Stainback and Tomaskovic-Devey 2012). Occupational segregation is the consequence of many factors sorting women and men into different fields. This includes the tendency for women and men to prefer different careers, the chilly climate women often experience in male-dominated fields that causes them to leave, and hiring discrimination where men are preferred over equally or more qualified women (Alegria 2019; Cech 2014; Correll, Benard, and Paik 2007).

The second mechanism contributing to gender wage gaps is rooted in unequal *valuation* of women's and men's labor. In this mechanism, women and men may work in the same occupation and hold similar qualifications, but women are paid less than men because their contributions are perceived as less valuable. Whereas sorting operates between occupations, valuation occurs within occupations. Different valuation resulting in within-occupation wage gaps may result from men's wage premiums in jobs that are stereotypically viewed as masculine. Because the stereotypical computer scientist is a man, managers may perceive them as more deserving of higher pay than equally qualified and performing women. Claudia Goldin (2014a, 2014b) argues that these within-occupation processes related to valuation now constitute the most important contributor to gender wage gaps.

In what follows, I investigate the mechanisms underlying the relationship between local norms and gender wage gaps. I first examine whether gender norms relate to wage gaps through shaping how women and men are sorted into different occupations. It is possible, for example, that places with egalitarian norms have a higher percentage of women in well-paying occupations, therefore reducing the gender wage gap. After investigating the relationship between norms and occupational sorting, I then examine the role of valuation by testing whether wages between women and men in the same occupation vary as a function of local gender norms, reflecting systematic differences in the value placed on women's work relative to men's.

Local Gender Norms and Occupational Sorting

Women more often work in lower-paying jobs than men. This is particularly evident at the extremes. Analyzing data from the ACS, Will McGrew (2016) uncovered that none of the ten highest paying occupations are majority women. The closest is financial managers, where women make up just under half of all workers. In every other high-paying occupation, women make up between 10 and 40 percent of workers. They account for about 10 percent of architects and engineers, a quarter of dentists, and around a third of all lawyers. The highest rank is overwhelmingly male dominated: Women make up only 21 percent of all executive-level managers. Representation in high-paying occupations is even lower for women of color, who account for only 3 percent of all executive-level managers (Krivkovich et al. 2020).

Not only are women *underrepresented* in the highest-paying occupations, but they are also *overrepresented* in the lowest-paying ones. McGrew's analysis found that women make up the majority of workers in seven of the ten lowest-paying occupations. Women are over 90 percent of all childcare workers, more than 75 percent of all personal care aids, and over 60 percent of fast-food counter workers and retail cashiers. Analysis conducted by the National Women's Law Center found that women workers make up 65 percent of those employed in low-wage occupations that pay less than $10.50 an hour (Morrison and Robbins 2015). Black and Hispanic women are even more likely than White women to be employed in low-wage jobs. Relative to their share of the labor force, Black and Hispanic women are about twice as likely as White women to be working in low-wage occupations.

The uneven distribution of women and men across occupations with varying pay is not only present at the extremes. Research has long established that occupational gender segregation is a widespread and enduring feature of the U.S. labor market. In 1970, it was extremely rare for women and men to work in the same occupations. Paula England, Andrew Levin, and Emma Mischel (2020) estimate that nearly 70 percent of all workers would have had to change occupations at that time in order for gender integration to be achieved. Today, segregation has declined but remains at high levels, with just over 40 percent of all workers needing to change occupations to achieve occupational gender integration. In other words, it continues to be rare for women and men to be equally represented within occupations. Drawing from surveys of a representative sample of U.S. employees, Kim Parker (2018) found that only about a third of women and men report that their workplace is balanced in terms of gender.

The persistence of occupational gender segregation is a driving factor behind gender wage gaps because the occupations where women tend to be employed generally have lower pay. Analyzing data from the Panel Study of Income Dynamics, Francine Blau and Lawrence Kahn (2017) estimate that approximately a third of the gender wage gap in the United States is due to the segregation of women in lower-paying occupations than men. Two primary factors sustain this pattern. The first relates to economic contexts. Over the past four decades, the U.S. service sector has grown at the same time that women's educational attainment and labor force participation has increased (Albrecht and Albrecht 2010). Consequently, women entering the labor force throughout this period are more likely to work in service-providing occupations such as education and healthcare support, rather than integrate long-standing male-dominated jobs in architecture, engineering, and blue-collar occupations such as construction (England 2010). By influencing the types of opportunities available, economic contexts foster labor market conditions that are conducive to ongoing gender segregation when an increased supply of women job seekers is met by a growing number of job opportunities in sectors of the economy traditionally associated with feminine characteristics, such as care and customer service.

The second factor sustaining occupational gender segregation relates to gender norms. If economic structures shape the types of opportunities available to women and men in the labor force, cultural norms influence how these opportunities are distributed and rewarded. Gender stereotypes toward the types of jobs women and men are best suited for often creates barriers for women and advantages for men in accessing well-paying masculine-typed occupations when hiring managers implicitly perceive their ideal candidate as a man based on the view that men, on average, are more likely to hold qualities associated with the position. This process is commonly referred to as statistical discrimination (Bielby and Baron 1986; Stainback and Tomas-kovic-Devey 2012). At the same time, these cultural gender stereotypes are also reflected in job seekers' socialized preferences. Research has found that women more often pursue careers in lower-paying caregiving fields than men (Cech 2013). In contrast, many men expressly avoid employment in fields associated with feminine characteristics (Yavorsky, Ruggs, and Dill 2021). Bias among hiring managers and socialized preferences among job seekers work in tandem to sustain the sorting of women and men into different fields. Socialization functions to steer women and men into gender-typical professions. But those who break socializing norms face additional barriers stemming from bias and hiring discrimination that may sort them into gender-conventional occupations despite personal efforts otherwise.

Stereotypes channeling women and men into gender-typical occupations and women's and men's developed preferences for different types of work do not occur in isolation. Instead, the logics individuals use to navigate their job search and the criteria used by managers in hiring decisions are informed by local norms. Individuals develop their ideas about their personal careers and the qualifications of others for certain jobs by drawing upon common understandings for the type of work women or men generally do, the tasks women or men are usually good at, and the jobs that are appropriate for women or men. An experiment by Shelley Correll and colleagues (2017) provides a clear example of how local cultural contexts shape individuals' perceptions of women and men job candidates. These researchers asked study participants to review two candidates' resumes and select one to be hired as a police chief in a U.S. town. After their selection, they were informed that they chose the woman candidate for the job and that the other resume belonged to a man candidate. One randomly selected group of participants was told at this point that the police chief position was located in a traditional town in Kansas, while another group was told the job was in a progressive town in Massachusetts. Study participants were then given the opportunity to change their selection. Those informed that the job was located in a traditional Kansas town were twice as likely to change their decision and select the man candidate than those who were told they were recommending a hire for a progressive Massachusetts town.

Correll's experiment provides strong evidence that people use their understanding of local norms to inform their decisions around the types of jobs women and men are suited for. Through learning only that their decision was made in the context of a place with traditional norms, study participants commonly adjusted their views to align with those conventional expectations. Consequently, they were less likely to recommend a woman candidate for the male-dominated position of police chief. Results from this study affirm key findings from Chapter 4: local norms have contextual effects that shape individuals' attitudes and behaviors. Correll and colleagues' study also shows how these contextual effects contribute to patterns of inequality. When local norms influence attitudes and behaviors in ways that pose barriers for women's access to male-dominated jobs, they contribute to ongoing patterns of occupational gender segregation.

Cultural contexts can influence hiring managers' perceptions and decision-making in ways that contribute to or challenge occupational gender segregation. Other research, however, also shows how gender norms operate through shaping workers' job preferences. Following graduates from four universities throughout the United States, Erin Cech (2013) found that individuals' perceived personal strengths were the largest predictor of whether they pursued employment in a female- or male-dominated occupation. Respondents who felt they were emotional, unsystematic, and people oriented were more likely to pursue work in female-dominated occupations that were traditionally associated with these feminine characteristics. Importantly, women respondents were more likely to hold these self-conceptions than men. As a result, these gender differences in self-conceptions are a major driver of occupational sorting where women tend to pursue jobs in majority-women occupations with a perceived match between job qualifications and personal traits. Similar patterns were observed among men in Cech's study: Those who felt that they possessed masculine-typed traits, such as being systematic and unemotional, were more likely to pursue careers in male-dominated technical or blue-collar occupations. Men more commonly perceived themselves as holding these strengths and were therefore more likely than women to pursue work in majority-men careers.

Central to Cech's study was the idea that individuals' self-conceptions were much more influential in determining their career pursuits than their personal attitudes about gender equality. Participants in her study may have felt women and men were equally suitable for different types of jobs but nonetheless perceived themselves as having gender-typical qualities. Cech argues that this reflects the influence of cultural norms. By residing in a particular context with norms that convey messages about women's and men's essential difference and suitability for different types of work, individuals internalize these expectations to form self-conceptions consistent with predominant norms. At the same time, they may occasionally form reactionary attitudes that challenge traditional gender roles while also possessing gender-typical personality traits that shape their occupational pursuits in ways that sustain segregation.

Economic context and cultural conditions operate together to sustain occupational gender segregation. Economic contexts set the structure of opportunity, while cultural norms provide the logic individuals use to navigate the labor market. Research on these two processes, however, has generally occurred at different levels of analysis. Sociologists and economists have studied the role of economic context by comparing industry composition across local labor markets and testing its relationship to occupational gender segregation (Kongar 2008; McCall 2001). These studies have found that service sector expansion facilitates women's labor force participation but also reinforces occupational gender segregation because women's employment gains are primarily made in feminine-typed occupations within the service industry (Charles and Grusky 2004). In contrast, studies of cultural processes have generally focused on the way norms shape individual-level attitudes that influence job-seeking and hiring behavior (Cech 2013; Correll et al.

2017). This body of research has inferred the influence of local norms on individuals but has not examined how these norms vary systematically across the United States.

In the following section, I explore how local variation in gender norms across the United States relates to the sorting of women and men into different occupations. I draw from studies focusing on economic context and apply a macro-comparative approach that tests whether spatial differences in local gender norms are associated with women's and men's varying representation across a set of occupations that have different pay and emphasize either feminine or masculine characteristics. In doing so, I explore whether local gender norms relate to gender wage gaps through influencing the types of occupations where women and men are typically employed.

Testing the Relationship of Local Gender Norms and Occupational Sorting

Occupations hold distinct cultural associations that advantage women or men for some roles and disadvantage them for others. The prototypical blue-collar worker possesses physical strength, hand-eye coordination, and mechanical skills—traits typically associated with men, who make up the vast majority of these employees. Men also make up over two-thirds of workers in STEM occupations, but the traits associated with these jobs are very different from blue-collar positions. STEM workers are expected to be analytic, systematic, and possess technical skills. Although these attributes differ from those required in blue-collar occupations, they are also stereotypically associated with men. Management is yet another occupation historically associated with an additional masculine-typed trait of leadership. However, recent research shows that public attitudes have grown increasingly supportive of women in leadership, a trend that corresponds to the dramatic rise in women's managerial representation over the past four decades (Scarborough, Sin, and Risman 2019).

Just as the cultural associations linking occupational characteristics to gender stereotypes are diverse, patterns of occupational gender segregation are multidimensional. One dimension of segregation captures gender differences in representation at managerial and executive ranks. Maria Charles and David Grusky (2004) refer to this as *vertical* segregation because it pertains to gender disparities in how workers climb occupational ladders. Another dimension of segregation is a *horizontal* component that describes a pattern where women and men work in different jobs that occupy similar positions in the workplace hierarchy (Charles and Grusky 2004). For example, women are more likely to be office administrators, and men are more commonly blue-collar workers. These jobs offer similar pay but have very different responsibilities. A third dimension of occupational gender segregation pertains to women's and men's representation in jobs requiring technical skills. Here, men most commonly make up the majority of workers in occupations requiring computer skills, mathematics proficiency, or analytic expertise, whereas women are more commonly employed in fields that emphasize people skills and relationships.

Occupational segregation has multiple dimensions that correspond to the diverse array of gender norms associating women and men with separate skills and characteristics. To capture these dynamic patterns, I examine the relationship of local gender norms to women's and men's employment in four key occupations that reflect different cultural associations. Characteristics of these occupations are reported in Table 5.1. First, I examine the relationship of local norms to women's and men's employment in management.[1] This occupation emphasizes leadership skills and decision-making, characteristics historically associated with men but increasingly applied to women in recent decades. Consistent with this, women now make up nearly half (43 percent) of all managers. Yet, as prior chapters have shown, gender norms are multidimensional and vary spatially. Therefore, it is possible that women have made fewer inroads in management in places with more conventional norms toward women's advancement or workplace leadership. In addition, a focus on management may shed light on whether the relationship of gender norms to local wage gaps, illustrated earlier in this chapter in Fig-

TABLE 5.1 CHARACTERISTICS OF MAJOR OCCUPATIONS

	Occupations				
	Management	STEM	Office administration	Blue collar	Total labor force
Percent women	43.0%	29.8%	73.3%	16.5%	47.5%
Percent men	57.0%	70.2%	26.7%	83.5%	52.5%
Median hourly wage	$30.77	$34.62	$17.16	$16.94	$20.19
Share of labor force	10.8%	9.3%	11.2%	22.0%	100.0%
Gender wage gap	19.9%	16.1%	13.5%	26.2%	19.8%

Note: Gender wage gaps calculated with independent linear regression models for each occupation predicting logged hourly wages with individual- and commuting-zone-level controls and with varying intercepts by commuting zone. Individual controls include race, age, age squared, education, marital status, work experience, work experience squared, and hours worked. Commuting-zone controls include the share of workers in the service sector, the share employed in management or professional occupations, the unemployment rate, the percentage of residents with a college degree, the percent foreign born, and the racial composition.

ure 5.2, is driven by occupational sorting. The median wage of managers is over thirty dollars an hour, about 50 percent higher than the median wage of workers in the total labor force. Therefore, egalitarian gender norms may reduce gender wage gaps by sorting women into better-paid managerial roles.

Second, I examine the relationship of local norms to women's and men's employment in STEM occupations to capture the dimension of segregation related to technical skills.[2] Women make up less than a third of all workers in STEM fields. Their underrepresentation in this occupation is a contributing factor to the overall gender wage gap because the median wage in STEM is nearly fifteen dollars an hour higher than the median wage for all workers. Local gender norms may therefore relate to gender wage gaps through an association with women's representation in high-paying STEM occupations.

Management and STEM are two high-wage occupations emphasizing different characteristics conventionally associated with men. I also examine the relationship of gender norms to women's and men's representation in two low-wage positions: office administration and blue-collar occupations.[3] Median wages in these jobs are less than half the median wages in STEM and about three dollars an hour less than the median wage for all workers. Beyond similar wages, however, office administration and blue-collar occupations have little in common. Office administration requires organization and people skills, which are commonly associated with women. Consistent with this, women make up about three-fourths of office administrators. In contrast, blue-collar work requires mechanical skills and hand-eye coordination—traits more often associated with men, who make up over 80 percent of these workers. Although sharing similar pay, office administration and blue-collar jobs are highly segregated from one another, making them ideal to explore the horizontal dimension of segregation.

In the following section, I examine the relationship of local gender norms to the sorting of women and men across these four occupations. For my analyses, I used data from the 2018 ACS, which is the most comprehensive source of information on U.S. labor markets and families (Ruggles et al. 2021). I restricted my sample to the employed population aged twenty-five to fifty-four, which included 993,471 respondents. With these data, I examined whether women's and men's probability of employment in each occupation depended on the local gender norms in their commuting zone. I conducted a series of hierarchical logistic regression models predicting employment in each occupation with a set of controls for individual and commuting zone characteristics.[4] Each equation also included an interaction term between gender and local norms to capture whether local gender norms affect the sorting of women and men into different occupations. From this interaction term, I calculated how the probability of employment in each occupation varies for women and men when we compare places that differ by one unit of egalitarianism in a dimension of local gender norms. This difference is equal to comparing commuting zones with very traditional to traditional, traditional to average, average to egalitarian, or egalitarian to very egalitarian norms.

I conducted independent models predicting the relationship of each dimension of gender norms to the probability of employment in each of the four selected occupations. If the effect of gender norms is significantly different for women and men, there is strong evidence that local norms have a meaningful and important relationship to occupational sorting. If local egalitarianism improves women's probability of employment in high-paying management and STEM jobs relative to men, this will also help reduce overall gender wage gaps. The sorting of women and men between low-paying office administration and blue-collar jobs may not affect gender wage gaps because these occupations have similar pay. Nonetheless, an analysis of these patterns may shed important insight on the reasons why these occupations are so heavily segregated. In the following four sections, I report the results of these analyses by focusing on how gender norms relate to the sorting of women and men across management, STEM, office administration, and blue-collar occupations.

Management

Figure 5.4 illustrates the relationship of each dimension of gender norms to women's and men's representation in management. The length of each line represents how a difference in one unit of egalitarianism in local gender norms relates to a shift in the probability of employment in management for women (dark line) and men (light line). Lines to the right of center reflect a higher probability of employment with more egalitarian gender norms, whereas those to the left reflect a lower probability of employment. The capped line between those representing women and men corresponds to the difference in the relationship of gender norms to managerial employment for these two groups. A dashed capped line means that the difference in the probability of employment is not significant and, therefore, the corresponding dimension of gender norms does not relate to the occupational sorting of women and men in management positions. A solid capped line means the opposite: that the association of gender norms to managerial employment is significantly different between women and men, representing a meaningful relationship between local norms and occupational sorting.

Figure 5.4 shows that local norms of public sphere gender essentialism have a stronger relationship to women's employment in management than all other dimensions of gender norms. Comparing commuting zones that differ by one unit in local gender norms (e.g., average to egalitarian), women's likelihood of employment in management increases by 0.2 percentage points in a more egalitarian context. Comparing extreme cases, this means

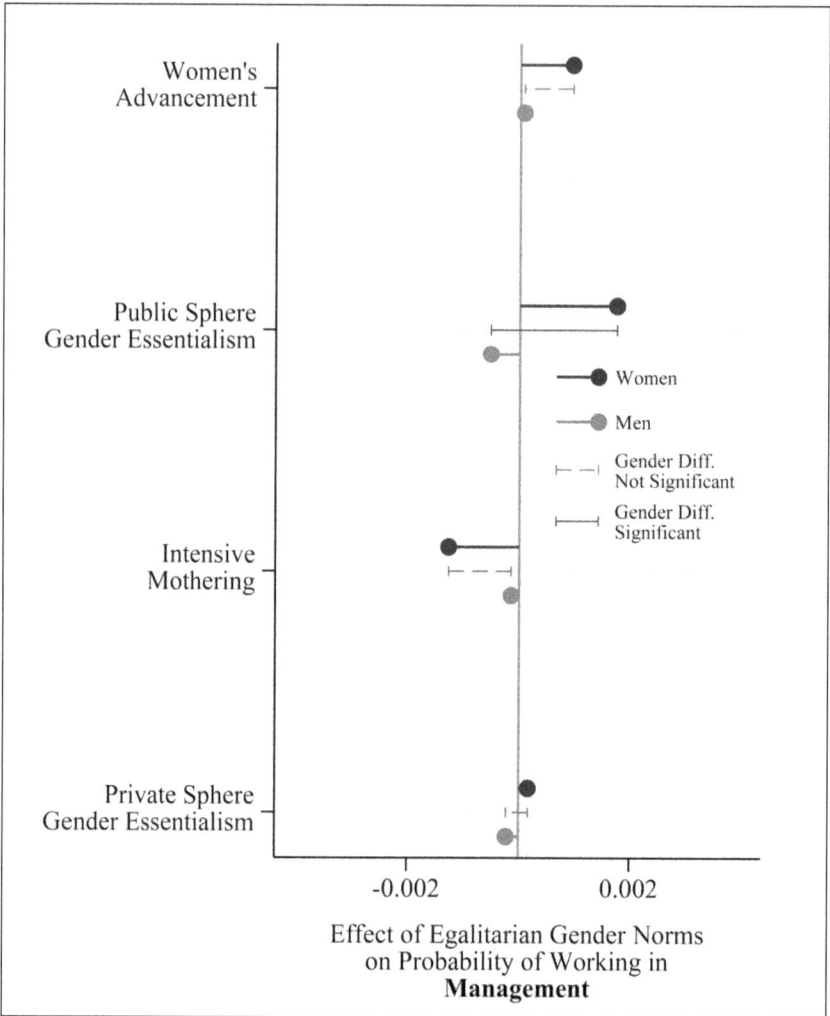

Figure 5.4 Relationship of Local Gender Norms to Women's and Men's Probability of Employment in Management

Note: Results calculated from independent hierarchical logistic regression models predicting employment in management with individual-level (race, age, age squared, education, marital status, work experience, work experience squared, and work hours) and commuting zone-level (share of workers in the service sector, share employed in management or professional occupations, unemployment rate, percentage of residents with a college degree, percent foreign born, and racial composition) controls. Intercepts were specified to vary by commuting zone. An interaction between gender and local norms was used to calculate the average marginal effects of one unit in egalitarian norms on the probability of employment in management for women and men.

that women residing in very traditional commuting zones on the dimension of norms related to public sphere gender essentialism are 0.8 percentage points less likely to work in management than those in very egalitarian commuting zones. Whereas egalitarian norms on this dimension facilitate women's managerial employment, they have a slightly negative association with men's employment in management. The difference between women and men in the relationship of local norms toward public sphere gender essentialism is significant, indicating that this dimension of local norms has a meaningful relationship to the occupational sorting of women and men in management positions that operates to increase women's representation in these high-paying roles.

Besides norms toward public sphere gender essentialism, no other dimension of gender norms was significantly related to the occupational sorting of women and men in management. Norms toward women's advancement and private sphere gender essentialism had a positive relationship between cultural egalitarianism and women's managerial employment, but the effect was not significantly different from men. Egalitarian norms toward intensive mothering have a negative association with managerial employment for both women and men, suggesting that these norms prevail in areas where employment in management is less likely regardless of gender.

STEM Occupations

The relationship of local gender norms to women's and men's probability of employment in STEM occupations is illustrated in Figure 5.5. Again, public sphere gender essentialism has the largest effect. Women in very egalitarian commuting zones on this dimension are 0.2 percentage points more likely to work in a STEM occupation than those in an egalitarian area, 0.4 percentage points more likely than those in an average area, 0.6 percentage points more likely than those in a traditional location, and 0.8 percentage points more likely than residents in a very traditional commuting zone. This positive effect is significantly greater than the relationship of public sphere gender essentialism to men's STEM employment, which is slightly negative. Therefore, these results indicate that egalitarian gender norms of public sphere gender essentialism promote women's representation in STEM, helping to desegregate this high-paying occupation.

The three remaining dimensions of local gender norms did not have a meaningful relationship to the occupational sorting of women and men in STEM occupations. Egalitarian norms of women's advancement and private sphere gender essentialism were predicted to have a positive relationship to women's STEM employment and a slightly negative relationship to men's STEM employment, but the size of this relationship was minimal and not significant. Egalitarian norms of intensive mothering predicted lower prob-

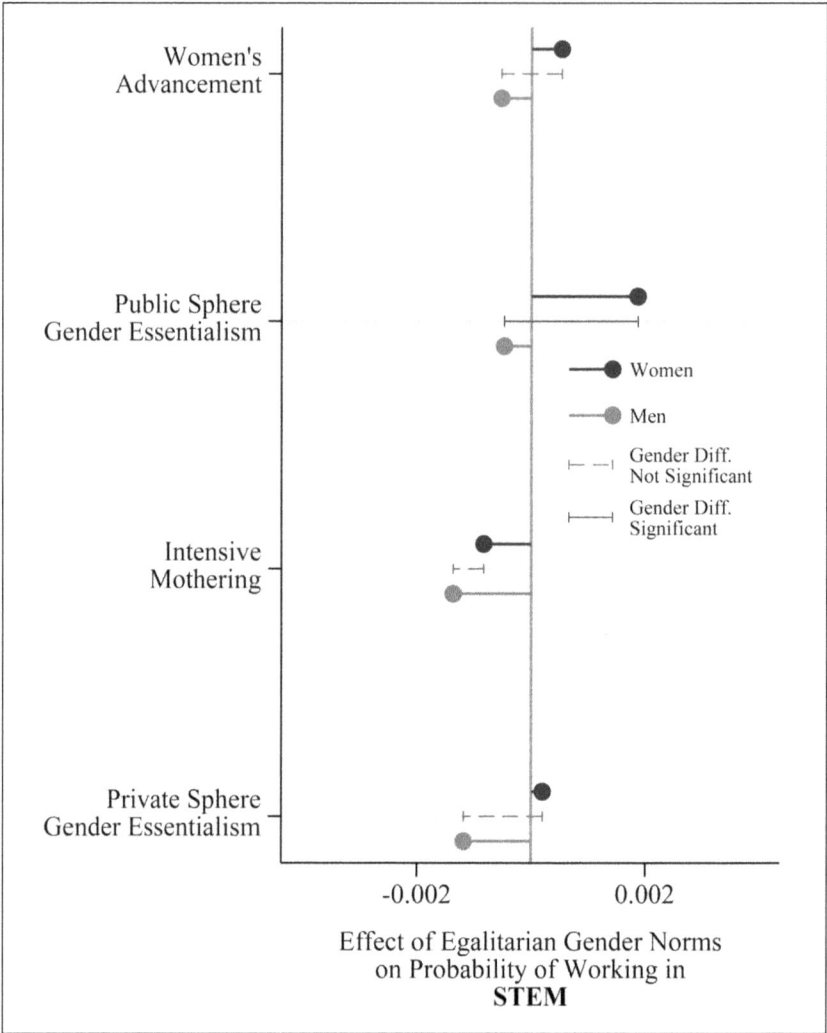

Figure 5.5 Relationship of Local Gender Norms to Women's and Men's Probability of Employment in STEM Occupations

Note: Results calculated from independent hierarchical logistic regression models predicting employment in STEM with individual-level (race, age, age squared, education, marital status, work experience, work experience squared, and work hours) and commuting zone-level (share of workers in the service sector, share employed in management or professional occupations, unemployment rate, percentage of residents with a college degree, percent foreign born, and racial composition) controls. Intercepts were specified to vary by commuting zone. An interaction between gender and local norms was used to calculate the average marginal effects of one unit in egalitarian norms on the probability of employment in STEM for women and men.

abilities of employment for both women and men, suggesting that STEM employment is universally less common in areas with egalitarian norms toward intensive mothering.

Office Administration

Figure 5.6 shows that gender norms across all four dimensions have a substantial relationship to the representation of women and men in office administration. Across each dimension, women are less likely, and men more likely, to work in office administration when local gender norms are more egalitarian. Although each dimension of gender norms has significant effects, the largest patterns are again observed in norms toward public sphere gender essentialism. On this dimension, a one-unit difference in local egalitarianism relates to a 0.3 percentage point reduction in women's likelihood of employment in office administration and a 0.4 percentage point increase in men's probability of employment in this role. Combining men's increased representation with women's decreased representation, women's probability of working in office administration relative to men reduces by nearly 1 percentage point between commuting zones that differ in only one unit of local egalitarianism on this dimension. The size of this combined effect is only slightly smaller for private sphere gender essentialism (0.5 percentage points) and women's advancement (0.5 percentage points). Egalitarian norms toward intensive mothering relate to lower odds of employment in office administration for both women and men, but the relationship is significantly larger for women, meaning that men make up a larger share of office administrators in commuting zones with egalitarian norms on this dimension.

Women make up the majority of workers in office administration. However, the results from Figure 5.6 show that this occupation is more integrated in commuting zones with egalitarian gender norms across each of the four dimensions. When local gender norms convey women and men as more equal and as possessing similar skills and characteristics, men account for a larger share of positions in conventionally feminized occupations like office administration.

Blue-Collar Occupations

The relationship of local gender norms to women's and men's employment in blue-collar occupations is in the opposite direction than what was observed with respect to office administration (see Figure 5.7). This corresponds to the fact that office administration jobs are mostly held by women, whereas blue-collar occupations are held mostly by men. Egalitarian norms toward women's advancement, public sphere gender essentialism, and private sphere gender essentialism have a positive relationship to women's employment in blue-collar occupations and a negative relationship to men's

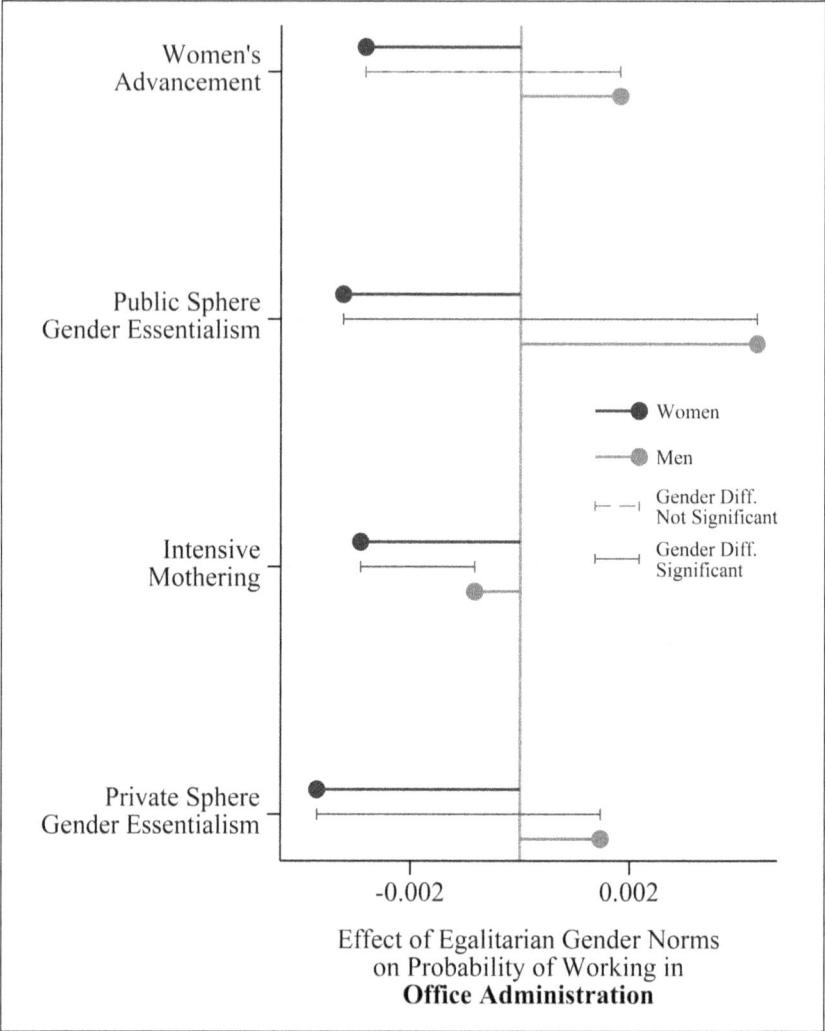

Figure 5.6 Relationship of Local Gender Norms to Women's and Men's Probability of Employment in Office Administration

Note: Results calculated from independent hierarchical logistic regression models predicting employment in office administration with individual-level (race, age, age squared, education, marital status, work experience, work experience squared, and work hours) and commuting zone-level (share of workers in the service sector, share employed in management or professional occupations, unemployment rate, percentage of residents with a college degree, percent foreign born, and racial composition) controls. Intercepts were specified to vary by commuting zone. An interaction between gender and local norms was used to calculate the average marginal effects of one unit in egalitarian norms on the probability of employment in office administration for women and men.

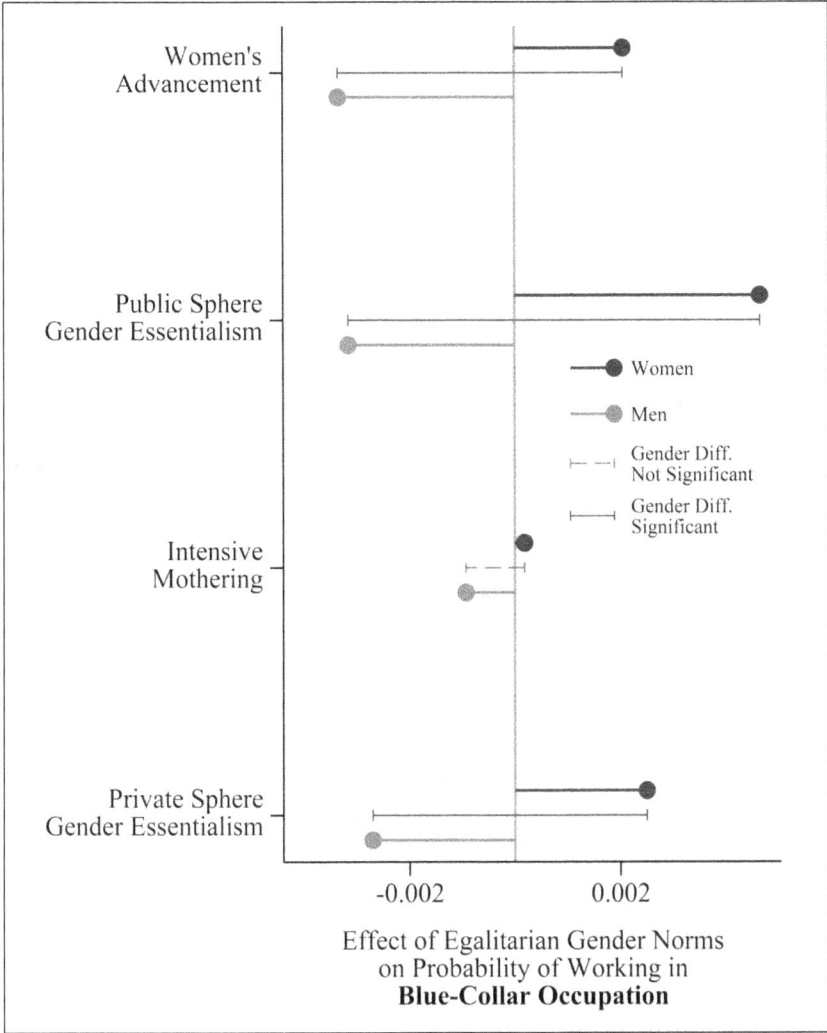

Figure 5.7 Relationship of Local Gender Norms to Women's and Men's Probability of Employment in Blue-Collar Occupations

Note: Results calculated from independent hierarchical logistic regression models predicting employment in blue-collar occupations with individual-level (race, age, age squared, education, marital status, work experience, work experience squared, and work hours) and commuting zone-level (share of workers in the service sector, share employed in management or professional occupations, unemployment rate, percentage of residents with a college degree, percent foreign born, and racial composition) controls. Intercepts were specified to vary by commuting zone. An interaction between gender and local norms was used to calculate the average marginal effects of one unit in egalitarian norms on the probability of employment in blue-collar occupations for women and men.

employment in these roles. This means that egalitarian gender norms across these dimensions operate to desegregate blue-collar jobs.

The largest effects are again observed on the dimension of local norms related to public sphere gender essentialism. For each unit difference in local egalitarianism, women are 0.5 percentage points more likely to work in blue-collar occupations while men are 0.3 percentage less likely. This relates to a combined shift of 0.8 percentage points favoring women's representation in blue-collar jobs. In addition to public sphere gender essentialism, egalitarian norms toward women's advancement and private sphere gender essentialism also have a strong relationship to women's integration in blue-collar occupations. For each of these dimensions, a one-unit difference in local egalitarianism relates to about a 0.5 percentage point increase in the probability of women's employment in blue-collar occupations relative to men. Gender norms toward intensive mothering were not significantly related to the sorting of women and men in blue-collar occupations.

Summary of Results: Occupational Sorting

Gender norms are related to the sorting of women and men across occupations. But not all dimensions of gender norms play an equal role or have consistent relationships with women's and men's employment. Norms of public sphere gender essentialism were associated with the sorting of women and men across each of the four occupations analyzed. In each case, egalitarianism on this dimension was related to lower levels of occupational segregation. Egalitarianism was associated with a higher probability of employment for women relative to men in majority-men management, STEM, and blue-collar occupations. It was also associated with a lower probability of employment for women relative to men in the majority-women occupation of office administration.

Other dimensions of gender norms were only relevant for the sorting of women and men in some occupations. Egalitarian norms of women's advancement and private sphere gender essentialism were associated with employment patterns in office administration and blue-collar occupations. Egalitarian norms on these dimensions related to a lower probability of women's employment in office administration and a higher probability of women's employment in blue-collar roles. The opposite pattern was observed for men. Consequently, egalitarianism on these norms was associated with reduced segregation in these low-wage occupations. Norms of intensive mothering had the weakest relationship to occupational sorting. However, intensive mothering was associated with employment in office administration. Women in places with greater support for working mothers were less likely to work in office administrative positions.

Although all four dimensions of gender norms related to the sorting of women and men workers across at least one of the four occupations analyzed, public sphere gender essentialism had the strongest and most consistent effects. This is likely related to the orientation of this dimension of gender norms. Public sphere gender essentialism conveys expectations about the types of jobs women and men are suited for. In places with egalitarian norms on this dimension, women and men are viewed as similarly qualified for occupations with varying characteristics, such as leadership, technical skills, or people skills. This was reflected in the aforementioned findings, where women were much more likely to work in majority-men management, STEM, and blue-collar occupations when norms toward public sphere gender essentialism were egalitarian. Importantly, this dimension of norms not only operates to increase women's representation in majority-men occupations. The analysis also revealed that egalitarianism in public sphere gender essentialism relates to greater representation of men in majority-women office administration roles. This indicates that these egalitarian norms help remove the salience of gender in segregated occupations, increasing the likelihood that men work in conventionally feminine, or women work in conventionally masculine, roles.

The previous chapter showed that local gender norms have contextual effects shaping individuals' attitudes and behaviors. Here, we have reviewed evidence that these contextual effects also play out in labor market processes. Local gender norms provide the logic individuals use when navigating the labor market and the criteria hiring managers apply when evaluating job candidates. When norms are more traditional, job seekers may be more likely to view their personal skills and interests as aligning with conventional ideas about the types of jobs women and men are essentially suited for. In contrast, under egalitarian contexts job seekers may have more varied assessments of their skills and interests because they are not influenced by local gender expectations about the type of work women and men should do. Similarly, hiring managers in traditional contexts may be more likely to express preferences (implicit or not) for a worker of a particular gender to match the requirements of the job opening. In egalitarian environments, the association of job requirements to candidates' gender would be far less salient, reducing the chances that hiring managers draw on these gendered logics when evaluating applicants.

Contextual effects of local gender norms may shape patterns of occupational segregation. However, these forms of occupational segregation may also reinforce local gender norms in a reciprocal fashion. By virtue of greater exposure to women in STEM and blue-collar roles and men in office administration positions, commuting zone residents may increasingly adopt views that reject gender essentialism and endorse beliefs that women and men hold similar skills and characteristics. From this perspective, prevailing patterns of occupational segregation shape local gender norms just as gender norms shape patterns of occupational segregation.

Establishing the causal direction between norms and occupational segregation is not possible in the current analysis. In addition, I do not believe it would be very helpful because empirically modeling causality would obscure the more complex reciprocal relationship between occupational structure and local norms. Local norms may be informed by prevailing patterns of occupational gender segregation that are themselves reinforced by predominant cultural norms. Rather than descending into arguments over which came first, or which is exogenous, we can instead conceptualize them as two components of a feedback loop driving local gender structures. Under periods of stability, norms and occupational segregation reinforce one another. But a change in one component could create change in the other. Public policies that improve women's representation in STEM occupations could alter local gender norms as more people are exposed to women in conventionally male-dominated roles. Conversely, social movements advocating for greater equality of women and men may alter local norms that inspire a larger number of women to pursue male-dominated roles. From this perspective, change can start on either component—occupational representation or norms—and lead to shifts in the other. However, another possibility is that shifts in one aspect generate a backlash in the other. For example, policies that improve occupational gender integration may be met with resistance from those adhering to local norms of traditionalism. Under these unstable conditions, either norms will change or occupational segregation will revert to previous patterns.

The relationship of local norms to occupational sorting is dynamic and complicated. But do these relationships have anything to do with gender wage gaps? The analyses presented prior provide evidence that egalitarian norms of public sphere gender essentialism may operate in this way, but not the other dimensions of gender norms. Public sphere gender essentialism was the only aspect of local gender norms that was associated with women's representation in high-paying management and STEM jobs. By supporting women's employment in these types of occupations, egalitarian norms on this dimension help reduce gender wage gaps via occupational sorting. Egalitarianism on the other dimensions of gender norms had important relationships to occupational sorting with respect to office administration and blue-collar occupations, but these two types of jobs have similar levels of pay that are relatively low. Therefore, although local norms of egalitarianism may help integrate these segregated occupations, this would not help reduce local wage gaps.

Gender norms are related to the sorting of women and men across occupations. In some cases, these patterns relate to the representation of women and men workers in similarly paid roles, such as office administration and blue-collar jobs. In other cases, particularly with respect to norms toward public sphere gender essentialism, the relationship of norms to occupational sorting has implications on the gender wage gap through the association of local egalitarianism to women's employment in high-paying management and STEM roles. The question remains, then, of why norms toward women's advancement and private sphere gender essentialism were related to lower commuting zone wage gaps, as illustrated earlier in this chapter (Figure 5.2). It is possible that public sphere gender essentialism may also be associated with gender wage gaps through additional mechanisms. In particular, local gender norms may relate to wage gaps through dynamics occurring between women and men in the same occupation.

Local Gender Norms and Within-Occupation Valuation

In addition to between-occupation sorting, mechanisms occurring within occupations have also been found to be major contributors to the gender wage gap. Whereas occupational sorting refers to the mechanisms driving women's underrepresentation, and men's overrepresentation, in high-paying roles, within-occupation mechanisms behind the gender wage gap capture the varying experiences of women and men who hold the same occupation. Research has shown, for example, that women are more likely than equally ranked men to face criticism at work for taking sick days or requesting time off to care for their children (Luhr 2020). Other studies show that men are often assumed to be workplace leaders even when they hold the same position as women colleagues (Martin 2003). This can result in men being evaluated more favorably, receiving higher wages, forming stronger relationships with company higher-ups, and obtaining privileged access to professional opportunities (Alegria 2019).

Although sociologists and economists have historically argued that occupational gender segregation is the largest contributing factor to the gender wage gap (Blau and Kahn 2017), recent studies show that the influence of this between-occupation mechanism is waning, while the importance of within-occupation dynamics is increasing. Claudia Goldin (2014b), for example, has found that as women's educational attainment increases, the role of within-occupational contributors to the gender wage gap has grown because of men's efforts to retain higher status than women at work. When men are paid more than equally ranked women, gender hierarchies are maintained even when occupational integration is achieved.

Gender wage gaps within occupations provide clear evidence that within-occupation processes play a large role in sustaining wage inequality between women and men. If gender wage gaps could be fully explained by the sorting of women into lower-paid jobs, within-occupation wage gaps would not exist. Yet, as illustrated in Figure 5.8, wage gaps within occupations can be just as bad, or even worse, than the overall gender wage gap. The wage gap for the entire labor force is 19.8 percent, meaning that women are paid nearly 20 percent less than men. Comparing women and men employed in blue-collar occupations, however, the wage gap grows to over 26 percent. This suggests that women face particularly extreme barriers to wage equity in blue-collar jobs. The gender wage gap in management is no better than the overall wage gap. Although median wages in management may be higher than the average job, women in this role are still paid less than similarly positioned men. Wage gaps in STEM and office administration positions are lower than the overall wage gap in the labor force but remain high. Women are paid 16 percent less than men in STEM and 13.5 percent less than men in office administration. In short, women are not only paid less than men in the labor force at large, but they are even paid substantially less than men when working in the same occupation.

Research has identified two primary factors driving these within-occupation wage gaps. The first relates to individual-level behaviors. Studying shifts occurring in male-dominated fields where women have made major inroads in recent decades, Claudia Goldin (2014b) found that men in these occupations increase their hours substantially in order to maintain a higher status than their new women colleagues. In many workplaces, excessive work hours receive wage premiums over and above the amount based on the extra time alone because supervisors view overwork as exhibiting productivity and a greater commitment to the company (Weeden, Cha, and Bucca 2016). Men have more time to put in these extra hours because they contribute less to household labor and childcare than women (Bianchi, Robinson, and Milke 2006). Whereas mothers may end work at five in the evening to pick up their children and cook dinner, men less commonly hold these family responsibilities and so commit longer and more continuous days. Although many mothers may resume work after their kids are put to bed, these hours are not in the office and therefore are invisible to supervisors and less likely to be rewarded (Goldin 2014b).

Other individual-level factors have also been found to affect wage disparities between women and men. Women's rising educational attainment was a major force reducing the gender wage gap from the 1970s through the early 2000s. As women surpassed men in college degree attainment, they

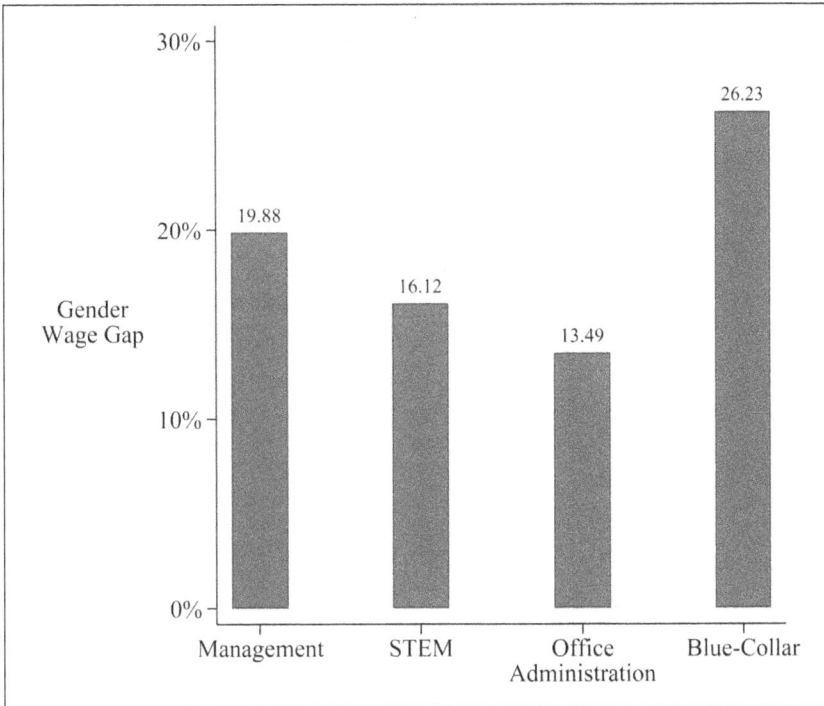

Figure 5.8 Gender Wage Gaps within Management, STEM, Office Administration, and Blue-Collar Occupations

Note: Gender wage gaps calculated with independent linear regression models for each occupation predicting logged hourly wages with individual- and commuting zone-level controls and specifying intercepts to vary by commuting zone. Individual controls include race, age, age squared, education, marital status, work experience, work experience squared, and work hours. Commuting zone controls include the share of workers in the service sector, the share employed in management or professional occupations, the unemployment rate, the percentage of residents with a college degree, the percent foreign born, and the racial composition.

were more qualified for high-paying jobs and increasingly eligible for better pay. Yet women reached parity with men in college degree attainment in 1981 and today account for nearly 60 percent of college graduates (National Center for Education Statistics 2021). Nonetheless, gender wage gaps remain, largely because men with college degrees are still paid more than women with college degrees. Research by Anthony Carnevale, Nicole Smith, and Artem Gulish (2018) shows that women college graduates earn an average of $26,000 less than men who have graduated from college. This is true even among women and men who study the same topics in university. Kyung Min Lim (2016) found that, among those who majored in a STEM field in college, women earn 22 percent less than men. Although education plays a major role in workers' wages, researchers have collectively observed that its contributions to the gender wage gap have diminished in recent decades as women's education surpassed men's while wage gaps persisted among college degree holders, even those majoring in the same field (Blau and Kahn 2017).

Differences in individual-level characteristics and behaviors between women and men, particularly work hours, are important factors driving the gender wage gap within occupations. An additional factor relates to cultural norms that place greater value on men's work over women's in the same occupation. Cultural norms can shape managers' perceptions and evaluations of employees with major implications for performance-based pay. These norms also influence interactions among colleagues. In environments with more conventional norms, women face exclusion from powerful networks of male colleagues and are expected to perform mundane office tasks unrelated to their position, which undermines their career advancement.

A widely cited study by Shelley Correll, Stephen Benard, and In Paik (2007) highlights how norms shape wages through influencing individuals' assessments of performance and worth. These researchers designed a set of resumes that were essentially identical but differed only in gender (indicated by first name) and parental status (reflected by listing "parent-teacher association coordinator" on resume). Participants in this study were told to evaluate the resumes for a marketing position at a new East Coast communications company. They were asked to rank the fictional candidates' strengths and estimate how much they should be paid. Comparing evaluations, Correll and colleagues found that mothers were perceived as less committed and competent than fathers. They were also perceived as less likely to be promoted in the future, considered less suitable for managerial grooming, and were less likely to be selected as a preferred candidate for hire. When estimating starting salaries, study participants offered mothers $13,000 less (8.7 percent) than what was offered to fathers.

Correll, Benard, and Paik's study used an experiment to highlight the way gender bias influences evaluations in ways that disadvantage women, particularly mothers. Although cognitive gender bias operates within individuals, social psychologists emphasize that these implicit views reflect local cultural environments where norms associate women and men with different attributes (Jost 2019). Prevailing norms provide a set of values for individuals to base their judgments on. Research has found, for example, that people exhibit lower levels of implicit racial prejudice in settings where racial equity and inclusion are emphasized (Lowery, Hardin, and Sinclair 2001). Studies on gender bias have uncovered similar trends, with hiring bias against women most pronounced in areas known for being traditional (Correll et al. 2017) and when evaluators are primed to think about conventional husband-breadwinner wife-homemaker family models (Hoyt 2012). Although implicit attitudes may operate beyond individuals' immediate perception, they mirror local value systems and norms.

Cultural norms are expressed in subtle ways within implicit attitudes that can devalue women's work and place a premium on men's, even when performance is equal. In other circumstances, gender norms are expressed more explicitly in workplace interactions. In interviews with women at major tech companies, Sharla Alegria (2019) found that they were more commonly asked to perform organizational roles that emphasized planning and project management, rather than technical roles that would have used their training in STEM fields such as computer science and math. As a result, many women in tech have fewer opportunities for professional development to keep up with new advances in their field. Lauren Alfrey and France Winddance Twine (2017) also conducted interviews with women in the tech industry and found that the work of their respondents was put under greater scrutiny because they were often the only woman in their department. These women also reported barriers to communicating with their male colleagues who did not value their contributions to team initiatives and often discussed major projects without including women who held key roles.

The tech sector has been the focus of several studies examining the challenges women face in majority-men workplaces where technical skills are highly valued. Yet expressions of conventional gender norms have also been documented more broadly. In interviews with professional women from a range of occupations including lawyers, professors, and scientists, Joan Williams and Rachel Dempsey (2014) found that, despite their career success, they were still expected to perform the majority of "office housework." Men commonly expected equally-ranked women colleagues to decorate for the office party, make coffee in the break room, and take notes during meetings. In a separate study, Patricia Martin (2003) clearly documented how gender norms operate in interactions between colleagues in ways that undermine women's authority:

> Tom and Betsy, both vice-presidents in a Fortune 100 company, stood talking in a hallway after a meeting. Along the hallway were offices but none was theirs. A phone started to ring in one office and after three or so rings, Tom said to Betsy, "Why don't you get that?" Betsy was surprised by Tom's request but answered the phone anyway and Tom returned to his office. (Martin 2003: 346)

Both employees were vice presidents of equal rank. But when a nearby phone was ringing, Tom habitually assumed that Betsy should answer it, reflecting conventional norms that women are responsible for "office housework." After hearing Tom's request, Betsy had the difficult choice of either confronting Tom and potentially souring a relationship with a colleague or conceding to conventional gendered practices and answering the telephone. The easiest choice was to answer the phone. This exchange, and the countless others that occur in workplaces each day, both reflect and reinforce conventional gender norms that protect men's time and authority while delegating "office housework" and other undervalued tasks to women.

Exchanges such as those between Betsy and Tom are not mundane workplace annoyances but instead have major impacts on women's careers. Time spent on office housework is time taken away from activities that may lead directly to raises and promotions. Although assisting colleagues and chipping in around the office may help build workers' reputation as a "team player," research has shown that women do not benefit from such altruistic behavior. Testing the effects of office altruism on worker performance evaluations, Madeline Heilman and Julie Chen (2005) found that only men were viewed more favorably for helping a colleague prepare copies or double-checking a presentation for errors and typos. Men performing these tasks were viewed as more deserving of raises, promotions, and bonus pay. In contrast, Heilman and Chen found that perceptions of women workers were unchanged if they performed these tasks. Worse yet, women who refused to help a colleague with office work were penalized and viewed as substantially less deserving of raises, promotions, and bonus pay than men who refused to help.

Other studies have shown how conventional gender norms often operate to devalue women's contributions in team meetings. Not only are women's opinions solicited less than equally ranked men, but studies show that men often interrupt, spend more time talking, and speak at higher volumes than equally ranked women (Lee and Mccabe 2021). When women exhibit these speaking patterns, they face backlash as colleagues view them as overbearing for behaving in the same manner viewed as acceptable for men (Brescoll 2011).

Through numerous practices, women's work is frequently valued less than men who hold the same position. When hired, women receive lower starting salaries than equally qualified men (Correll, Benard, and Paik 2007). Once in the job, they are more commonly expected to perform "office housework," reflecting assumptions that women's time is valued less than men's, whose hours are protected and devoted to activities that lead to promotions and raises. Further yet, in collaborative settings, women's contributions are undermined by men who interrupt and speak louder and more often. Collectively, these patterns indicate that women's access to high-paying occupations is not enough to achieve pay equality. Instead, gender norms that devalue women's contributions continue to sustain gender wage gaps even between employees who hold the same occupations.

Norms that devalue women's workplace contributions are not uniform, however. As we have reviewed throughout this book, commuting zones across the United States have distinct configurations of norms across four separate dimensions. Chapter 4 showed that these norms also have contextual effects that shape individuals' attitudes and behaviors. It is therefore possible that workplace interactions are conditioned by local norms in ways that affect the extent that women's contributions are devalued relative to men. In what follows, I test this hypothesis by examining whether the four dimensions of local gender norms predict wage gaps occurring within the four occupations examined earlier: management, STEM, office administration, and blue-collar work.

Testing the Relationship of Local Gender Norms to Within-Occupation Wage Gaps

The varying experiences of women and men in the same occupation have been shown to be an important contributor to gender wage gaps. Studies suggest that women's work is frequently undervalued relative to men in the same occupation: They receive less recognition for their contributions and are expected to perform additional "office housework" that is outside of their job description. In short, women's work receives less value than work performed by equally positioned men. To test whether this pattern of valuation is related to local gender norms, I focus on gender wage gaps within management, STEM, office administration, and blue-collar occupations. Although there are several more occupations in the U.S. labor force, I examine these four because they capture important variation across occupational characteristics. Management and STEM occupations are both high wage, whereas office administration and blue-collar occupations are low-wage jobs. Among high-wage occupations, STEM is overwhelmingly composed of men while management is more gender balanced, with women making up nearly half of all workers. STEM occupations also emphasize technical skills, compared to management, which prioritizes leadership. Among low-wage positions, blue-collar jobs are overwhelmingly composed of men and are characterized by manual labor. In contrast, office administration jobs require people skills and the vast majority of workers in these roles are women. Collectively, these four occupations capture diversity in wages, gender composition, and work characteristics that represent broader variation in the labor force as a whole. In additional analyses, I examined within-occupation wage gaps for a more expansive and detailed set of occupations. General findings remained the same. Therefore, I focus on these four occupations to parsimoniously illustrate key findings.

Women are paid less than men in all four occupations (see Figure 5.8), indicating that occupational sorting cannot fully account for wage gaps because women are consistently paid less than men in the same occupation. Instead, these patterns reflect the devaluation of women's work compared to equally positioned men. However, the extent of these wage gaps varies widely. The wage gap is smallest in office administration, a low-wage majority-women occupation, and largest in blue-collar roles that are also low-wage but majority men. In fact, the wage gap is nearly twice as large in blue-collar occupations as it is in office administration. This suggests that women's contributions may be particularly undervalued in majority-men environments where stereotypically masculine characteristics, such as manual labor, are emphasized. Among the two high-wage jobs, wage gaps are worse in management (19.9 percent) than STEM (16.1 percent), but both are near the overall average for the labor force (19.8 percent).

To test the relationship of local gender norms to within-occupation wage gaps representing differences in the valuation of women and men in the same roles, I again used data from the 2018 ACS and created independent samples of respondents employed in management (110,064 respondents), STEM (91,846), office administration (112,997) and blue-collar (221,003) occupations. For each sample, I applied a series of independent hierarchical linear regression models (with a varying intercept by commuting zone) that predicted hourly wage (logged) with the same individual- and commuting zone-level variables used earlier in equations examining occupational sorting. These control variables are standard in studies examining the gender wage gap (Cha and Weeden 2014; Mandel and Semyonov 2014). I also added an additional control for more detailed occupations within the four broad categories of management (27 detailed occupations), STEM (46), office administration (42), and blue collar (126).[5] This accounts for the possibility that wage gaps within occupations are due to women and men holding different types of detailed positions, such as women more commonly working as human resource managers whereas men are overrepresented among purchasing managers (Scarborough 2018b). Each equation estimates the difference in wages between women and men within management, STEM, office administration, and blue-collar occupations, controlling for covariates. I interact this gender difference in wages with each dimension of local gender norms to test whether within-occupation wage gaps vary depending on the gender norms in the commuting zone where workers reside. The resulting coefficients represent how a one-unit change in local gender egalitarianism relates to levels of the gender wage gap for each of the four occupations. A coefficient of −0.05, for example, means that each unit increase in egalitarian norms, such as moving from very traditional to traditional, traditional to average, average to egalitarian, or egalitarian to very egalitarian, predicts a 5 percentage point decrease in the within-occupation gender wage gap.

In the following four sections, I report the results of these analyses, focusing on how gender norms relate to the different valuation of women and men within the same occupation. If local gender norms are associated with smaller within-occupation wage gaps, this provides evidence that these cultural features shape the valuation of women's and men's work in the same position. I focus on wage gaps for each occupation separately, starting with management, then STEM, before turning my attention to office administration and blue-collar roles.

Management

Figure 5.9 reports the relationship of each of the four dimensions of local norms to wage gaps between women and men managers. Egalitarianism across each of the four dimensions relates to lower gender wage gaps, but the size of the effect varies substantially. The strongest relationship is observed with respect to norms toward public sphere gender essentialism. Comparing commuting zones that differ in one unit on gender egalitarianism (e.g., average areas to egalitarian ones), the gender wage gap is smaller by 2 percentage points in places with more egalitarian norms toward public sphere gender essentialism. At the extremes, this translates to wage gaps in very traditional areas that are over 8 percentage points worse than wage gaps in very egalitarian locales. The size of this relationship is notably large. For comparison, the gender wage gap has fallen by only 0.4 percentage points in the last decade for the United States as a whole (Hegewisch and Barsi 2020). This means that a woman manager who remains in the same commuting zone would have to wait fifty years (assuming the pace of longitudinal change remains) for the gender wage gap to reduce by the equivalent amount that it would decline if she moved to a location where local gender norms toward public sphere gender essentialism were more egalitarian by only one unit.

Other dimensions of gender norms also had strong relationships to wage gaps within management occupations. Commuting zones with egalitarian norms toward private sphere gender essentialism have lower gender wage gaps. Although the effect is smaller than that observed for public sphere gender essentialism, it remains substantial. A difference of one unit in local egalitarianism toward private sphere gender essentialism relates to a reduction in the management gender wage gap of 1.22 percentage points.

Norms toward women's advancement were also related to lower gender wage gaps within management. Commuting zones where local norms support women's advancement and leadership have lower gender wage gaps in management by about one percentage point for every one unit difference in

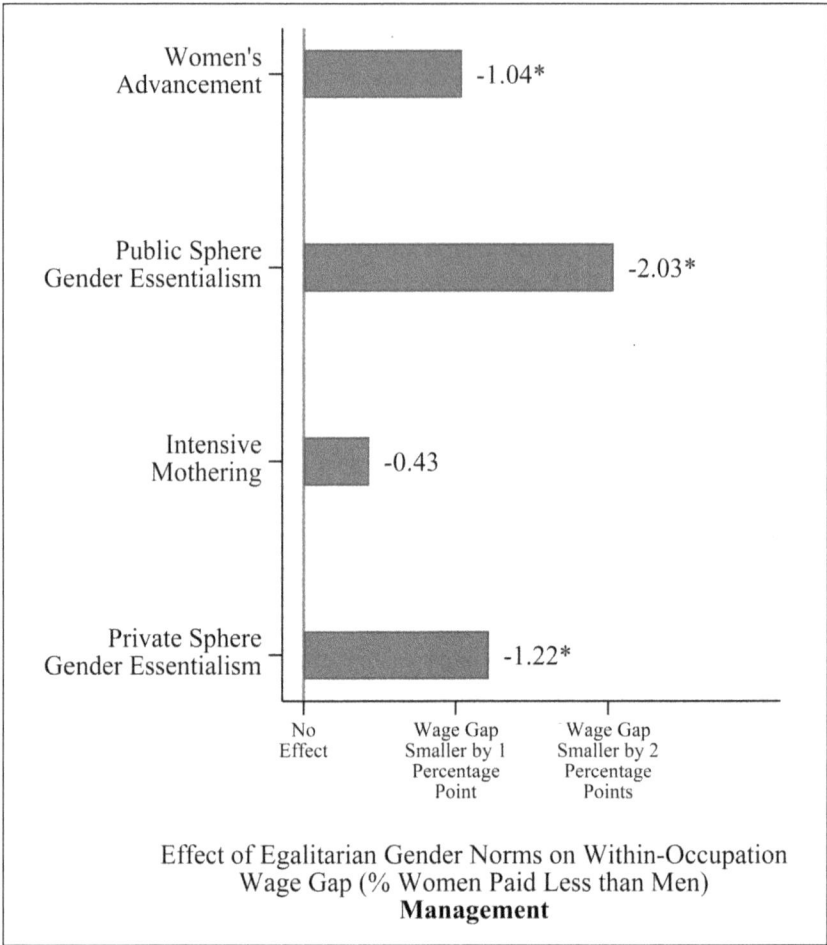

Figure 5.9 Relationship of Local Gender Norms to Within-Occupation Wage Gaps: Management

Note: Results calculated from hierarchical linear regression model predicting logged hourly wages with individual-level (race, age, age squared, education, marital status, work experience, work experience squared, work hours, and detailed occupation) and commuting zone (share of workers in the service sector, share employed in management or professional occupations, unemployment rate, percentage of residents with a college degree, percent foreign born, and racial composition) controls. Intercepts were specified to vary by commuting zone. An interaction between gender and local norms was used to determine whether wage gaps between women and men varied by local levels of egalitarianism. * indicates relationship of norms and wage gap significant at p < 0.05 level.

local egalitarianism. The fourth dimension of local norms, intensive mothering, was not significantly associated with wage gaps. Here, we see that places that support working mothers have lower gender wage gaps, but the relationship is too small to make any confident claims.

Overall, there is strong evidence that women's work in management is perceived as more equal to men's in places with more egalitarian gender norms on three of the four dimensions. Surprisingly, norms toward women's advancement did not have the strongest relationship, despite being directly related to expectations of women's leadership capabilities that are emphasized in management. Although egalitarian norms toward women's advancement did relate to lower within-management wage gaps, the size of this relationship was smaller than what was observed for norms toward public sphere gender essentialism and private sphere gender essentialism. This suggests that norms conveying women and men as naturally oriented toward different tasks are a major factor driving wage penalties for women in management. As discussed previously, in many workplaces women are expected to do the "office housework," which can detract from their performance and, consequently, career advancement. These patterns may be driven by norms of public and private sphere gender essentialism that convey women as oriented toward these interpersonal and caregiving tasks. In contexts with egalitarian norms on these dimensions, expectations for office housework would be equally directed toward women and men managers. With such burdens shared, women managers have greater opportunity to focus on tasks that more directly translate to raises, bonuses, and promotions.

STEM

Turning to STEM occupations, Figure 5.10 reports that local gender norms do not have a meaningful relationship to wage gaps within STEM occupations. Egalitarianism on each dimension of gender norms relates to lower gender wage gaps, but the relationship is too small to draw any confident conclusions. Instead, the evidence suggests that gender wage gaps within STEM occupations are similar regardless of commuting zone gender norms.

Local gender norms relate to wage gaps within management but not STEM. This difference likely reflects characteristics of each occupation that make it more or less influenced by local norms. Whereas management occupations emphasize leadership and have near parity in the representation of women and men, STEM occupations require technical skills in engineering, mathematics, and science and are composed mostly of men workers. It is possible that either the technical nature or the male-dominated setting of STEM occupations makes them resistant to greater equity in egalitarian contexts. The emphasis on technical skills may provide criteria for workers to discriminate against women because these qualifications are stereotypi-

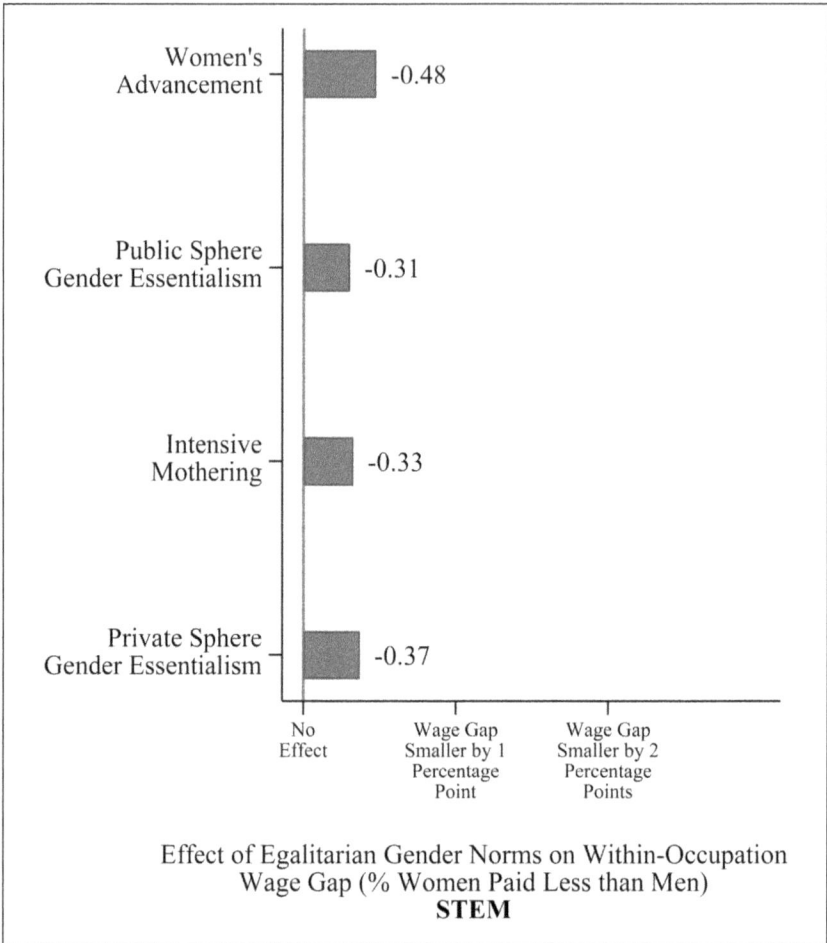

Figure 5.10 Relationship of Local Gender Norms to Within-Occupation Wage Gaps: STEM

Note: Results calculated from hierarchical linear regression model predicting logged hourly wages with individual-level (race, age, age squared, education, marital status, work experience, work experience squared, work hours, and detailed occupation) and commuting zone (share of workers in the service sector, share employed in management or professional occupations, unemployment rate, percentage of residents with a college degree, percent foreign born, and racial composition) controls. Intercepts were specified to vary by commuting zone. An interaction between gender and local norms was used to determine whether wage gaps between women and men varied by local levels of egalitarianism.

cally associated with men. As documented by Lauren Alfrey and France Winddance Twine (2017), women's contributions in technical settings are often incorrectly attributed to men who are assumed to possess greater technical knowledge. Another possibility is that the male-dominated setting of STEM occupations isolates workers from the influence of local gender norms. Men in STEM may be resistant to local egalitarianism because they benefit from traditional norms that offer them additional, unearned, credit and wage premiums (Goldin 2014b). As documented earlier, women are more likely to work in STEM in places with egalitarian norms toward public sphere gender essentialism. It is possible that men in STEM are reacting against women's rising representation by maintaining wage discrimination.

At this point, we are unable to determine whether STEM occupations' resistance to local norms is due to their technical or male-dominated features. However, in the space that follows, I also examine blue-collar occupations, which are male -dominated but require a completely different set of job skills than STEM. If within-blue-collar-occupation wage gaps are also unrelated to local norms, this would suggest that these patterns are driven by men's resistance rather than technical job requirements because STEM and blue-collar jobs require different qualifications, but each are dominated by men.

Office Administration

As noted previously, women are paid an average of 13.5 percent less than men in office administration occupations. However, Figure 5.11 shows that this wage gap is substantially higher in places with traditional norms toward women's advancement, public sphere gender essentialism, and private sphere gender essentialism. Across each of these three dimensions, women residing in traditional environments face greater wage inequality than women residing in areas with more traditional norms.

The strongest relationship is found in the dimension of local norms related to public sphere gender essentialism. Gender wage gaps are predicted to be 2.7 percentage points smaller in a commuting zone that is just one unit more egalitarian. Comparing the extremes, gender wage gaps are over 10 percentage points lower in very egalitarian than very traditional commuting zones on this dimension. The size of this relationship is even larger than what was observed for within-management wage gaps, suggesting that the benefits of local egalitarianism on wage equity are greatest in majority-women occupations such as office administration.

Norms toward women's advancement and private sphere gender essentialism also had substantial relationships with gender wage gaps in office administration. A difference of one unit in local egalitarianism toward women's advancement relates to a reduction of office administration wage gaps by 1.76 percentage points. The same difference with respect to norms toward private

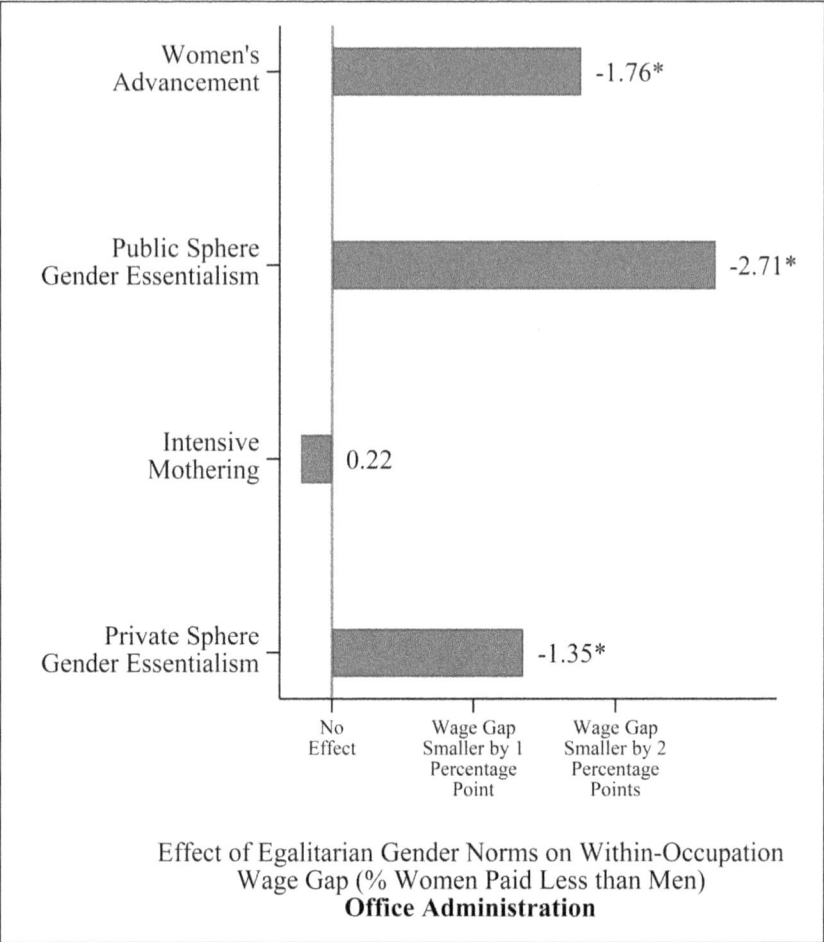

Figure 5.11 **Relationship of Local Gender Norms to Within-Occupation Wage Gaps: Office Administration**

Note: Results calculated from hierarchical linear regression model predicting logged hourly wages with individual-level (race, age, age squared, education, marital status, work experience, work experience squared, work hours, and detailed occupation) and commuting zone (share of workers in the service sector, share employed in management or professional occupations, unemployment rate, percentage of residents with a college degree, percent foreign born, and racial composition) controls. Intercepts were specified to vary by commuting zone. An interaction between gender and local norms was used to determine whether wage gaps between women and men varied by local levels of egalitarianism. * indicates relationship of norms and wage gap significant at $p < 0.05$ level.

sphere gender essentialism is related to a reduction in within-occupation wage gaps by 1.35 percentage points. As with management, norms of intensive mothering were unrelated to within-occupation wage gaps in office administration. This is consistent with the patterns illustrated earlier in the chapter (Figures 5.2 and 5.3) showing that this dimension of gender norms does not have a meaningful relationship with wage gaps.

Overall, the analysis of wage gaps within office administration indicates that women's work is valued more equally to men's in places with egalitarian norms. This is particularly true when women and men are viewed as similarly suited for different types of work. In these environments, supervisors may more readily see women office administrators' broader contributions to the workplace, rather than only those that are associated with femininity and undervalued (Levanon, England, and Allison 2009).

Blue-Collar Occupations

Last, the results of my analysis of blue-collar wage gaps are reported in Figure 5.12. None of the four dimensions of local gender norms have a substantial relationship to wage gaps within blue-collar occupations. Some dimensions even report an association where egalitarianism predicts worse wage gaps, but the relationship is nonsignificant and far too small to confidently support this claim. Instead, the dominant trend reported in Figure 5.12 is that local norms have no effect on pay equality between women and men who work in blue-collar occupations.

Office administration and blue-collar occupations have similar wages, but the relationship of gender norms to wage gaps is very strong in office administration and absent in blue-collar roles. There are two key differences between these occupations that may help explain this pattern. First, the nature of the work is dramatically different. Office administration requires people skills and organization, characteristics stereotypically associated with women. In contrast, blue-collar occupations emphasize manual labor and hand-eye coordination, two traits more commonly associated with men. It may be that jobs requiring skills in manual labor are less sensitive to local gender norms. Yet the skills required in blue-collar jobs are also very different from those in STEM, where within-occupation wage gaps were similarly resistant to the influence of local norms. Therefore, we can rule out the possibility that the particular skills required in STEM or blue-collar occupations make them resistant to the equalizing effects of local egalitarian norms.

Instead, the common feature of both STEM and blue-collar occupations is that they are both dominated by men. Seven out of ten workers in STEM and over four out of five blue-collar workers are men. These male-dominated settings may foster subcultures that are resistant to egalitarian gender norms, particularly if those subcultures operate to maintain the status and

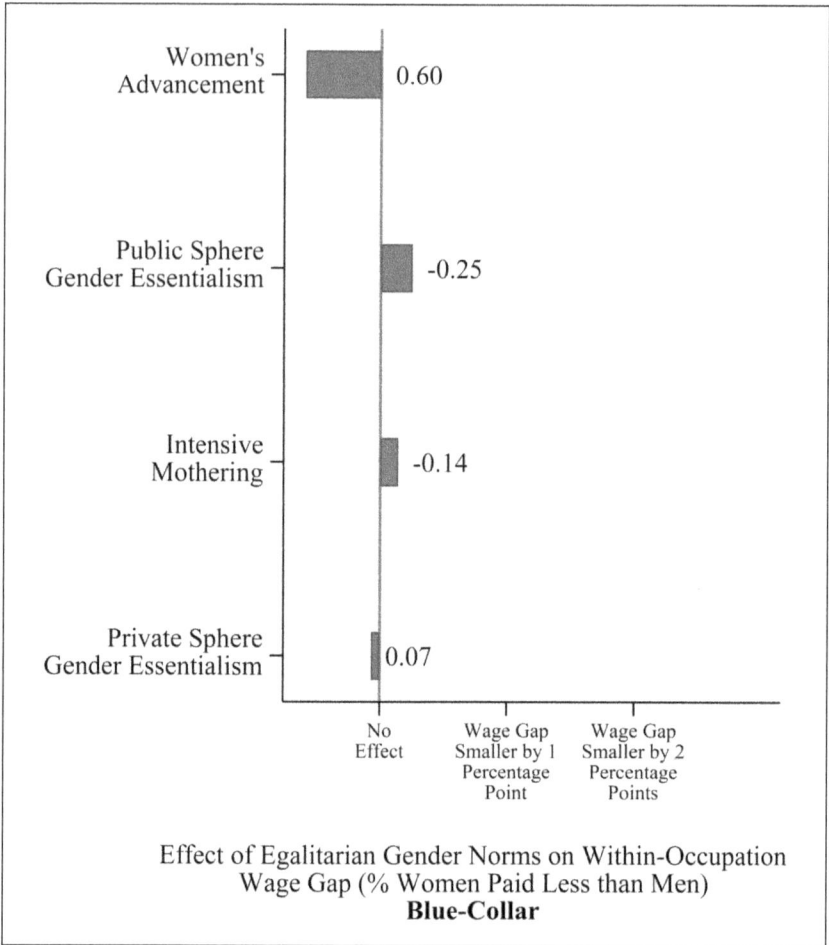

Figure 5.12 Relationship of Local Gender Norms to Within-Occupation Wage Gaps: Blue-Collar Occupations

Note: Results calculated from hierarchical linear regression model predicting logged hourly wages with individual-level (race, age, age squared, education, marital status, work experience, work experience squared, work hours, and detailed occupation) and commuting zone (share of workers in the service sector, share employed in management or professional occupations, unemployment rate, percentage of residents with a college degree, percent foreign born, and racial composition) controls. Intercepts were specified to vary by commuting zone. An interaction between gender and local norms was used to determine whether wage gaps between women and men varied by local levels of egalitarianism.

privilege of men, who make up the majority of workers. In contrast, about three out of four office administrators, and nearly half of managers, are women, who have a direct interest in reducing gender wage gaps and may draw on local norms to do so.

Summary of Results: Within-Occupation Valuation

Wage gaps within occupations reflect a lower value placed on women's work relative to men in the same position. Prior research has shown that these processes of valuation occur through biased assessments of women's work performance as well as interactions between colleagues where women's contributions are stifled or they are expected to perform tasks that do not lead to career progress, bonuses, or raises. The results here indicate that such gender differences in valuation are often conditioned by local gender norms. Wage gaps are smaller in management and office administration occupations in areas with more egalitarian norms toward women's advancement, public sphere gender essentialism, and private sphere gender essentialism. The size of these relationships was substantial for each dimension, with a one-unit difference in local egalitarianism relating to at least a one percentage point reduction in within-occupation wage gaps. The strongest relationship was observed for norms toward public sphere gender essentialism. In both management and office administration, a difference of one unit in local egalitarianism on this dimension was associated with lower gender wage gaps by between two and three percentage points. This strong relationship reflects the nature of this dimension of gender norms. In places where women and men are viewed as equally suited for different types of work, women's contributions are visible and valued. Expectations for doing the "office housework" would be shared by both women and men in these settings. As a result, women are more equally paid in places with egalitarian norms toward public sphere gender essentialism.

In contrast to office administration and management, local gender norms were unrelated to wage gaps within STEM and blue-collar occupations. These jobs differ in both function and gender composition from managerial and office administration roles. However, STEM and blue-collar occupations differ in function from each other as well. Instead, a common driver of resistance to local gender norms in these two occupations is the fact that each are overwhelmingly composed of men. In these occupational settings, the devaluation of women's labor relative to men may persist even in egalitarian commuting zones as men workers resist cultural pressure to relinquish their privileges. As women gain employment in STEM and blue-collar occupations, particularly in areas with egalitarian gender norms (see Figures 5.5 and 5.7), men in these roles may seek to maintain their advantages through direct wage discrimination in pay setting or indirectly through neglecting women's workplace contributions and expecting them to undertake "office housework."

Conclusion: Culture's Consequences on Occupational Sorting and Within-Occupation Valuation

In the beginning of this chapter, I posed the question, does place matter for gender equality? In the aggregate, places with more egalitarian gender norms have lower gender wage gaps, suggesting that there is a meaningful relationship between local norms and equality between women and men. This general association tells us little, however, about what is driving this association or how gender norms facilitate more equal pay. For these deeper questions, I drew upon sociological theories of gender to identify two possible mechanisms underlying the relationship between local norms and gender wage gaps. First, local gender norms may relate to wage gaps through shaping the sorting of women and men into different occupations with varying pay. Overall, women are more likely to work in low-paying jobs, and men are more likely to work in high-paying jobs. If local norms facilitate women's employment in high-paying occupations, this will lead to reductions in the gender wage gap through decreasing segregation. The second mechanism relates to the different value placed on women's and men's work in the same occupation. Studies have shown that equally ranked women and men face very different opportunities and constraints at work, with women more likely to be assigned mundane and nonwork-related tasks than men (Williams and Dempsey 2014). Women's workplace contributions also receive less praise and often go unnoticed (Alfrey and Twine 2017). These barriers may be particularly pronounced in areas with traditional gender norms that devalue women's work.

I tested whether the relationship of gender norms to gender wage gaps is driven by (1) occupational sorting or (2) within-occupation valuation. My analyses focused on four major occupations that represent a cross-section of high- and low-paying jobs that are gender integrated, male dominated, or female dominated and require different sets of skills. Among high-paying occupations, I focused on management as a role that requires leadership and is nearly gender integrated and STEM as a technical field that is composed primarily of men workers. The two low-paying occupations I analyzed were office administration and blue-collar jobs. Both have similar wages, but office administration is female dominated and requires organization and people skills whereas blue-collar jobs are male dominated and require manual labor and hand-eye coordination.

This chapter shows that gender norms operate through both occupational sorting and valuation, but under certain conditions. Table 5.2 summarizes key results. The most consistent pattern was that occupations are more gender integrated in commuting zones with egalitarian norms toward public sphere gender essentialism. Women were more likely to work in high-paying management and STEM occupations in areas where norms conveyed more equal expectations for the types of work women and men are suited for. In these settings, men were also more likely to work in low-paying female-dominated office administration occupations. Together, this translates to lower gender wage gaps in places with egalitarian norms toward public sphere gender essentialism because women have greater representation in high-paying jobs and are less concentrated in low-paying feminized roles. Egalitarian norms toward public sphere gender essentialism also related to women's employment in male-dominated blue-collar occupations, but this would not translate to lower gender wage gaps via occupational sorting because these positions generally have low pay. Nonetheless, it does suggest that prevailing gender norms play an important role in maintaining segregation in blue-collar roles.

Norms of public sphere gender essentialism were not the only dimension related to occupational sorting. Egalitarianism toward private sphere gender essentialism was also associated with a higher proportion of women in blue-collar occupations, as well as greater representation of men in office administration. This suggests that broader norms conveying women and men as essentially different, spanning work and home, contribute to occupational gender segregation. Norms toward women's advancement did not relate to women's representation in high-paying management or STEM occupations but did help desegregate low-paying office administration and blue-collar positions. This is counterintuitive because leadership skills are an important part of being a manager. It is possible that leadership expectations play a smaller role at job entry in management than they do in shaping performance evaluations and raises once in the position. Instead, norms of essential difference are more central at job entry, where expectations around candidates' "fit" for the job are prominent and rooted in notions of the type of work women and men are best suited for. Gender norms toward intensive mothering had the weakest relationship to gender wage gaps. Across all analyses, support for working mothers was only related to greater representation of men in female-dominated office administration occupations. This may play a small role in reducing gender wage gaps by reducing the concentration of women in this low-paying position.

The sorting of women and men in all four occupations was related to at least one dimension of gender norms. In contrast, the relationship of norms

TABLE 5.2   SUMMARY OF RESULTS: THE RELATIONSHIP OF LOCAL EGALITARIANISM TO OCCUPATIONAL SORTING AND WITHIN-OCCUPATION WAGE GAPS

| | Occupation | | | | | | | |
| | Management | | STEM | | Office administration | | Blue collar | |
	Sorting	Valuation	Sorting	Valuation	Sorting	Valuation	Sorting	Valuation
Women's advancement	–	Yes	–	–	Yes	Yes	Yes	–
Public sphere gender essentialism	Yes	Yes	Yes	–	Yes	Yes	Yes	–
Intensive mothering	–	–	–	–	Yes	–	–	–
Private sphere gender essentialism	–	Yes	–	–	Yes	Yes	Yes	–

Note: Contents of table report whether each dimension of gender norms predicts the sorting of women and men into different occupations or the differential valuation of women's and men's work as indicated by within-occupation wage gaps.

to within-occupation valuation (measured by occupation-specific wage gaps) was observed only in management and office administration. Places with egalitarian norms toward women's advancement, public sphere gender essentialism, and private sphere gender essentialism had lower gender wage gaps in management and office administration positions.

Gender norms did not relate to within-occupation wage gaps in STEM or blue-collar occupations. These two roles require very different skills and have vastly different pay. One common feature, however, is that they are both overwhelmingly composed of men. Over 70 percent of workers in STEM and over 80 percent of workers in blue-collar occupations are men. This highlights an important feature of gender norms: Although they relate to behavior and attitudes in the aggregate, their influence is not universal and can often be resisted. Male-dominated STEM and blue-collar occupations appear to be a site where egalitarian gender norms, which would otherwise improve gender equality between workers, are resisted. As women's employment slowly increases in these occupations, men seek to attain, or maintain, higher status by discriminating against women colleagues (Goldin 2014a, 2014b). When men are the vast majority in an occupation, they may face little resistance in these efforts. Male-dominated occupations appear to be a shelter for discrimination against women workers, even in commuting zones that have egalitarian norms. In contrast, integrated occupations, such as management, where 43 percent of workers are women, or female-dominated occupations, such as office administration (73 percent women), are much more sensitive to local gender norms. In egalitarian contexts, women's work is valued more equally to men's, and within-occupation pay gaps are significantly smaller. In these contexts, men who benefit from gender discrimination and traditional norms make up a smaller portion of workers and therefore constitute less resistance to egalitarianism.

Collectively, these aggregate relationships between commuting zone characteristics and occupations are sustained by patterns of interaction at more micro levels among supervisors, workers, and job applicants. Although I did not examine these detailed ways that norms shape individuals and their relationships, existing research can shed light on how micro-level dynamics operate to form the aggregate patterns observed in this chapter. On the side of job seekers, research by Erin Cech (2013) has shown how individuals often pursue careers that are consistent with expectations conveyed by prevailing gender norms. Women more commonly view themselves as excelling in interpersonal relations and caregiving, whereas men more often see their strengths as technical and systematic. These perceptions reflect predominant norms of gender essentialism and result in the sorting of women into lower-paying care-sector occupations. Other work has focused on the role of norms in shaping how hiring managers evaluate candidates. Shelley Correll and colleagues

(2017) have found that cognitive gender bias against women applying for male-dominated occupations is more pronounced in traditional settings than in places with progressive reputations. This suggests that hiring managers take cues from the local culture to evaluate whether women and men candidates are an "ideal fit" for their position. When local norms convey traditional expectations about the types of jobs women and men are suited for, women face significant barriers in access to male-dominated jobs. As a result, they are more likely to end up working in a female-dominated occupation, which, on average, offers lower wages (Levanon, England, and Allison 2009).

Even after being hired, gender norms shape interactions between workers and supervisors. Women and men of equal rank are often treated differently in ways that reflect prevailing norms. In traditional settings, women are expected to perform "office housework" tasks that can detract from productive activities directly related to promotion and pay (Williams and Dempsey 2014). Other research has shown that gender norms shape supervisors' evaluations of workers. Social psychology research has documented that women employees are often viewed as less worthy of raises or promotion than equally performing men (Correll, Benard, and Paik 2007). These patterns of interaction and cognitive bias are most pronounced in traditional settings where prevailing norms both reflect and reinforce workplace dynamics that disadvantage women.

Although this chapter conceptualizes norms as influencing patterns of inequality, this relationship is not unidirectional. Instead, cultural norms and forms of gender inequality such as the gender wage gap are linked in reciprocal feedback loops (Calnitsky 2019). Gender norms may shape levels of the gender wage gap, but the gender wage gap itself can shape gender norms by conferring a higher value on men's work than contributions made by equally positioned women. It is therefore difficult, and even unproductive, to try and identify which of these components—norms or wage gaps—is the primary cause because changes in one aspect can lead to changes in the other. Social movements and public discourse may slowly shift collective norms in ways that foster more equitable access to high-paying occupations and facilitate fair assessments of women's and men's contributions in the same role. Alternatively, gender wage gaps may slowly decline as a result of regulatory pressure aimed at addressing wage discrimination. Under these circumstances, the presence of equally paid women in the workplace may shift individuals' gender attitudes in ways that alter collective norms.

Gender norms and forms of inequality are reciprocal and operate to sustain one another. Gender norms influence wage gaps, and wage gaps influence gender norms. However, an advantage of focusing on the half of this feedback loop where norms shape wage gaps is that it allows us to see whether efforts to change local norms would be effective in reducing levels of gender inequality. The evidence presented in this chapter clearly shows that commuting zones with egalitarian norms have more women in higher-paying jobs and more equitable dynamics between women and men within several occupations. In other words, fostering egalitarian gender norms is a useful strategy for improving gender equality. How we change local norms is a different question entirely—and not one I explore in this book. Nonetheless, the evidence presented here shows that such efforts would be effective.

Place matters. Where you live can shape the opportunities available to you or the barriers you encounter. It also influences the degree to which you are affected by gender inequality. Although women are paid less than men in every commuting zone in the United States, this wage gap is far worse in places like Oklahoma City than Burlington. Underlying these different patterns of inequality are distinct configurations of gender norms. This chapter has reviewed how these norms shape the sorting of women and men into different occupations and the valuation of women's and men's work in the same role. Yet norms are not fixed entities. They are subject to contestation and change, particularly when we recognize instances where they create unfair and challenging conditions.

6

Conclusion

Advancing Equality at the Local Level

W hile writing this book, I have presented research to scholars and community leaders across the United States. In each talk, I started by reporting the local wage gap in the city where I was presenting and comparing it to neighboring cities and similar places in the country. Observers in Chattanooga, Tennessee, were shocked to hear that women were paid over 20 percent less than men in their community. Many in Washington, D.C., were concerned about their 17.5 percent local gender wage gap but proud that this was lower than the average commuting zone. Across the many locales and audiences, however, I soon learned that prior to my presentation, nearly all those attending my talk were unfamiliar with the levels of gender inequality in their community. This juxtaposed starkly with their involvement in local organizations and commitment to gender equality more broadly. Instead, it highlighted the fact that gender inequality in the United States is almost never framed as a local issue. Instead, it is primarily discussed on a national scale. This is particularly true with regards to the gender wage gap, where regular news coverage focuses almost exclusively on national trends.

The themes from this book underscore the importance of focusing on our local communities as a primary terrain where gender inequality is reproduced. Not only do gender wage gaps vary across the United States to a similar extent as they do throughout European nations (see Chapter 1), but the different cultural environments across U.S. commuting zones play a fundamental role in shaping these more detailed spatial patterns. While it has been documented elsewhere that commuting zones have different economic specializations (McCall 2001), these locales also have unique cultural environments that convey varying expectations for women and men. These local gender norms are composed of four dimensions relating to women's advancement, public sphere gender essentialism, intensive mothering, and private sphere gender essentialism. Together, these norms provide the logic people use when navigating social life—they influence how women and men perceive their personal strengths and interests, as well as frame our perceptions of others. In Milwaukee, for example, women's educational and occupational advancement is supported, but they are still expected to be primarily responsible for domestic labor. Meanwhile, in Grand Rapids, women and men have more equal contributions to family life, but norms toward women's advancement in the public sphere remain constraining for women.

Across the United States, commuting zone residents experience the gender structure in different ways. All feel the effects of gender inequality, but some experience it more than others depending on the local norms where they reside. Instead of playing out on a national stage, patterns of gender inequality are much more localized. This localism in the gender structure corresponds to increased localism observed in other social domains. Regional policy has long been crucial for attracting business through incentives or appealing tax structures (Roy 1999). Recent scholarship has shown that local cultural assets such as nightlife, museums, and art also play a large role in enticing tech development (Florida 2012). Increasingly, municipalities have enacted policies that have typically been the domain of the federal government (Katz and Nowak 2017). For example, in the area of immigration, many municipalities have implemented "Sanctuary City" ordinances that protect undocumented residents from deportation. In contrast, the federal government has failed for decades to pass any sort of comprehensive immigration policy. At the time of writing, the U.S. Congress is debating a new bill that could potentially provide universal pre-K and paid parental leave for families across the United States. However, these policies were first administered in states and municipalities long before they were taken seriously at the federal level. Places like Oklahoma have had universal pre-K for four-year-olds since 1998. New York City and Washington, D.C., also instituted universal public pre-K in 2014 and 2009, respectively. Although few federal representatives currently advocate for similar levels of public support for university education, cities like Kalamazoo, Michigan, have established programs that fund public university education for all graduates of local high schools.[1]

Bruce Katz and Jeremy Nowak (2017) have described the growing influence of local government as *new localism*. The smaller scale of cities compared to nations allows for greater flexibility and ease of passing legislative agendas. Meanwhile, urban markets with concentrated industries have a growing influence on the global economy. As a result, Katz and Nowak argue that local actions are not only highly impactful for the immediate residents of municipalities and metro areas but are increasingly shaping the direction of federal policy. Local governments provide a natural "testing ground" where innovative policy solutions can be piloted before being implemented on a national scale. Indeed, it was Berkeley, California, that passed the first domestic partnership ordinance in 1984 that spread to same-sex marriage laws across several U.S. states and eventually led to the national recognition of same-sex marriage in 2015. Presently, local legislation is leading the way toward universal public health care, with San Francisco successfully implementing this program as it gains momentum on the national stage (Seipel 2017).

This book shows that new localism also applies to gender inequality, as local environments play a fundamental role in gender relations and the opportunities or barriers experienced by women and men. Local gender norms shape the attitudes and behaviors of residents, which, in turn, sustain ongoing patterns of occupational gender segregation and the gender wage gap. Recognizing the role of local norms in the reproduction of inequality provides new opportunities to address these patterns and foster fair and equitable communities. By virtue of being smaller than nations or states, commuting zones have more flexibility in successfully implementing creative policy. They also have the ability to change more rapidly. The fact that commuting zones consist of individuals who reside, work, and play alongside one another may accelerate cultural change when/if it begins.

In this concluding chapter, I summarize key contributions of the book. Along the way, I highlight how we can use these insights to improve gender equality in our communities. I also discuss how gender norms intersect with other dimensions of local culture and inequality in proposing future research building from the topics covered here. Last, I argue that a focus on local communities provides new opportunities to implement policies that advance gender equality. I highlight several local governments that have successfully done this and conclude with a call for greater attention to be devoted to the communities where we live, work, and play. Joining our neighbors to create local change can be an effective strategy to build toward broader and collective progress.

The Structure, Causes, and Consequences of Local Gender Norms

Chicago is the City of Big Shoulders, New Orleans is known as the Big Easy, and Detroit is revered as the Motor City. Places throughout the United States have unique cultural reputations that are often a source of pride for residents. Within these well-known characterizations, however, exist a highly influential layer of gender norms that shape residents' attitudes and local patterns of gender inequality. The primary contribution of this book is that it brings this layer into focus. Examining the way eight indicators of local gender norms vary systematically across U.S. commuting zones reveals that places not only have distinct gender norms but that these norms are composed of four separate dimensions. The first, *women's advancement*, relates to support for women's careers and leadership. Second, *public sphere gender essentialism* describes the extent to which people believe women and men are naturally suited for different types of work. The third dimension is referred to as *intensive mothering* and captures local expectations toward mothers' balance of careers and childcare. Finally, the fourth dimension, *private sphere gender essentialism*, pertains to expectations toward the gendered division of labor in the family.

Identifying the four dimensions of gender norms makes it possible to chart how places can be egalitarian in some respects while exhibiting traditional norms in others. Milwaukee, for example, is fairly egalitarian with respect to women's advancement but has traditional norms toward intensive mothering. In contrast, Grand Rapids is somewhat egalitarian across all dimensions except women's advancement, where norms convey men as better suited for leadership than women. In other instances, places that trend egalitarian or traditional show variation in the intensity of each dimension. Indianapolis is egalitarian across all dimensions, but particularly in norms toward private sphere gender essentialism, which convey expectations of equal caregiving for both women and men. Norms in Houston trend traditional across all four dimensions but are closer to average for public sphere gender essentialism.

Mapping the distribution of these local configurations of gender norms across the United States revealed significant spatial variation. Places in close proximity commonly have very different cultural environments. Madison and Milwaukee are separated by less than eighty miles, but gender norms in Madison are far more egalitarian, particularly with respect to the family. In Kentucky, Lexington and Louisville are neighboring commuting zones, but norms in Louisville are more egalitarian than Lexington in all four dimensions. Across the United States, one need not travel very far to experience a distinct set of local gender norms.

The diversity of gender norms in the United States is striking, particularly considering how advances in technology, social media, and transportation make it easier than ever to communicate or regularly visit places across the country. If spatial divides are shrinking in many respects, how do local gender norms remain distinct, even between neighboring commuting zones? To examine this question, I tested two possible reasons. First, local gender norms could be sustained by differences in the types of people who live there—otherwise known as *compositional effects*. Research shows that highly educated individuals, for example, tend to have more egalitarian gender attitudes. If these individuals make up a larger share of the population in some areas than others, this may contribute to local gender norms through differences in demographic composition. The second possible mechanism is *contextual effects*, where the experience of residing in places with certain norms influences individuals' behaviors and attitudes. From this perspective, residents' sense of identity, preferences, and perceptions of others are shaped by the local norms in the geographic environment where they live and work.

Both compositional and contextual effects help sustain local gender norms, but contextual effects play a larger role. The demographic, economic, and cultural composition of residents across commuting zones accounted for only 23 to 38 percent of spatial variation in local gender norms. Compositional effects do contribute to local norms, but their influence is limited. Instead, contextual effects of local norms on individuals' attitudes are much more consequential. I identified contextual effects by comparing whether the education and religion gaps in gender attitudes varied across places with different gender norms. On average, the college educated hold greater support for gender equality than those with lower levels of education. But this attitudinal gap disappears in places with traditional gender norms toward women's advancement and public sphere gender essentialism. This indicates that traditional gender norms cause the college educated, who would otherwise hold much greater support for equality, to possess conventional views no different from the less educated. A parallel pattern was observed for religion. On average, individuals affiliated with liberal (e.g., United Methodist) or moderate (e.g., Lutheran) religions hold greater support for gender equality than those affiliated with fundamentalist (e.g., Southern Baptist) religions. Yet this gap disappears in traditional contexts, particularly among religious moderates and in attitudes toward working mothers and the family division of labor. This indicates that the contextual experience of residing in places with traditional norms causes religious moderates and liberals, who would otherwise hold greater support for gender equality, to possess conventional views that align with local traditionalism.

Recognizing the role of contextual effects in sustaining local gender norms reveals the importance of space in persistent gender traditionalism. Scholars have long been puzzled by the lack of progress in support for gender equality since the mid-1990s, a pattern referred to as the "stalled gender revolution" (England 2010). The findings presented here suggest that a major source of this stall stems from the contextual effects of traditional communities throughout the United States. In these environments where traditional gender norms prevail, conventional attitudes are supported and reinforced.

This is true even among those whom we would expect to hold egalitarian views, such as the college educated or religious liberals. Instead of changing local norms, these individuals develop personal attitudes that align with, and therefore reinforce, such traditional environments.

If gender norms are sustained by shaping individuals' attitudes, it is therefore possible that they also shape local patterns of gender inequality. Indeed, I found that gender norms are strongly correlated to levels of the gender wage gap in commuting zones across the United States, with more egalitarian places having lower gender wage gaps. This was true across the dimensions of norms related to women's advancement, public sphere gender essentialism, and private sphere gender essentialism. Norms toward intensive mothering did not relate to gender wage gaps, although previous research has shown that this dimension is associated with women's employment (Ruppanner et al. 2021).

Two mechanisms underlie the relationship of local gender norms to gender wage gaps. First, norms operate through influencing the *occupational sorting* of women and men into different jobs with varying pay. Scholars have shown that occupational gender segregation is a major contributor to the gender wage gap because women more commonly work in jobs with lower pay than men (Blau and Kahn 2017). Focusing on four occupations with different pay, job requirements, and gender compositions reveals that places with more egalitarian gender norms had a higher concentration of women in high-paying management and STEM jobs as well as a lower concentration of women in low-paying office administration jobs. The strongest effects were observed for the dimension of norms related to public sphere gender essentialism, indicating that norms that convey women and men as essentially different play a major role in the sorting of women into lower-paying occupations. Local egalitarianism also improved women's representation in low-paying, male-dominated, blue-collar jobs. This shows that local norms shape occupational sorting more generally and not only in ways that reduce the gender wage gap.

A second mechanism underlying the relationship of local norms to gender wage gaps is *within-occupation valuation*, where women's work is commonly valued and rewarded less than men who hold the same job. Scholars such as Claudia Goldin (2014a, 2014b) have argued that these differences in valuation reflect men's efforts to retain privilege in occupations that are becoming more gender integrated. To examine this mechanism, I tested whether local gender norms predicted wage gaps between women and men workers in the same occupation. In general, within-occupation valuation was fairer, with women being paid more similarly to men in the same position, in places with more egalitarian gender norms. However, these patterns were not universal. Only in management and office administration roles did egalitarian norms toward women's advancement, public sphere gender essentialism, and private sphere gender essentialism predict lower within-occupation wage gaps. Women make up a substantial share of workers in each of these two occupations, accounting for 43 percent of managers and 73 percent of office administrators. In contrast, local norms did not relate to within-occupation valuation in male-dominated STEM (70 percent men) and blue-collar (83 percent men) roles. Here, wage gaps remained high regardless of local norms. This pattern highlights a crucial point about local gender norms: Their influence is not deterministic and can be resisted. In male-dominated STEM and blue-collar occupations where men have an interest in maintaining their privilege, local norms of egalitarianism are resisted as men retain wage premiums.

To briefly summarize, there are three major contributions of this book. First, commuting zones have distinct configurations of gender norms across four dimensions: women's advancement, public sphere gender essentialism, intensive mothering, and private sphere gender essentialism. Second, these distinct configurations of local gender norms are sustained largely by contextual effects where exposure to local norms shapes individuals' attitudes to align with prevailing values. Contextual effects are most pronounced in places with traditional norms, where individuals we would expect to hold more egalitarian views, such as the college educated and religiously moderate/liberal, espouse conventional gender attitudes. Third, local gender norms are strongly related to patterns of gender inequality. They shape the sorting of women and men into different occupations with varying pay, as well as the unfair valuation of women and men in the same occupation. Yet local norms of egalitarianism have less influence in male-dominated occupations where men have an interest in maintaining wage premiums.

Where new insight is drawn, new questions develop. With the recognition that places have distinct gender norms, we can now investigate how these norms are resisted and how they can be changed. We can explore their intersection with other dimensions of culture and stratification, such as systems of racism and heterosexism. Questions also remain about how local norms relate to local policies, as well as how norms operate in reciprocal relationships with levels of inequality and women's labor force participation. I now consider these future pursuits.

The Path Forward and Intersectional Dimensions of Inequality

Throughout the preceding pages, I have focused almost exclusively on gender inequality and gender norms. Yet gender intersects with other forms of inequality that also vary across the United States. Many places experiencing economic booms in recent decades have also had unprecedented growth in class inequality between the poor and the rich (Reardon and Bischoff 2011). Research on racial segregation has long recognized that cities have different patterns of racial inequality sustained through discrimination, residential segregation, and the uneven distribution of public resources (Massey and Denton 1993; Quillian 2012). Studies on space and sexuality have established that places convey different cultural values that embrace or sanction lesbian, gay, bisexual, transgender, and queer (LGBTQ) identities and expressions (Ghaziani 2015). My focus on gender norms throughout this book adds a vital, if ultimately incomplete, layer to the expansive literature on space and inequality. In addition to being characterized by patterns of inequality across race, class, and sexuality, I have shown that places also contain distinct configurations of gender norms.

We know many of the local features that shape residents' lives and patterns of inequality. What we need now is an understanding of how these components interact, co-construct, or contradict one another. Places have distinct gender norms. Previous research has also highlighted how places have distinct patterns of racial inequality. How are these related? Do egalitarian gender norms help reduce racial inequality? Or does their effect depend on local levels of racism and racial discrimination that influence whether gender-egalitarian logics are used for equitable ends or, rather, as liberal justification for white people's resource accumulation?

There are no clear answers at this point, but the findings presented here, as well as existing research, suggest that intersecting patterns may shed important light on the mechanisms sustaining social inequality in U.S. commuting zones. There is some evidence that egalitarian norms may reduce gender inequality across race. The examination of wage gaps in Chapter 5 revealed that local egalitarianism was associated with smaller gender wage gaps for Black, Hispanic, and White residents. Other research also indicates that traditional gender norms may worsen levels of racial inequality. Focusing on Toronto, Leslie Kern (2020) found that traditional gender norms can be a driver of gentrification that displaces low-income residents who are disproportionately Black and Hispanic. In some neighborhoods, Kern observed that middle-class White parents draw on traditional norms of intensive mothering in demands for upscale resources, such as high-end shopping and children's stores, that are unaffordable and inaccessible for longtime residents. In other instances, conventional tropes of women's vulnerability are used by gentrifying residents who request greater police presence and security. Such tropes have historically been applied to White women and used to justify racial violence, particularly against Black men (Hamilton et al. 2019). Kern draws parallels between this history and her observations in gentrifying neighborhoods as both White women and White men petition for greater police presence that disproportionately targets Black residents on the basis of White women's perceived need for protection.

Although there is good reason to expect that traditional gender norms worsen other forms of inequality, whereas egalitarian norms improve them, it is also possible that egalitarian gender norms are strategically used to sustain power disparities along other axes of inequality. As discussed in Chapter 2, individuals are not "cultural dopes" but instead recognize prevailing norms and adopt strategies of action to navigate complex interactions (Swidler 2001). In places where gender egalitarianism prevails, individuals may express feminist attitudes in order to acquire resources and further their privilege on another dimension of inequality. These dynamics were observed in a recent study by Joanna Pepin, Danny Lambouths III, Ronald Kwon, Ronaldo Monasterio and I (Scarborough, Pepin, et al. 2021) where we found that White men commonly hold anti-sexist attitudes alongside regressive racial attitudes that view African Americans in a negative light. The consequence of holding anti-sexist but not anti-racist attitudes is that White men's superficially feminist opinions operate as a form of racial resource hoarding. Because White men are most commonly partnered with White women, they often benefit from White women's advances in the labor market and additional contributions to household income. Therefore, the combination of anti-sexist views alongside regressive racial attitudes means that they only support gender equality for White women, from whom they are more likely to indirectly benefit. These findings illustrate how gender egalitarian attitudes can be used as a mechanism sustaining racial inequality. Similar trends may play out at the aggregate level of commuting zones in instances where egalitarian gender norms prevail but occur alongside high levels of racism. In such settings, the benefits of gender egalitarian norms would be primarily observed among White women and associated with worsening racial inequality.

No single book or research project can answer every relevant question on a topic. The best aim is instead to make a clear contribution that generates a new set of valuable questions. By highlighting distinct configurations of gender norms and their relationship to social life, this book provides a firm foundation for research devoted more directly to multiple intersecting features of local communities. We can proceed with an understanding that places have distinct gender norms. What we need next is to understand whether they also have racial norms or environments that convey different configurations of racism. A great deal of research has uncovered how levels of racial inequality and patterns of residential racial segregation vary across the United States (Massey and Denton 1993; Quillian 2012). Considering how these structural conditions co-occur with varying cultural features may add important insight to our understanding of how local forms of racial inequality are sustained. From this point, we can further investigate how local gender norms and racisms interrelate and their dynamic configurations. This type of research would provide valuable insight on the ways local norms may be mutually constitutive if, for instance, traditional gender norms are used to justify regressive racial norms. Such a research agenda would also uncover faults in progressive racial and gender norms if, in some instances, egalitarian gender norms co-occurred alongside regressive racisms. This would add crucial insight to our understanding of how contradictory norms may operate to sustain intersecting systems of power.

Additional limitations of this book offer important opportunities for future research. My primary goal was to map local gender norms across the United States and identify their general patterns with individuals' attitudes, behaviors, and local levels of gender inequality. This goal required quantitative analysis that used large-scale nationally comprehensive data across all U.S. commuting zones. As discussed in Chapter 1, such an approach excels at breadth—describing broad and generalizable trends—but not depth, which would uncover greater detail in local norms and the way they are experienced in individuals' lives. Characterizing each commuting zone's local culture with the four dimensions of gender norms allowed me to make general comparisons between places and chart their relationship to individuals' attitudes and levels of inequality. But it also obscured each place's unique history and context. It was not possible, for example, to discuss the long history of radical feminist organizing in Dayton, Ohio (Ezekiel 2002) or the role of conservative groups such as the Tea Party in opposing gender equality and women's rights in places like Tallahassee (Rohlinger and Brown 2009). These are important details of each place's local culture but aspects that are not readily comparable to other locations and therefore given less attention in the large-scale comparative approach used here. Future research drawing from residents' experiences and the history of places across the United States will add valuable nuance to our understanding of how local norms originate and their dynamic impact on individuals' lives.

Finally, future research may devote greater attention to understanding the dynamic relationship between local norms and patterns of inequality. As discussed in Chapter 5, norms and levels of inequality are reciprocal and mutually reinforcing. Further disentangling this relationship will help shed light on the ways we may address levels of inequality and foster more egalitarian norms. For example, future research may investigate the conditions where cultural change leads to improvements in local gender equality and other instances where it may be resisted. Results from Chapter 5 show that male-dominated subcultures, such as those in STEM and blue-collar occupations, may actively resist egalitarian norms that would otherwise promote equality. Additional research is needed to investigate whether there are conditions where these occupations may be more embracing of egalitarian norms as well as the role of additional subcultures that actively resist egalitarian norms or those that actively promote them.

The Promise of Local Culture

One conspicuous feature of the feminist movement in the United States is that it has had limited impact on federal policy that would support gender equality. The United States remains the only industrialized nation without paid parental leave and is one of only a few nations without publicly supported childcare. At the time of writing, the U.S. Congress is debating an expansive bill that would include paid parental leave, universal pre-K, childcare subsidies, and child allowance benefits. The odds are slim that all policies will be approved. Instead, legislators are likely to select only one, keeping the United States far behind other developed nations in terms of family policy that would support mothers and gender equality.

The absence of public policy that would support gender equality is even more surprising when we consider recent research showing that over 80 percent of Americans support policies like paid family leave and a substantial share endorse gender equality in the home and workplace (Horowitz, Parker, and Livingston 2017; Scarborough, Sin, and Risman 2019). Why, then, has the United States failed to institute popular policies that would help achieve the common aim of gender equality? Recall the spatial distribution of gender norms illustrated in Chapter 3. Although there was significant variation within regions, the East and West Coasts generally had more egalitarian norms, whereas the central and southern regions were more traditional. This corresponds closely to electoral maps where coastal states have liberal politics and are democratic leaning, whereas inland states are the opposite. These inland states have smaller populations but nonetheless have an equal number of senators and greater per capita influence in the Electoral College than coastal states with larger populations that also tend to have more egalitarian norms. This means that power in the federal government is weighted in favor of places in the United States where traditional gender norms prevail. As a result, federal policy is often more regressive in terms of gender equality than the nation's population as a whole.

I am not suggesting that efforts to change federal policy are a waste of time. It is crucial that we preserve existing protections and continue to push for the expansion of policy that promotes gender equality. I am suggesting, however, that efforts to change policy will be more successful and prompt quicker change if directed at the local levels of commuting zones and municipalities.

Municipalities are ideally positioned to take the lead on policy that would promote gender equality. Many places in the United States already have highly egalitarian gender norms and would have little trouble gathering support for policies that support equality between women and men. Once these places implement policy, surrounding areas may follow. To begin to gather support for local policy, it is crucial that more attention be directed to local levels of inequality. Merely by documenting levels of the gender wage gap across cities in the United States, researchers and journalists provide a level of accountability that forces public leaders to respond and take action to ameliorate gender inequality. Although this approach may be more effective for cities with higher-than-average gender wage gaps, even leaders in places like San Francisco and Washington, D.C., can be held accountable by tracking whether progress is being maintained over time or if gender wage gaps have remained unchanged or worsened.

Local leaders can start, therefore, by bringing attention to the state of gender inequality in their area. Then, they can suggest effective policy to address inequities. This strategy has already taken shape in some places across the United States. Leaders in the city of Chattanooga, for example, took immediate action after the Institute for Women's Policy Research (2015) ranked Tennessee as the forty-ninth worst state in the country for the status of women. The Women's Fund of Greater Chattanooga established the "49 to 1" campaign with the goal of improving Tennessee's ranking to the best in the nation. As part of the campaign, they advocate for specific bills to be passed in the state legislature that would improve local levels of gender equality. These bills include the Tennessee Pay Equality Act that forbids gender wage discrimination and the Pregnancy Workers Fairness Act designed to ensure pregnant workers receive necessary accommodations. At the municipal level, the city of Chattanooga has established the Mayor's Council on Women that conducts research on local issues related to women and gender with the purpose of providing direct recommendations to the mayor and city council on policies that will improve women's lives in the city.

Those who have been working to support gender equality in their community will have the best idea of what policies may be most effective at improving local conditions. To assist in those efforts, here are a few local policies that have surfaced across the United States that serve as examples of initiatives with the potential to support equality.

Policies to Remedy Gender Pay Gaps: Several cities and states across the United States have instituted policies aimed at removing hiring practices that have been found to increase gender wage gaps. Chicago, New Orleans, New York City, and Massachusetts, for example, have banned employers from asking job applicants about previous pay history. The practice of using pay history to set initial salary offers exacerbates gender wage disparities because wage gaps in previous positions end up depressing wages in future jobs. Other states, such as California, Colorado, and Michigan, have banned employers from enforcing pay secrecy policies where workers are forbidden from disclosing their salaries. These regulations improve wage transparency and keep employers accountable to fair wage regulations.

Paid Parental Leave: Paid parental leave is gaining support in cities and states across the country. In 2020, Washington, D.C., instituted a parental leave policy that provides new mothers and fathers eight weeks of leave while receiving up to 90 percent of their salary. On a smaller scale, city workers in Austin receive thirty days of paid parental leave. While not as generous or comprehensive as the leave policies in Washington, D.C., parental leave in Austin is a step in the right direction and provides a foundation for further expansion. It also illustrates how municipalities can institute progressive policies even in locations where state governments are heavily Republican and opposed to these types of initiatives.

Public-Sponsored/Subsidized Childcare: In 2014, New York City made history by providing free universal preschool for children in the city. Following New York, Seattle passed legislation to heavily subsidize preschool. Policies to support childcare for infants and children aged three and younger have been more difficult to pass due to the fact that early childcare facilities are rarely associated with public schools (as preschools are) and can be much more expensive due to the lower teacher-to-child ratios. Nonetheless, the Kids First Childcare Financial Assistance Program in Aspen, Colorado, subsidizes childcare for families who are financially eligible and also helps parents identify and enroll children in a licensed daycare. This program is funded by a local sales tax, benefiting from the high levels of tourism in the region. While few cities may have such massive flows of revenue from outside visitors, other areas may learn from the program in Aspen by leveraging their unique economic assets to generate the public funds necessary to support early childcare.

Conclusion

In the preceding pages, I have made three primary arguments. First, commuting zones across the United States have different gender norms. These norms are composed of four dimensions related to women's advancement, public sphere gender essentialism, intensive mothering, and private sphere gender essentialism. Second, these norms are sustained through shaping individuals' attitudes and behaviors in ways that align with prevailing cultural values. Through exposure to local norms, individuals come to align their personal views with common expectations. This is particularly true in places with traditional gender norms. Third, gender norms are highly related to patterns of inequality. Gender wage gaps are lower in more egalitarian environments and higher in more traditional ones. This pattern is driven by the relationship of local norms to occupational sorting as well as within-occupation gender differences in valuation. In egalitarian commuting zones, women have greater access to high-paying occupations and are less concentrated in low-paying positions. Within the same occupation, women's work is valued more equally to men in egalitarian commuting zones than in traditional ones. However, exceptions to this pattern were found in male-dominated STEM and blue-collar occupations where men incumbents resist egalitarian pressures that may limit their unearned privileges.

All of us live within an environment of norms that convey particular messages about gender. Our consciousness of these norms can empower us to be active agents in changing them. We can realize how gendered logics shape, often unconsciously, whom we consider to be appropriate for certain occupations and qualified to hold leadership positions. We can continue to talk about gender inequality, raising consciousness of the gender structure and building support for policies that advance equality. We can join public demonstrations advocating for women's rights or engage in online discussions about the state of gender inequality. All these actions, and many more, contribute to cultural change. I suggest we should continue to bring attention to patterns of inequality and their causes in whatever way possible. Then, we can translate those concerns into policy, both at the federal level and locally. Valuable opportunities for equitable progress can be found at the local level of city governments where change is most feasible. Realizing the tremendous role of local norms in social life, we can join our neighbors to build a more equitable future, starting with our own communities.

Notes

CHAPTER 1

1. See Amazon HQ2 request for proposal, available at https://images-na.ssl-images -amazon.com/images/G/01/Anything/test/images/usa/RFP_3._V516043504_.pdf.

CHAPTER 2

1. Some of the data used in this analysis are derived from Sensitive Data Files of the GSS, obtained under special contractual arrangements designed to protect the anonymity of respondents. These data are not available from the author. Persons interested in obtaining GSS Sensitive Data Files should contact the GSS at GSS@NORC.org.

2. Generally, between one thousand and two thousand respondents are surveyed by the GSS every two years. This means that in any given survey year, there are not enough respondents in each commuting zone to produce reliable aggregate estimates. Therefore, I follow methods from prior research in combining surveys across years of data and adjusting for potential longitudinal change (Ruppanner et al. 2021; Scarborough and Sin 2020). I pooled all available survey years from 2000 through 2018 to increase sample sizes within each commuting zone. Respondents were matched to commuting zones by county because counties do not intersect commuting zone boundaries. Commuting zones with less than thirty GSS respondents were recoded as missing, and full information maximum likelihood was used to retain these missing cases in the confirmatory factor analysis (discussed later in the chapter as the method for measuring gender norms). The total sample for this item includes 13,549 respondents across eighty-four commuting zones. Previous research has shown that gender attitudes have generally stalled since the mid-1990s after a period of more rapid change in the 1980s (England 2010; Scarborough, Sin, and Risman 2019). This suggests that the gender attitudes measured here from 2000 through 2018 were relatively stable. Nonetheless, to account for

potential shifting conditions during the span of time covered by the data, I used a varying intercept (by commuting zone) logistic regression equation with fixed effects for survey year. The resulting estimate is the year-adjusted proportion of respondents in each commuting zone who disagree with the statement that men are better suited for politics than women. This approach has been used and validated in previous research (Ruppanner et al. 2021; Scarborough and Moeder 2022; Scarborough and Sin 2020).

3. See the Project Implicit website, available at https://implicit.harvard.edu/implicit /index.jsp. To take an IAT, select "Project Implicit Social Attitudes" and follow the prompts.

4. I used data from 2005 (when the Gender-Career IAT was first available) through 2018 to increase sample sizes within commuting zones. The total sample was 945,181 respondents. To adjust for the multiple years represented in the data, I used a varying intercept (by commuting zone) regression model with fixed effects for year to calculate the adjusted average of commuting zone implicit attitudes. Respondents were matched to commuting zones by county because counties do not intersect commuting zone boundaries.

5. I used data spanning 2003 (when the Gender-Science IAT was first available) through 2018. The total sample included 625,576 respondents. A varying intercept regression model (by commuting zone) with fixed effects for year was used to calculate commuting zone-adjusted average implicit attitudes toward women in science. Respondents were matched to commuting zones by county because counties do not intersect commuting zone boundaries.

6. The ACS is the most comprehensive source of sociodemographic data available among nationally representative surveys. The ACS is conducted annually, and the U.S. Census Bureau recommends using five-year samples when generating spatial estimates. Five-year samples pool consecutive years of the ACS, which are intentionally sampled to ensure that no respondents are surveyed twice and are weighted to be nationally representative. I use ACS individual-level microdata from the Integrated Public Use Microdata Series (Ruggles et al. 2020) and assign respondents to commuting zones by geospatially matching Public Use Microdata Areas (PUMAs, the most detailed spatial unit identified in the microdata) to commuting zones. In the few instances where PUMAs straddle the borders of commuting zones, I adopted the approach used in previous research (Autor and Dorn 2013; Dorn 2009; Scarborough and Sin 2020) and weighted respondents based on the likelihood of belonging to a commuting zone, calculated from the proportion of PUMA population residing in each commuting zone, determined at the census-block level with the Geocorr application from the Missouri Census Data Center (2018) (see Scarborough and Sin 2020). The ACS sample is restricted to those with a college degree and included a total of 3,719,804 respondents.

7. The index of dissimilarity is calculated as the summed absolute difference in the number of women and men across fields of study relative to their overall population among college degree holders. Estimates from the index are interpreted as the proportion of women and men who would have to change educational fields for there to be perfect gender integration, with a score of zero indicating perfect integration and a score of one reflecting absolute segregation.

8. I used the same procedure discussed in note 2 to aggregate responses on this GSS survey question to commuting zones. The total sample for this item was 14,402 respondents across eighty-nine commuting zones.

9. Note 2 discusses the method used to aggregate this GSS item to commuting zones. The total sample was 14,274 respondents across eighty-eight commuting zones.

10. I use the methods discussed in note 2 to aggregate this item to commuting zones. The total sample included 14,298 respondents across eighty-six commuting zones.

11. A detailed discussion of the data collection, coding, and validation of these tweets is provided in my 2018 article in the journal *Socius* (see Scarborough 2018a). Briefly, I used the search Twitter API to collect a sample of 118,793 tweets about feminism that were matched to U.S. commuting zones using the stated location in each user's bio. I used Botometer (Varol et al. 2017) to identify and remove tweets produced by bots, which reduced the sample to 105,066. Of these, about half (51,562) were retweets consisting of 3,605 unique texts. I qualitatively coded these as either holding positive or negative sentiment toward feminism. The remaining 53,504 tweets were unique texts. To code these, I used naive Bayes sentiment analysis with supervised learning. First, I developed a training set using a 5 percent sample of the unique tweets. I used this training set to generate a lexicon of one-word and two-word sets (also known as tokens) found in positive and negative tweets about feminism. In these sets, each one- and two-word token has a probability of being found in a negative or positive tweet toward feminism. I applied these tokens and associated probabilities to the naive Bayes equation to calculate the full probability of a tweet being negative or positive. Tweets were assigned as either positive or negative depending on which sentiment was more probable as determined by the product of probabilities assigned to the one- and two-word tokens it contained.

12. Because the two variables from Project Implicit come from the same source of nonrepresentative data and may be correlated due to shared sampling biases, I have specified their error terms to be correlated. For illustrative clarity, this is not specified in Figure 2.1.

CHAPTER 3

1. Best Buy has since stopped ROWE, citing financial concerns during the 2007–2009 recession. ROWE expert and sociologist Phyllis Moen described the decision to end ROWE as a reversion to conventional practices that often occurs when companies experience tough times. Although ROWE is no longer official Best Buy policy, Moen also reported that many offices in the company continue to operate according to its structure (Stevenson 2014).

CHAPTER 4

1. The model used to calculate full effects includes a fixed effect for year because data are from the pooled GSS spanning years 2000 through 2018.

CHAPTER 5

1. I identified management occupations using the Standard Occupational Classification (SOC) coding structure from the Bureau of Labor Statistics. Respondents classified as employed in a management occupation (SOC code 11) were coded as managers.

2. I identify STEM occupations according to the Bureau of Labor Statistics classification that includes roles related to computing, mathematics, architecture, engineering, life sciences, and physical sciences (see U.S. Bureau of Labor Statistics 2021).

3. Office administrators include those classified as "office and administrative support occupations" (SOC code 43) in the Bureau of Labor Statistics SOC structure. Blue-

collar occupations are classified in ways consistent with prior research (Joseph et al. 2016) that include farming/fishing/forestry, construction/extraction, installation/maintenance/repair, production, and transportation/material moving jobs (SOC codes 45, 47, 49, 51, and 53).

4. Each model includes controls for the following individual-level characteristics: gender, race (White, Black, Hispanic, and other race), age, age squared, education (less than high school, high school degree, some college, college degree or more), marital status (married/unmarried), work experience (age minus years in school minus 6), work experience squared, and hours worked (less than thirty-five, thirty-five to forty-nine, fifty or more). I also include controls for commuting zone characteristics to ensure that the predicted relationship of norms to employment is not driven by spurious observed characteristics of localities. These include the share of workers in the service industry, managerial/professional intensity (share of total jobs that are managerial or professional), the unemployment rate, the share of residents with a college degree, the percent foreign born, and the racial composition (percent Black, percent Hispanic, percent Asian, percent other race). Because respondents are clustered by commuting zones, the intercept in each equation varies by commuting zone. Each equation also included an interaction term between gender and local norms to capture whether local gender norms affect the sorting of women and men into different occupations. From this interaction term, I calculated how the probability of employment in each occupation shifted for women and men when we compare places that differ by one unit of egalitarianism on a dimension of local gender norms. This difference is equal to comparing egalitarian to very egalitarian places or traditional locales to average ones.

5. I included a fixed effect for respondents' five-digit SOC occupation within each of the four general occupations of management, STEM, office administration, and blue collar.

CHAPTER 6

1. See the Kalamazoo Promise website, available at https://www.kalamazoopromise.com/.

References

Abelson, Miriam. 2019. *Men in Place: Trans Masculinity, Race, and Sexuality in America*. Minneapolis: University of Minnesota Press.

Acock, Alan C. 2013. *Discovering Structural Equation Modeling Using Stata: Revised Edition*. 1st ed. College Station, TX: Stata Press.

Adams, Jimi. 2007. "Stained Glass Makes the Ceiling Visible: Organizational Opposition to Women in Congregational Leadership." *Gender & Society* 21 (1): 80–105.

Albrecht, Don, and Carol Albrecht. 2010. "Economic Restructuring and Education in the Nonmetropolitan United States." *Journal of Rural Social Sciences* 25 (1): 60–89.

Alegria, Sharla. 2019. "Escalator or Step Stool? Gendered Labor and Token Processes in Tech Work." *Gender & Society* 33 (5): 722–45.

Alexander, C. J. 2020. "Alexander: The LDS Church Needs to Step Back from Influencing State Policy." *Daily Utah Chronicle*, September 20, 2020. Available at https://dailyutah chronicle.com/2020/09/19/alexander-church-state/.

Alfrey, Lauren, and France Winddance Twine. 2017. "Gender-Fluid Geek Girls: Negotiating Inequality Regimes in the Tech Industry." *Gender & Society* 31 (1): 28–50.

Arkes, Hal R., and Philip E. Tetlock. 2004. "Attributions of Implicit Prejudice, or 'Would Jesse Jackson "Fail" the Implicit Association Test?'" *Psychological Inquiry* 15 (4): 257–78.

Autor, David H, and David Dorn. 2013. "The Growth of Low-Skill Service Jobs and the Polarization of the US Labor Market." *American Economic Review* 103 (5): 1553–97.

Berenson, Barbara F. 2018. *Massachusetts in the Woman Suffrage Movement: Revolutionary Reformers*. Charleston, SC: History Press Library Editions.

Bettie, Julie. 2003. *Women without Class: Girls, Race, and Identity*. Oakland: University of California Press.

Bianchi, Suzanne M., John P. Robinson, and Melissa A. Milke. 2006. *The Changing Rhythms of American Family Life*. Russell Sage Foundation.

Bielby, William T., and James N. Baron. 1986. "Men and Women at Work: Sex Segregation and Statistical Discrimination." *American Journal of Sociology* 91 (4): 759–99.

Blau, Francine D., and Lawrence M. Kahn. 2017. "The Gender Wage Gap: Extent, Trends, and Explanations." *Journal of Economic Literature* 55 (3): 789–865.

Bloom, Joshua, and Waldo E. Martin. 2016. *Black against Empire: The History and Politics of the Black Panther Party*. Oakland: University of California Press.

Boeckmann, Irene, Joya Misra, and Michelle J. Budig. 2015. "Cultural and Institutional Factors Shaping Mothers' Employment and Working Hours in Postindustrial Countries." *Social Forces* 93 (4): 1301–33.

Boltanski, Luc, and Laurent Thévenot. 2006. *On Justification*. Princeton, NJ: Princeton University Press.

Bolzendahl, Catherine I., and Daniel J. Myers. 2004. "Feminist Attitudes and Support for Gender Equality: Opinion Change in Women and Men, 1974–1998." *Social Forces* 83 (2): 759–89.

Bourdieu, Pierre. 1984. *Distinction: A Social Critique of the Judgement of Taste*. Cambridge, MA: Harvard University Press.

———. 1990. *The Logic of Practice*. Stanford, CA: Stanford University Press.

Brescoll, Victoria L. 2011. "Who Takes the Floor and Why: Gender, Power, and Volubility in Organizations." *Administrative Science Quarterly* 56 (4): 622–41.

Brewster, Karin L., and Irene Padavic. 2000. "Change in Gender-Ideology, 1977–1996: The Contributions of Intracohort and Change in Population Turnover." *Journal of Marriage and Family* 62 (2): 477–87.

Brooks, Clem, and Catherine Bolzendahl. 2004. "The Transformation of US Gender Role Attitudes: Cohort Replacement, Social-Structural Change, and Ideological Learning." *Social Science Research* 33 (1): 106–33.

Brown, Timothy A. 2015. *Confirmatory Factor Analysis for Applied Research*. 2nd ed. New York: Guilford Press.

Brown-Saracino, Japonica. 2017. *How Places Make Us: Novel LBQ Identities in Four Small Cities*. Chicago, IL: University of Chicago Press.

Bruch, Elizabeth E., and M.E.J. Newman. 2018. "Aspirational Pursuit of Mates in Online Dating Markets." *Science Advances* 4 (8). Available at https://doi.org/10.1126/sciadv .aap9815.

Budig, Michelle J., Joya Misra, and Irene Boeckmann. 2012. "The Motherhood Penalty in Cross-National Perspective: The Importance of Work–Family Policies and Cultural Attitudes." *Social Politics: International Studies in Gender, State & Society* 19 (2): 163–93.

Calnitsky, David. 2019. "The High-Hanging Fruit of the Gender Revolution: A Model of Social Reproduction and Social Change." *Sociological Theory* 37 (1): 35–61.

Campbell, Colin, and Jonathan Horowitz. 2016. "Does College Influence Sociopolitical Attitudes?" *Sociology of Education* 89 (1): 40–58.

Carnevale, Anthony P., Nicole Smith, and Artem Gulish. 2018. "Women Can't Win: Despite Making Educational Gains and Pursuing High-Wage Majors, Women Still Earn Less than Men." Washington, DC: Georgetown University Center on Education and the Workforce.

Catalyst. 2020. "Women in Science, Technology, Engineering, and Mathematics (STEM): Quick Take." *Catalyst*. Available at https://www.catalyst.org/research/women-in-science -technology-engineering-and-mathematics-stem/.

Catsambis, Sophia. 1994. "The Path to Math: Gender and Racial-Ethnic Differences in Mathematics Participation from Middle School to High School." *Sociology of Education* 67 (3): 199–215.

Cech, Erin A. 2013. "The Self-Expressive Edge of Occupational Sex Segregation." *American Journal of Sociology* 119 (3): 747–89.

———. 2014. "Culture of Disengagement in Engineering Education?" *Science, Technology, & Human Values* 39 (1): 42–72.

Cech, Erin A., Mary Blair-Loy, and Laura E. Rogers. 2018. "Recognizing Chilliness: How Schemas of Inequality Shape Views of Culture and Climate in Work Environments." *American Journal of Cultural Sociology* 6 (1): 125–60.

Cha, Youngjoo, and Sarah Thébaud. 2009. "Labor Markets, Breadwinning, and Beliefs: How Economic Context Shapes Men's Gender Ideology." *Gender & Society* 23 (2): 215–43.

Cha, Youngjoo, and Kim A. Weeden. 2014. "Overwork and the Slow Convergence in the Gender Gap in Wages." *American Sociological Review* 79 (3): 457–84.

Charles, Maria, and Karen Bradley. 2009. "Indulging Our Gendered Selves? Sex Segregation by Field of Study in 44 Countries." *American Journal of Sociology* 114 (4): 924–76.

Charles, Maria, and David B. Grusky. 2004. *Occupational Ghettos: The Worldwide Segregation of Women and Men*. Stanford, CA: Stanford University Press.

Chetty, Raj, Nathaniel Hendren, and Lawrence F. Katz. 2016. "The Effects of Exposure to Better Neighborhoods on Children: New Evidence from the Moving to Opportunity Experiment." *American Economic Review* 106 (4): 855–902.

Christofferson, D. Todd. 2013. "The Moral Force of Women." *Ensign* 43:29–33.

Christopherson, Susan, Harry Garretsen, and Ronald Martin. 2008. "The World Is Not Flat: Putting Globalization in Its Place." *Cambridge Journal of Regions, Economy and Society* 1 (3): 343–49.

Clampet-Lundquist, Susan, and Douglas S. Massey. 2008. "Neighborhood Effects on Economic Self-Sufficiency: A Reconsideration of the Moving to Opportunity Experiment." *American Journal of Sociology* 114 (1): 107–43.

Cleave, Evan, and Godwin Arku. 2017. "Putting a Number on Place: A Systematic Review of Place Branding Influence." *Journal of Place Management and Development* 10 (5): 425–46.

Coleman, James S. 1994. *Foundations of Social Theory*. Cambridge, MA: Harvard University Press.

Collins, Caitlyn. 2019. *Making Motherhood Work: How Women Manage Careers and Caregiving*. Princeton, NJ: Princeton University Press.

Collins, Caitlyn, Liana Christin Landivar, Leah Ruppanner, and William J. Scarborough. 2021. "COVID-19 and the Gender Gap in Work Hours." *Gender, Work & Organization* 28 (1): 101–12.

Collins, Patricia Hill. 2008. *Black Feminist Thought: Knowledge, Consciousness, and the Politics of Empowerment*. New York: Routledge.

Combahee River Collective. (1978) 2014. "A Black Feminist Statement." *Women's Studies Quarterly* 42 (3/4): 271–80.

Connell, Raewyn. 1995. *Masculinities*. Cambridge, UK: Polity.

———. 2013. *Gender and Power: Society, the Person and Sexual Politics*. Cambridge, UK: Polity.

Connell, Raewyn, and James W. Messerschmidt. 2005. "Hegemonic Masculinity: Rethinking the Concept." *Gender & Society* 19 (6): 829–59.

Cooper, Marianne. 2000. "Being the 'Go-To Guy': Fatherhood, Masculinity, and the Organization of Work in Silicon Valley." *Qualitative Sociology* 23 (4): 379–405.

Correll, Shelley J. 2001. "Gender and the Career Choice Process: The Role of Biased Self-Assessments." *American Journal of Sociology* 106 (6): 1691–730.

Correll, Shelley J., Stephen Benard, and In Paik. 2007. "Getting a Job: Is There a Mother-hood Penalty?" *American Journal of Sociology* 112 (5): 1297–339.

Correll, Shelley J., Cecilia L. Ridgeway, Ezra W. Zuckerman, Sharon Jank, Sara Jordan-Bloch, and Sandra Nakagawa. 2017. "It's the Conventional Thought That Counts: How Third-Order Inference Produces Status Advantage." *American Sociological Review* 82 (2): 297–327.

Correll, Shelley J., Katherine R. Weisshaar, Alison T. Wynn, and JoAnne Delfino Wehner. 2020. "Inside the Black Box of Organizational Life: The Gendered Language of Per-formance Assessment." *American Sociological Review* 85 (6): 1022–50.

Cotter, David, Joan M. Hermsen, and Reeve Vanneman. 2011. "The End of the Gender Revolution? Gender Role Attitudes from 1977 to 2008." *American Journal of Sociology* 117 (1): 259–89.

Crawley, Sara L. 2011. "Visible Bodies, Vicarious Masculinity, and 'The Gender Revolu-tion': Comment on England." *Gender and Society* 25 (1): 108–12.

Crossley, Alison Dahl. 2017. *Finding Feminism: Millennial Activists and the Unfinished Gender Revolution*. New York: New York University Press.

Daminger, Allison. 2020. "De-Gendered Processes, Gendered Outcomes: How Egalitar-ian Couples Make Sense of Non-Egalitarian Household Practices." *American Socio-logical Review* 85 (5): 806–29.

Darity, William A., and Patrick L. Mason. 1998. "Evidence on Discrimination in Employ-ment: Codes of Color, Codes of Gender." *Journal of Economic Perspectives* 12 (2): 63–90.

Davis, Angela Y. 1983. *Women, Race, & Class*. New York: Vintage.

Davis, Donald R., and Jonathan I. Dingel. 2019. "A Spatial Knowledge Economy." *Amer-ican Economic Review* 109 (1): 153–70.

Dernberger, Brittany N., and Joanna R. Pepin. 2020. "Gender Flexibility, but Not Equal-ity: Young Adults' Division of Labor Preferences." *Sociological Science* 7:36–56. Avail-able at https://doi.org/10.15195/v7.a2.

DiMaggio, Paul. 1997. "Culture and Cognition." *Annual Review of Sociology* 23 (1): 263–87.

Dorn, David. 2009. *Essays on Inequality, Spatial Interaction, and the Demand for Skills*. PhD diss., University of St. Gallen, no. 3613.

Eagly, Alice H. 2007. "Female Leadership Advantage and Disadvantage: Resolving the Contradictions." *Psychology of Women Quarterly* 31 (1): 1–12.

Earl, Jennifer, and Katrina Kimport. 2011. *Digitally Enabled Social Change: Activism in the Internet Age*. Cambridge, MA: MIT Press.

England, Paula. 2005. "Gender Inequality in Labor Markets: The Role of Motherhood and Segregation." *Social Politics: International Studies in Gender, State & Society* 12 (2): 264–88.

———. 2010. "The Gender Revolution: Uneven and Stalled." *Gender & Society* 24 (2): 149–66.

———. 2016. "Sometimes the Social Becomes Personal: Gender, Class, and Sexualities." *American Sociological Review* 81 (1): 4–28.

England, Paula, Andrew Levine, and Emma Mishel. 2020. "Progress toward Gender Equal-ity in the United States Has Slowed or Stalled." *Proceedings of the National Academy of Sciences* 117 (13): 6990–97.

Evans, Alice. 2019. "How Cities Erode Gender Inequality: A New Theory and Evidence from Cambodia." *Gender & Society* 33 (6): 961–84.

Ezekiel, Judith. 2002. *Feminism in the Heartland*. Columbus: Ohio State University Press.

Florida, Richard. 2002a. "Bohemia and Economic Geography." *Journal of Economic Geog-raphy* 2 (1): 55–71.

———. 2002b. "The Economic Geography of Talent." *Annals of the Association of American Geographers* 92 (4): 743–55.

———. 2012. *The Rise of the Creative Class, Revisited*. New York: Basic Books.

———. 2017. "Where's the Real 'Next Silicon Valley'?" *Bloomberg*, June 20, 2017. Available at https://www.bloomberg.com/news/articles/2017-06-20/where-america-s-high-tech-cities-are-and-will-be.

Fowler, Christopher S., Leif Jenson, and Danielle Rhubart. 2019. "Assessing U.S. Labor Market Delineations for Containment, Economic Core, and Wage Correlation." Available at https://Osf.Io/T4hpu/.

Fritsch, Michael, and Michael Wyrwich. 2018. "Regional Knowledge, Entrepreneurial Culture, and Innovative Start-Ups over Time and Space—an Empirical Investigation." *Small Business Economics* 51 (2): 337–53.

Garcia, Lorena. 2012. *Respect Yourself, Protect Yourself: Latina Girls and Sexual Identity*. New York: New York University Press.

Garfinkel, Harold. 1991. *Studies in Ethnomethodology*. 1st ed. Cambridge, UK: Polity.

Gauchat, Gordon, Maura Kelly, and Michael Wallace. 2012. "Occupational Gender Segregation, Globalization, and Gender Earnings Inequality in U.S. Metropolitan Areas." *Gender & Society* 26 (5): 718–47.

Gerson, Kathleen. 2009. *The Unfinished Revolution: Coming of Age in a New Era of Gender, Work, and Family*. Oxford, UK: Oxford University Press.

Ghaziani, Amin. 2015. *There Goes the Gayborhood?* Reprint ed. Princeton, NJ: Princeton University Press.

Gilchrist, Karen. 2019. "This US City Ranks the Best in the World to Be a Woman Entrepreneur." *CNBC*, July 16, 2019. Available at https://www.cnbc.com/2019/07/16/san-francisco-bay-ranks-the-best-city-for-women-entrepreneurs-dell.html.

Givhan, Robin. 2007. "Hillary Clinton's Tentative Dip into New Neckline Territory." *Washington Post*, July 20, 2007. Available at https://www.washingtonpost.com/wp-dyn/content/article/2007/07/19/AR2007071902668.html.

Glauber, Rebecca. 2011. "Limited Access: Gender, Occupational Composition, and Flexible Work Scheduling." *Sociological Quarterly* 52 (3): 472–94.

Goldin, Claudia. 2014a. "A Grand Gender Convergence: Its Last Chapter." *American Economic Review* 104 (4): 1091–1119.

———. 2014b. "A Pollution Theory of Discrimination: Male and Female Differences in Occupations and Earnings." In *Human Capital in History: The American Record*, edited by Leah P. Boustan, Carola Frydman, and Robert A Margo, 313–48. Chicago, IL: University of Chicago Press.

Goldin, Claudia, and Cecilia Rouse. 2000. "Orchestrating Impartiality: The Impact of 'Blind' Auditions on Female Musicians." *American Economic Review* 90 (4): 715–41.

Goldscheider, Frances, Eva Bernhardt, and Trude Lappegård. 2015. "The Gender Revolution: A Framework for Understanding Changing Family and Demographic Behavior." *Population and Development Review* 41 (2): 207–39.

Greenwald, Anthony G., Debbie E. McGhee, and Jordan L. K. Schwartz. 1998. "Measuring Individual Differences in Implicit Cognition: The Implicit Association Test." *Journal of Personality and Social Psychology* 74 (6): 1464–80.

Griswold, Wendy. 1994. *Cultures and Societies in a Changing World*. New York: Sage.

———. 2008. *Regionalism and the Reading Class*. Chicago, IL: University of Chicago Press.

Guenther, Katja. 2010. *Making Their Place: Feminism after Socialism in Eastern Germany*. Stanford, CA: Stanford University Press.

Hamilton, Laura T., Elizabeth A. Armstrong, J. Lotus Seeley, and Elizabeth M. Armstrong. 2019. "Hegemonic Femininities and Intersectional Domination." *Sociological Theory* 37 (4): 315–41.

Harrison, Scott. 2014. "California Retrospective: In 1938, L.A. Woman Went to Jail for Wearing Slacks in Courtroom." *Los Angeles Times*, October 23, 2014. Available at https://www.latimes.com/local/california/la-me-california-retrospective-20141023-story.html.

Hays, Sharon. 1998. *The Cultural Contradictions of Motherhood*. New Haven, CT: Yale University Press.

Healy, Kieran. 2017. "Fuck Nuance." *Sociological Theory* 35 (2): 118–127.

Hegewisch, Ariane, and Zohal Barsi. 2020. "The Gender Wage Gap by Occupation 2019 and by Race and Ethnicity." C490. Washington, DC: Institute for Women's Policy Research.

Hegewisch, Ariane, and Heidi Hartmann. 2019. *The Gender Wage Gap: 2018 Earnings Differences by Race and Ethnicity*. Washington, DC: Institute for Women's Policy Research.

Heilman, Madeline E. 2001. "Description and Prescription: How Gender Stereotypes Prevent Women's Ascent up the Organizational Ladder." *Journal of Social Issues* 57 (4): 657–74.

Heilman, Madeline E., and Julie J. Chen. 2005. "Same Behavior, Different Consequences: Reactions to Men's and Women's Altruistic Citizenship Behavior." *Journal of Applied Psychology* 90 (3): 431–41.

Hofstede, Geert. 1984. *Culture's Consequences: International Differences in Work-Related Values*. New York: Sage.

Hooper, Daire, Joseph Coughlan, and Michael Mullen. 2008. "Structural Equation Modeling: Guidelines for Determining Model Fit." *Electronic Journal of Business Research Methods* 6 (1): 53–60.

Horne, Christine, and Stefanie Mollborn. 2020. "Norms." *Annual Review of Sociology* 46 (4): 1–21.

Horowitz, Juliana Menasce, Kim Parker, and Gretchen Livingston. 2017. "Americans Widely Support Paid Family and Medical Leave, but Differ Over Specific Policies." Washington, DC: Pew Research Center. Available at https://www.pewresearch.org/social-trends/2017/03/23/americans-widely-support-paid-family-and-medical-leave-but-differ-over-specific-policies/.

Hoyt, Crystal L. 2012. "Gender Bias in Employment Contexts: A Closer Examination of the Role Incongruity Principle." *Journal of Experimental Social Psychology* 48 (1): 86–96.

Inglehart, Ronald, and Pippa Norris. 2003. *Rising Tide: Gender Equality and Cultural Change around the World*. Cambridge: Cambridge University Press.

Institute for Women's Policy Research. 2015. "Status of Women in the States: The Best and Worst States Overall for Women in 2015." R#466. Washington, DC: Institute for Women's Policy Research.

International Labour Organization. 2018. "Global Wage Report 2018/19." Geneva, Switzerland: International Labour Organization.

Jackman, Mary R. 1994. *The Velvet Glove: Paternalism and Conflict in Gender, Class, and Race Relations*. Oakland: University of California Press.

Jago, Marian. 2017. "Towards a Spatial Reconsideration of 'West Coast' and 'East Coast' in Jazz: Hip Hop Parallels and Notions of the Local." *Jazz Perspectives* 10 (2–3): 123–40.

Jones, Nikki. 2010. *Between Good and Ghetto: African American Girls and Inner-City Violence*. New Brunswick, NJ: Rutgers University Press.

Joseph, Nataria T., Matthew F. Muldoon, Stephen B. Manuck, Karen A. Matthews, Leslie A. MacDonald, James Grosch, and Thomas W. Kamarck. 2016. "The Role of Occupational Status in the Association between Job Strain and Ambulatory Blood Pressure during Working and Nonworking Days." *Psychosomatic Medicine* 78 (8): 940–49.

Jost, John T. 2019. "The IAT Is Dead, Long Live the IAT: Context-Sensitive Measures of Implicit Attitudes Are Indispensable to Social and Political Psychology." *Current Directions in Psychological Science* 28 (1): 10–19.

Kane, Emily W. 2000. "Racial and Ethnic Variations in Gender-Related Attitudes." *Annual Review of Sociology* 26 (1): 419–39.

Katz, Lawrence, and Jeremy Nowak. 2017. *The New Localism: How Cities Can Thrive in the Age of Populism*. Washington, DC: Brookings Institution Press.

Kendall, Carl, Aimee Afable-Munsuz, Ilene Speizer, Alexis Avery, Norine Schmidt, and John Santelli. 2005. "Understanding Pregnancy in a Population of Inner-City Women in New Orleans—Results of Qualitative Research." *Social Science & Medicine* 60 (2): 297–311.

Kern, Leslie. 2020. *Feminist City: Claiming Space in a Man-Made World*. New York: Verso.

Kiley, Kevin, and Stephen Vaisey. 2020. "Measuring Stability and Change in Personal Culture Using Panel Data." *American Sociological Review* 85 (3): 477–506.

Kling, Jeffrey, Jeffrey Liebman, and Lawrence Katz. 2007. "Experimental Analysis of Neighborhood Effects." *Econometrica* 75 (1): 83–119.

Knight, Carly R., and Mary C. Brinton. 2017. "One Egalitarianism or Several? Two Decades of Gender-Role Attitude Change in Europe." *American Journal of Sociology* 122 (5): 1485–532.

Kongar, Ebru. 2008. "Is Deindustrialization Good for Women? Evidence from the United States." *Feminist Economics* 14 (1): 73–92.

Kremer, Alex. 2018. "Has Belarus Really Succeeded in Pursuing Gender Equality?" World Bank. Available at https://blogs.worldbank.org/europeandcentralasia/has-belarus-really-succeeded-pursuing-gender-equality.

Krivkovich, Alexis, Irina Starikova, Kelsey Robinson, Rachel Valentino, and Lareina Yee. 2020. "Women in the Workplace 2020." New York: McKinsey.

Lastoe, Stacey. 2019. "There's a New Bachelorette Capital, and It's Not Vegas." *CNN*, May 1, 2019. Available at https://www.cnn.com/travel/article/bachelorette-party-nashville-tennessee/index.html.

Leamaster, Reid J., and Mangala Subramaniam. 2016. "Career and/or Motherhood? Gender and the LDS Church." *Sociological Perspectives* 59 (4): 776–97.

Lee, Jennifer J., and Janice M. Mccabe. 2021. "Who Speaks and Who Listens: Revisiting the Chilly Climate in College Classrooms." *Gender & Society* 35 (1): 32–60.

Legerski, Elizabeth Miklya, and Marie Cornwall. 2010. "Working-Class Job Loss, Gender, and the Negotiation of Household Labor." *Gender & Society* 24 (4): 447–74.

Levanon, Asaf, Paula England, and Paul Allison. 2009. "Occupational Feminization and Pay: Assessing Causal Dynamics Using 1950–2000 U.S. Census Data." *Social Forces* 88 (2): 865–91.

Lim, Kyung Min. 2016. "Major Matters: Exploration of the Gender Wage Gap among STEM Graduates." PhD diss., University of California Los Angeles.

Listokin, David, Kaitlynn Davis, Michael Lahr, Orin Puniello, Garrett Hincken, Ningyuan Wei, and Marc Weiner. 2011. "Route 66 Economic Impact Study." New Brunswick, NJ: Rutgers University.

Lopata, Helena Z., and Barrie Thorne. 1978. "On the Term 'Sex Roles.'" *Signs: Journal of Women in Culture and Society* 3 (3): 718–21.

Lorber, Judith. 1995. *Paradoxes of Gender.* New Haven, CT: Yale University Press.

Lowery, Brian S., Curtis D. Hardin, and Stacey Sinclair. 2001. "Social Influence Effects on Automatic Racial Prejudice." *Journal of Personality and Social Psychology* 81 (5): 842–55.

Lucas, Robert E. 2009. "Ideas and Growth." *Economica* 76 (301): 1–19.

Luhr, Sigrid. 2020. "Signaling Parenthood: Managing the Motherhood Penalty and Fatherhood Premium in the U.S. Service Sector." *Gender & Society* 34 (2): 259–83.

Mandel, Hadas, and Moshe Semyonov. 2014. "Gender Pay Gap and Employment Sector: Sources of Earnings Disparities in the United States, 1970–2010." *Demography* 51 (5): 1597–618.

Martin, Patricia Yancey. 2003. "'Said and Done' Versus 'Saying and Doing': Gendering Practices, Practicing Gender at Work." *Gender & Society* 17 (3): 342–66.

Mason, Karen Oppenheim, John L. Czajka, and Sara Arber. 1976. "Change in U.S. Women's Sex-Role Attitudes, 1964–1974." *American Sociological Review* 41 (4): 573–96.

Mason, Karen Oppenheim, and Yu-Hsia Lu. 1988. "Attitudes toward Women's Familial Roles: Changes in the United States, 1977–1985." *Gender & Society* 2 (1): 39–57.

Massey, Douglas, and Nancy A. Denton. 1993. *American Apartheid: Segregation and the Making of the Underclass.* Cambridge, MA: Harvard University Press.

Maxwell, Rahsaan. 2019. "Cosmopolitan Immigration Attitudes in Large European Cities: Contextual or Compositional Effects?" *American Political Science Review* 113 (2): 456–74.

———. 2020. "Geographic Divides and Cosmopolitanism: Evidence From Switzerland." *Comparative Political Studies* 53 (13): 2061–90.

McCall, Leslie. 2001. *Complex Inequality: Gender, Class and Race in the New Economy.* New York: Routledge.

McGrew, Will. 2016. "Gender Segregation at Work: 'Separate but Equal' or 'Inefficient and Unfair.'" Washington, DC: Washington Center for Equitable Growth.

Meagher, Kelsey D., and Xiaoling Shu. 2019. "Trends in U.S. Gender Attitudes, 1977 to 2018: Gender and Educational Disparities." *Socius* 5 (January). Available at https://doi.org/10.1177/2378023119851692.

Mejova, Yelena, Ingmar Weber, and Michael W. Macy. 2015. *Twitter: A Digital Socioscope.* Cambridge: Cambridge University Press.

Messner, Michael A. 1990. "When Bodies Are Weapons: Masculinity and Violence in Sport." *International Review for the Sociology of Sport* 25 (3): 203–20.

Miller, Amanda J., and Daniel L. Carlson. 2016. "Great Expectations? Working- and Middle-Class Cohabitors' Expected and Actual Divisions of Housework." *Journal of Marriage and Family* 78 (2): 346–63.

Mills, C. Wright. 2000. *The Sociological Imagination.* Oxford: Oxford University Press.

Missouri Census Data Center. 2018. "Geocorr 2018." Columbia: University of Missouri.

Moen, Phyllis, and Erin L. Kelly. 2007. "Flexible Work and Well-Being Study." Minneapolis: Minnesota Population Center, University of Minnesota.

Molotch, Harvey, William Freudenburg, and Krista E. Paulsen. 2000. "History Repeats Itself, but How? City Character, Urban Tradition, and the Accomplishment of Place." *American Sociological Review* 65 (6): 791–823.

Morrison, Anne, and Katherine Gallagher Robbins. 2015. "Women's Overrepresentation in Low-Wage Jobs." Washington, DC: National Women's Law Center.

National Center for Education Statistics. 2021. "Undergraduate Degree Fields." Available at https://nces.ed.gov/programs/coe/indicator/cta.

Newport, Frank. 2013. "Provo-Orem, Utah, Is Most Religious U.S. Metro Area." *Gallup*, March 29, 2013. Available at https://news.gallup.com/poll/161543/provo-orem-utah -religious-metro-area.aspx.

Ottaviano, Gianmarco I. P., and Giovanni Peri. 2005. "Cities and Cultures." *Journal of Urban Economics* 58:304–37.

———. 2006. "The Economic Value of Cultural Diversity: Evidence from US Cities." *Journal of Economic Geography* 6 (1): 9–44.

Parker, Brenda. 2017. *Masculinities and Markets: Raced and Gendered Urban Politics in Milwaukee*. Athens: University of Georgia Press.

Parker, Kim. 2018. "Gender Discrimination More Common for Women in Mostly Male Workplaces." Washington, DC: Pew Research Center. Available at https://www.pewre search.org/fact-tank/2018/03/07/women-in-majority-male-workplaces-report-higher -rates-of-gender-discrimination/.

Parker, Kim, and Wendy Wang. 2013. *Modern Parenthood: Roles of Moms and Dads Converge as They Balance Work and Family*. Washington, DC: Pew Research Center.

Parsons, Talcott. (1951) 1991. *The Social System*. Hove, UK: Psychology Press.

Parsons, Talcott, and Robert Freed Bales. 1955. *Family, Socialization and Interaction Process*. New York: Free Press.

Paulsen, Krista E. 2004. "Making Character Concrete: Empirical Strategies for Studying Place Distinction." *City & Community* 3 (3): 243–62.

Pearse, Rebecca, and Raewyn Connell. 2016. "Gender Norms and the Economy: Insights from Social Research." *Feminist Economics* 22 (1): 30–53.

Peek, Lori, and Alice Fothergill. 2008. "Displacement, Gender, and the Challenges of Parenting after Hurricane Katrina." *NWSA Journal* 20 (3): 69–105.

Pepin, Joanna R., and David A. Cotter. 2018. "Separating Spheres? Diverging Trends in Youth's Gender Attitudes about Work and Family." *Journal of Marriage and Family* 80 (1): 7–24.

Perry, Samuel L., and Andrew L. Whitehead. 2015. "Christian Nationalism and White Racial Boundaries: Examining Whites' Opposition to Interracial Marriage." *Ethnic and Racial Studies* 38 (10): 1671–89.

Pessin, Léa, and Bruno Arpino. 2018. "Navigating between Two Cultures: Immigrants' Gender Attitudes toward Working Women." *Demographic Research* 38:967–1016.

Petersen, Trond, and Laurie A. Morgan. 1995. "Separate and Unequal: Occupation-Establishment Sex Segregation and the Gender Wage Gap." *American Journal of Sociology* 101 (2): 329–65.

Peterson, Anna. 2011. "Making Women's Suffrage Support an Ethnic Duty: Norwegian American Identity Constructions and the Women's Suffrage Movement, 1880–1925." *Journal of American Ethnic History* 30 (4): 5–23.

Porter, Michael E. 1998. "Clusters and the New Economics of Competition." *Harvard Business Review*, November 1, 1998. Available at https://hbr.org/1998/11/clusters-and -the-new-economics-of-competition.

Pratt, Michael G., and Eliana Crosina. 2016. "The Nonconscious at Work." *Annual Review of Organizational Psychology and Organizational Behavior* 3 (1): 321–47.

Putnam, Robert. 2001. "Social Capital: Measurement and Consequences." *Canadian Journal of Policy Research* 2 (1): 41–51.

Quillian, Lincoln. 2012. "Segregation and Poverty Concentration: The Role of Three Segregations." *American Sociological Review* 77 (3): 354–79.

Rakim. 2014. "Key Tracks: Rakim on 'In the Ghetto.'" *Red Bull Music Academy*, March 18, 2014. Available at https://daily.redbullmusicacademy.com/2014/03/key-tracks-rakim-in -the-ghetto.

Rao, Aliya Hamid. 2021. "Gendered Interpretations of Job Loss and Subsequent Professional Pathways." *Gender & Society* 35 (6): 884–909.

Reardon, Sean F., and Kendra Bischoff. 2011. "Income Inequality and Income Segregation." *American Journal of Sociology* 116 (4): 1092–153.

Reger, Jo. 2012. *Everywhere and Nowhere: Contemporary Feminism in the United States.* Oxford: Oxford University Press.

Rentfrow, Peter Jason. 2010. "Statewide Differences in Personality: Toward a Psychological Geography of the United States." *American Psychologist* 65 (6): 548–58.

Rentfrow, Peter J., Samuel D. Gosling, and Jeff Potter. 2008. "A Theory of the Emergence, Persistence, and Expression of Geographic Variation in Psychological Characteristics." *Perspectives on Psychological Science* 3 (5): 339–69.

Rice, Tom W., and Diane L. Coates. 1995. "Gender Role Attitudes in the Southern United States." *Gender & Society* 9 (6): 744–56.

Ridgeway, Cecilia L. 2011. *Framed by Gender: How Gender Inequality Persists in the Modern World.* Oxford: Oxford University Press.

Ridgeway, Cecilia L., and Shelley J. Correll. 2004. "Unpacking the Gender System: A Theoretical Perspective on Gender Beliefs and Social Relations." *Gender & Society* 18 (4): 510–31.

Risman, Barbara J. 2004. "Gender as a Social Structure: Theory Wrestling with Activism." *Gender & Society* 18 (4): 429–50.

———. 2018. *Where the Millennials Will Take Us: A New Generation Wrestles with the Gender Structure.* Oxford: Oxford University Press.

Ritzer, George. 2018. *The McDonaldization of Society: Into the Digital Age.* 9th ed. Los Angeles: Sage.

Robinson, Zandria F. 2014. *This Ain't Chicago: Race, Class, and Regional Identity in the Post-Soul South.* 1st ed. Chapel Hill: University of North Carolina Press.

Rohlinger, Deana A., and Jordan Brown. 2009. "Democracy, Action, and the Internet after 9/11." *American Behavioral Scientist* 53 (1): 133–50.

Roy, William B. 1999. *Socializing Capital.* Princeton, NJ: Princeton University Press.

Ruggles, Steven, Sarah Flood, Ronald Goeken, Jose Pacas, Megan Schouweiler, and Matthew Sobek. 2021. "IPUMS USA: Version 11.0." Minneapolis, MN: IPUMS.

Ruppanner, Leah. 2020. *Motherlands: How States in the U.S. Push Mothers Out of Employment.* Philadelphia, PA: Temple University Press.

Ruppanner, Leah, Caitlyn Collins, Liana Christin Landivar, and William J. Scarborough. 2021. "How Do Gender Norms and Childcare Costs Affect Maternal Employment Across US States?" *Gender & Society* 35 (6): 910–39.

Ryan, Camille L., and Kurt Bauman. 2016. "Educational Attainment in the United States: 2015." P20–578. Washington, DC: U.S. Census Bureau.

Scala, Dante J., and Kenneth M. Johnson. 2017. "Political Polarization along the Rural-Urban Continuum? The Geography of the Presidential Vote, 2000–2016." *Annals of the American Academy of Political and Social Science* 672 (1): 162–84.

Scarborough, William J. 2018a. "Feminist Twitter and Gender Attitudes: Opportunities and Limitations to Using Twitter in the Study of Public Opinion." *Socius* 4 (January): 1–16. Available at https://doi.org/10.1177/2378023118780760.

———. 2018b. "What the Data Says about Women in Management between 1980 and 2010." *Harvard Business Review*, February 23, 2018. Available at https://hbr.org/2018 /02/what-the-data-says-about-women-in-management-between-1980-and-2010.

———. 2019. "Choosing Schools, Reproducing Family Inequality? Race, Gender, and the Negotiation of a New Domestic Task." *Sociological Quarterly* 60 (1): 46–70.

Scarborough, William J., and Rowena Crabbe. 2021. "Place Brands across U.S. Cities and Growth in Local High-Technology Sectors." *Journal of Business Research* 130:70–85.

Scarborough, William J., and Allison Suppan Helmuth. 2021. "How Cultural Environments Shape Online Sentiment toward Social Movements: Place Character and Support for Feminism." *Sociological Forum* 36 (2): 426–47.

Scarborough, William J., and Jessica Moeder. 2022. "Culture's Gendered Consequences: The Relationship between Local Cultural Conditions and the Gender Wage Gap." *Social Currents*. Available at https://doi.org/10.1177/23294965211045088.

Scarborough, William J., Joanna R. Pepin, Danny L. Lambouths III, Ronald Kwon, and Ronaldo Monasterio. 2021. "The Intersection of Racial and Gender Attitudes, 1977 through 2018." *American Sociological Review* 86 (5): 823–55.

Scarborough, William J., and Ray Sin. 2020. "Gendered Places: The Dimensions of Local Gender Norms across the United States." *Gender & Society* 34 (5): 705–35.

Scarborough, William J., Ray Sin, and Barbara Risman. 2019. "Attitudes and the Stalled Gender Revolution: Egalitarianism, Traditionalism, and Ambivalence from 1977 through 2016." *Gender & Society* 33 (2): 173–200.

Scarborough, William J, Katherine Sobering, Ronald Kwon, and Mehr Mumtaz. 2021. "The Costs of Occupational Gender Segregation in High-Tech Growth and Productivity across US Local Labor Markets." *Socio-Economic Review*. Available at https://doi.org/10.1093/ser/mwab036.

Schnabel, Landon. 2016. "Gender and Homosexuality Attitudes across Religious Groups from the 1970s to 2014: Similarity, Distinction, and Adaptation." *Social Science Research* 55:31–47.

Schwartz, David G., and Alexis Rajnoor. 2021. "Las Vegas Strip Casino Employment: Productivity, Revenues, and Payrolls, a Statistical Study, 1990–2020." Las Vegas, NV: Center for Gaming Research, University Libraries, University of Nevada Las Vegas.

Seaver, Maggie. 2017. "The Top 10 Bachelor and Bachelorette Party Destinations 2019." *Real Simple*, 2017. Available at https://www.realsimple.com/weddings/weddings-planning/top-bachelorette-party-destinations.

Seipel, Tracy. 2017. "San Francisco's Universal Health Care Plan Eyed as Model for California." *Mercury News*, April 2, 2017. Available at https://www.mercurynews.com/2017/04/02/san-franciscos-universal-health-care-plan-eyed-as-model-for-california/.

Sewell, William H. 1992. "A Theory of Structure: Duality, Agency, and Transformation." *American Journal of Sociology* 98 (1): 1–29.

Shu, Xiaoling, and Kelsey D. Meagher. 2018. "Beyond the Stalled Gender Revolution: Historical and Cohort Dynamics in Gender Attitudes from 1977 to 2016." *Social Forces* 96 (3): 1243–74.

Siebens, Julie, and Camille L. Ryan. 2012. "Field of Bachelor's Degree in the United States: 2009." American Community Survey Reports. Washington, DC: U.S. Census Bureau.

Smith, Tom W. 1987. "GSS Methodological Report No. 43: Classifying Protestant Denominations." Chicago, IL: National Opinion Research Center.

Smith, Tom W., Michael Davern, Jeremy Freese, and Stephen Morgan. 2018. "General Social Surveys, 1972–2018 [Machine-Readable Data File]/Principal Investigator, Smith, Tom W.; Co-Principal Investigators, Michael Davern, Jeremy Freese, and Stephen Morgan; Sponsored by National Science Foundation.—NORC Ed.—." Chicago, IL: NORC at the University of Chicago. Available at http://gssdataexplorer.norc.org.

Spain, Daphne. 2011. "Women's Rights and Gendered Spaces in 1970s Boston." *Frontiers: A Journal of Women Studies* 32 (1): 152–78.

———. 2016. *Constructive Feminism: Women's Spaces and Women's Rights in the American City.* Ithaca, NY: Cornell University Press.

Stainback, Kevin, and Donald Tomaskovic-Devey. 2012. *Documenting Desegregation: Racial and Gender Segregation in Private Sector Employment since the Civil Rights Act.* New York: Russell Sage Foundation.

Stevenson, Seth. 2014. "Would You Do Your Job Better If Your Boss Didn't Care How You Did It?" *Slate,* May 12, 2014. Available at https://slate.com/business/2014/05/best-buys-rowe-experiment-can-results-only-work-environments-actually-be-successful.html.

Sutton, April, Amanda Bosky, and Chandra Muller. 2016. "Manufacturing Gender Inequality in the New Economy: High School Training for Work in Blue-Collar Communities." *American Sociological Review* 81 (4): 720–48.

Swidler, Ann. 1986. "Culture in Action: Symbols and Strategies." *American Sociological Review* 51 (2): 273–86.

———. 2001. *Talk of Love.* Chicago, IL: University of Chicago Press.

Taylor, Tiffany, Brianna Turgeon, Alison Buck, Katrina Bloch, and Jacob Church. 2019. "Spatial Variation in U.S. Labor Markets and Workplace Gender Segregation: 1980–2005." *Sociological Inquiry* 89 (4): 703–26.

Tomaskovic-Devey, Donald, and Kevin Stainback. 2007. "Discrimination and Desegregation: Equal Opportunity Progress in U.S. Private Sector Workplaces since the Civil Rights Act." *Annals of the American Academy of Political and Social Science* 609 (1): 49–84.

U.S. Bureau of Labor Statistics. 2021. "Occupational Employment and Wage Statistics: STEM." 2021. Available at https://www.bls.gov/oes/topics.htm.

U.S. Census Bureau. 2020. "Labor Force Participation Rate - Women [LNS11300002]." Available from FRED, Federal Reserve Bank of St. Louis, at https://fred.stlouisfed.org/series/LNS11300002.

Vaisey, Stephen. 2009. "Motivation and Justification: A Dual-Process Model of Culture in Action." *American Journal of Sociology* 114 (6): 1675–715.

Varol, Onur, Emilio Ferrara, Clayton A. Davis, Filippo Menczer, and Alessandro Flammini. 2017. "Online Human-Bot Interactions: Detection, Estimation, and Characterization." *Proceeding of the Eleventh International AAAI Conference on Web and Social Media* 11 (1): 289–289.

Weeden, Kim A., Youngjoo Cha, and Mauricio Bucca. 2016. "Long Work Hours, Part-Time Work, and Trends in the Gender Gap in Pay, the Motherhood Wage Penalty, and the Fatherhood Wage Premium." *RSF: The Russell Sage Foundation Journal of the Social Sciences* 2 (4): 71–102.

Whitehead, Andrew L., and Samuel L. Perry. 2019. "Is a 'Christian America' a More Patriarchal America? Religion, Politics, and Traditionalist Gender Ideology." *Canadian Review of Sociology/Revue Canadienne de Sociologie* 56 (2): 151–77.

Williams, Joan C., and Rachel Dempsey. 2014. *What Works for Women at Work: Four Patterns Working Women Need to Know.* New York: New York University Press.

Wrong, Dennis H. 1961. "The Oversocialized Conception of Man in Modern Sociology on JSTOR." *American Sociological Review* 26 (2): 183–93.

Wynn, Jonathan R. 2015. *Music/City: American Festivals and Placemaking in Austin, Nashville, and Newport.* Chicago, IL: University of Chicago Press.

Xu, Kaiyuan, Brian S. Nosek, Anthony G. Greenwald, Kate A. Ratliff, Yoav Bar-Anan, Emily Umansky, Mahzarin R. Banaji, Nicole Lofaro, and Colin Smith. 2018. "Project Im-

plicit Demo Website Datasets." Open Science Framework (OSF). Available at https://doi
.org/10.17605/OSF.IO/Y9HIQ.

Yavorsky, Jill E., Enrica N. Ruggs, and Janette S. Dill. 2021. "Gendered Skills and Unemployed Men's Resistance to 'Women's Work.'" *Gender, Work & Organization* 28 (4):
1524–45.

Index

William J. Scarborough is Assistant Professor of Sociology at the University of North Texas.

www.ingramcontent.com/pod-product-compliance
Lightning Source LLC
Chambersburg PA
CBHW050804270326
41926CB00025B/4537